The Open Door

The Open Door

Early Modern Wajorese Statecraft and Diaspora

KATHRYN ANDERSON WELLEN

NIU PRESS
DeKalb, IL

© 2014 by Northern Illinois University Press
Published by the Northern Illinois University Press, DeKalb, Illinois 60115
Manufactured in the United States using acid-free paper
All Rights Reserved

Library of Congress Cataloging-in-Publication Data

Wellen, Kathryn Anderson, author.
The open door : early modern Wajorese statecraft and diaspora / Kathryn Anderson Wellen.
    pages cm
Includes bibliographical references and index.
Summary: "The Wajorese people were one of many groups that spread across Indonesian during the early modern era. In the wake of the Makassar War (1666–1669), the Dutch took control of Makassar on the Indonesian island of Sulawesi and used it to consolidate their power in the region. Because the Wajorese had sided with the war's losers, they were treated very harshly and many opted to emigrate. They scattered far and wide across the Southeast Asian archipelago, settling in eastern Kalimantan, western Sumatra, the Straits of Malacca, and the Sulawesian port city of Makassar. Wellen reconstructs the fascinating and little-told story of the Wajorese diaspora. Wajorese migrants exhibited remarkable versatility in adapting to local conditions in the areas where they settled. They perpetuated their own culture overseas while simultaneously using various assimilation strategies such as intermarriage to thrive in their adopted homelands. Relations between Wajorese migrants and their homeland intensified in the early 18th century when successive rulers in Wajoq deliberately sought to harness the growing military and commercial potential of the migrant communities. This effort culminated in the 1730s when the exiled La Maddukelleng, an Indonesian national hero, returned to Makassar from neighboring eastern Kalimantan and attempted to expel the Dutch from South Sulawesi. His campaign exemplifies the manner in which overseas Wajorese remained an essential part of Wajoq long after they left home. The Open Door's strong thematic organization allows readers with specific interests such as commercial law, family networks, diaspora, and comparative politics to quickly find fascinating and relevant information about this lesser-known Southeast Asian society"— Provided by publisher.
ISBN 978-0-87580-712-6 (pbk : alk. paper) — ISBN 978-1-60909-170-5 (e-book)
1. Wajo (Indonesia : Kabupaten)—Politics and government. 2. Wajo (Indonesia : Kabupaten)—Emigration and immigration. I. Title.
DS646.49.W35W45 2014
959.8--dc23
2014033388

For Sandy

Contents

Acronyms

ANRI—Arsip Negara Republik Indonesia (Jakarta)

BKI—Bijdragen tot de Taal-, Land- en Volkenkunde van Nederlandsch-Indie

CRL—Center for Research Libraries (Chicago)

JAS—*Journal of Asian Studies*

JMBRAS—*Journal of the Malay Branch of the Royal Asiatic Society*

JSEAS—*Journal of Southeast Asian Studies*

KITLV—Koninklijk Instituut voor Taal-, Land- en Volkenkunde (Leiden)

NA—Nationaal Archief (The Hague)

RIMA—Review of Indonesian and Malaysian Affairs

TNI—Tijdschrijft voor Nederlandsch-Indie

SFR—Sumatra Factory Records

Acknowledgments

A historian's first book often takes a long time to produce and as such the debts accrued along the way are often particularly numerous. This is most definitely the case with *The Open Door*. I researched and wrote the first version of this book as a student at the University of Hawai'i. I would like to thank Cornelia Moore for helping me learn Dutch and the late Muhammad Salim for helping me learn Bugis, as well as my history teachers Leonard Y. Andaya, Barbara Watson Andaya, David A. Chappell, and the late Jerry Bentley. I would also like to thank the family of the late Buhari for extending hospitality to me in Makassar and to the many other Indonesians who welcomed and helped me during my long study of the Wajorese. Additionally I would like to acknowledge Thomas and Frances Blakemore, whose inspired generosity enabled me and many others to study an Asian language. To the many archivists and librarians who assisted me in my research, I am also truly grateful.

The Open Door assumed its present form while I was working as a researcher at the Royal Netherlands Institute for Southeast Asian and Caribbean Studies. Heather Sutherland inspired me to completely rework the study and Leonard and Barbara again offered valuable advice, this time regarding the identity and family chapters. I also would like to thank Campbell Macknight, Henk Schulte Nordholt, Jessica Roitman, Sharyn Graham Davies, Ariel Cusi Lopez, Jennifer Nourse and an anonymous Makassarese-speaking reviewer for reading chapters or the entire book and offering suggestions for improvement. I would also like to acknowledge the encouragement I received from Jim Collins, the assistance Nico van Rooijen gave me with the maps, the support I received from my family, and the help I received from Northern Illinois University Press. I could have never written this book all alone, but I alone am responsible for any errors.

The Open Door

Amongst Diasporas and States

The historiography of diaspora and other geographically dispersed social formations has advanced rapidly during the last decades. Conceptually diaspora provides a framework for understanding the experience of belonging to more than one society simultaneously; an experience that resonates widely with an ever-growing number of groups in the modern world. Upon looking back across the ages, historians see that what has been called "the exemplary condition of late modernity"[1] has always existed. However, while the concept of diaspora has been applied to a chronologically and geographically diverse variety of groups, the discourse about diaspora rests largely upon Western, post-Enlightenment notions of statecraft. These modern European concepts might serve as a valuable basis of comparison for understanding the relationship between late modern diaspora and nation states, but they are less valuable for understanding the historical experiences of groups beyond the scope of these influences.

This book attempts to examine the relationship between a state and a diaspora without undue reliance upon foreign notions of statecraft. Undeniably it is heavily influenced by the traditions and theories of the Western academic world in which it was produced. It is also tarnished by the absence of a Bugis word for "diaspora." Nevertheless, by examining the fluidity with which political, commercial, familial, and cultural practices transferred from a homeland to other locations this study challenges the conceptual boundary between a diaspora and a state, a boundary upon which so much of diaspora discourse is based.

The case in point is Wajoq and the Wajorese diaspora. A Bugis people hailing from South Sulawesi, Indonesia, the Wajorese are best known in the Western world through Joseph Conrad's novel *The Rescue*.[2] In Indonesia they are best known through the repatriate leader La Maddukelleng (ca. 1700–1765) who was proclaimed as a national hero in 1998.[3] This study details the interaction between Wajoq and the Wajorese diaspora through a thematic examination of four geographically distinct Wajorese settlements. In order of their proximity to Wajoq, these are Makassar, eastern Kalimantan, the Malay world, and western Sumatra. The bulk of the study is concerned with the period from the 1670s, when intolerable conditions in Wajoq added a new sense of urgency to emigration, until the 1730s when the exile La Maddukelleng returned from overseas and assumed the leadership of Wajoq, but the study extends chronologically into both earlier and later time periods. These extensions allow the description of essential aspects of Wajorese political history and the continuation of exemplary narratives. By focusing on a single, early modern society, this study offers both a diachronic example to the discourse on diaspora, and an innovative case study of an early modern Bugis state to the body of literature about traditional Southeast Asian statecraft.

Figuratively speaking, Wajoq had an open door that allowed people to come and go as they pleased. Indeed the right of people to enter and leave Wajoq is encoded in Wajorese foundational texts.[4] The Wajorese leader La Tiringeng To Taba is recorded as saying, "The door of Wajoq shall be open when they enter; the door of Wajoq shall be open when they leave; they enter on their own feet and they leave on their own feet."[5] This open door facilitated the establishment of a far-flung network of Wajorese migrants and merchants across the Southeast Asian archipelago. Furthermore, the government's passive encouragement of migration and active encouragement of overseas commerce enabled it to harvest the economic and military power of its emigrants to strengthen the state. Coupled with cultural and social cohesion, this combination produced a diaspora that cooperated synergistically with the state. While such an open door may not have been unique among Bugis states,[6] certain historical circumstances resulted in the formation of a unique, albeit not always distinct, diaspora.

Especially for the reader who is more interested in diaspora than in South Sulawesi, it is important to note at the outset that there are numerous Bugis polities. The result of this multiplicity, and of the propensity of Bugis people in general to migrate, is that numerous groups of Bugis have emigrated or circulated to different places across the archipelago and beyond at various times throughout history. This process also continues, albeit along very different lines, until present day. Given that they all share a common ethnonym (Bugis) and have more specific identities (such as Wajorese or Bonéan) as well, it is appropriate to refer to the Bugis diaspora in both the singular and the plural. It is also appropriate to refer to any individual group more specifically as this study does. Yet it should be noted that, except for the case of direct citations, this study refers to Wajo-rese groups as Wajorese even when describing instances in which they re-ferred to themselves with the more salient ethnonym of Bugis. This avoids confusion when discussing them alongside other Bugis groups, such as the Riau Bugis who were known according to their established stronghold in Riau in the western archipelago.

It is hoped that readers who are more familiar with early modern South-east Asia than with diaspora studies will appreciate the use of the concept of diaspora as a means of reframing the relationship between the local and the foreign. Southeast Asian historiography has long recognized the sig-nificance of the foreign to the dialectic of shaping the local. Indeed, there may be more room in Southeast Asian studies for a historiography that tran-scends geographical boundaries than in other area studies. Nevertheless, geographically dispersed communities functioning in concert push the lim-its of what is commonly considered to be a state. To contextualize this study it is worthwhile to briefly examine concepts of states and diaspora.

Concepts of States in Southeast Asia

Seventeenth-century states were very different from the system of na-tion-states that currently encompasses the globe. While Benedict Anderson has demonstrated the powerful hold that nation-states have on the imagina-tion,[7] the critical conceptual link between nation and territory upon which nation-states rest did not develop until the eighteenth century. Prior to that, the European political landscape consisted largely of absolutist monarchies such as France and Spain the sovereigns of which often claimed divine right to rule. It was only during the eighteenth century that Enlightenment ideals such as political equality, popular sovereignty, and liberty inspired political reform that, particularly but not exclusively in France, was ac-companied by the rise of nationalism. Whereas there had previously been communal sentiments based on a wide variety of cultural, religious and ethnic actors, there now developed nationalism, which was a revolutionary political plan for the construction of a homogenous, politically, and spiritu-ally unified nation.[8]

The historiographical tendency[9] has been to view this development as an exclusively European phenomenon fueled by exceptional develop-ments such as print capitalism and industrialization.[10] Recently, however, this approach has come under fire. Victor Lieberman argues that localized societies across Eurasia coalesced politically, culturally, and commercially from about 1450 to 1830.[11] While he notes that such integration was less significant in certain areas, especially insular Southeast Asia, he argues that even during the sixteenth through eighteenth centuries, this development transcends any East-West divide.[12] Yet the concept of a bounded nation-state developed along exceptionally rigid lines in Europe. A critical shift around the sixteenth century in which the public good became increasingly associated with the state pushed European states towards nation-states.[13] Gradually, the concept of a nation-state developed as a sharply delineated, territorial political unit, with uniform institutions and authority throughout, supposedly contiguous with the ancestral lands of a single people sharing a common heritage, language, and culture. This conceptualization was eventually exported to other parts of the world via European colonialists and later European-educated bilingual elites, which led to the expansion of the nation-state system. While it assumed distinct local forms, the nation-state system eventually encompassed the globe.

In the process, the nation-state system, with its boundaries of contiguous lands, standardized languages, and educational systems, butted heads with indigenous systems all over the world. Misunderstandings between European and Asian officials over the question of boundaries exemplify this clash perfectly. Thongchai Winichakul recounts the stunned, confused and annoyed responses of the Siamese government and people to British attempts at marking boundaries in the nineteenth century. Whereas Siamese concepts of political sovereignty included boundaries, these were much more flexible than the European system in which a state's sovereignty was coterminous with its borders.[14] Another example comes from South Sulawesi where Dutch officials tried to learn the precise borders of two countries from their respective rulers. When asked to which country certain mountains belonged, the rulers replied that they have much better things to fight about than scruffy hills.[15] Clearly political systems in Southeast Asia and their relations to territory confused colonial officials who were accustomed to the European system.

In efforts to understand these systems, scholars have developed a variety of models of statecraft and applied them to Southeast Asian states. A number of these models account for physically disparate constituents within a single state. The so-called cosmic polity models are of particular interest because they do not require a state to be physically contiguous. That being said, they are of limited usefulness for studying South Sulawesi because they often are based on Indic-concepts which were of only marginal influence in South Sulawesi.

The most widespread cosmic polity model is that of the *mandala*. Literally meaning circle, a mandala is a painted, engraved or carved configuration consisting of a central divinity encircled by other divinities. It was first applied to politics in the fourth-century Sanskrit political treatise *Arthasastra*. With reference to Southeast Asia, it is most commonly used with reference to Indianized societies on the mainland and in the western archipelago. O.W. Wolters, Benedict Anderson and S. J. Tambiah have all used this concept in different ways.[16]

Wolters describes the mandala as

> a particular and often unstable political situation in a vaguely definable geographical area without fixed boundaries and where smaller centers tended to look in all directions for security. Mandalas would expand and contract in a concertina-like fashion. Each one contained several tributary rulers, some of whom would repudiate their vassal status when the opportunity arose and try to build up their own networks of vassals.[17]

Thus his model is characterized by flexible polities consisting of multiple centers and rulers that look for security in a variety of directions, all underneath a mandala overlord. It aptly describes the late seventh- to early eleventh-century political situation in which Srivijaya from its center on the east coast of Sumatra near Palembang exerted influence over a variety of harbor principalities and hinterland chiefs on the Malay Peninsula and the north and northeastern coasts of Sumatra.[18] Wolters also applies the mandala concept to Angkor, Ayudhya, and Majapahit.

Anderson's version of the mandala polity, which relies heavily on Soemarsaid Moertono's study of early Javanese statecraft,[19] emphasizes the importance of the center. He uses the image of light from a reflector lamp as a metaphor for Javanese political influence. He equates the manner in which the lamp's brightness gradually and evenly diminishes with increased distance from the light source to the manner in which a ruler's power diminishes towards the periphery until it merges with the nearest neighbor's sphere of influence.[20] Anderson applies this to both Majapahit, which had widespread tributaries on diverse islands, and to the Republic of Indonesia. His approach differs from Wolters' in that the periphery does not replicate the center nor have its own brightness, but rather is subject to the center's diluted authority. While such an emphasis on the center may obscure politics and society on the periphery, the value of this image is that it clearly represents the diffuse nature of political influence. Anderson argues that the uneven application of authority stems from the Javanese conception of power as constant. Because there is a fixed amount of power in the universe, its concentration in one area results in dilution in another.[21]

Tambiah's galactic model draws on the concept of mandala, defined here as a core with an enclosing element, to describe a traditional form of statecraft that encodes political, economic, topographical, and cosmological features. A galactic polity has a complex of satellites surrounding a spiritually important center.[22] The satellites are small-scale replicas of the center that are created by the polity splitting into independent components through succession disputes, rebellions, and shifting capitals and territories.[23] The outlying territories are not firmly controlled; rather they are joined through a tributary and spiritual relationship,[24] which is reified through oaths of loyalty, marriage and messengers.[25] Tambiah argues that this model was pervasive in Southeast Asia.[26]

While not a cosmic polity, the segmentary state is another model of statecraft that allows for physically discontiguous constituents within a single state. The main feature of a segmentary state is a pyramidal social structure in which very similar powers are exercised at several different levels. In any segment at any given time there is "a certain degree of monopoly of political power, development of administrative staff and definition of territorial limits . . ."[27] While Aidan W. Southall developed this concept with reference to the Alur in highland East Africa, several scholars have used it as a means of understanding statecraft in Asia. Richard Fox has applied it to the Rajput polities in North India and Burton Stein has applied in to the Cholas of South India.[28] In Southeast Asia, Thomas Kiefer and James Warren have applied it to the Taosug of Sulu.[29] The political systems of these societies are composed of constituents that are structurally similar, the authority of which differed in extent rather than kind. In a sense, the segmentary state combines several important aspects of statecraft found in Southeast Asia such as the gradual diffusion of power from the center to the periphery (as seen in Anderson's concept of mandala) and the replication of the center's political system among its political constituents on the periphery (as seen in Wolters' concept of mandala or Tambiah's galactic polity's satellites).

The most striking feature that emerges from all of these models is the emphasis on the center rather than the periphery. This differs from the European emphasis on borders, which stems from the concept that sovereignty and territory are coterminous, at least in theory. The relationship between territory and borders also differs fundamentally from that of a European state because the total territory included in a given traditional Southeast Asian state is not necessarily contiguous. While there have been strong objections to the application of models based on Indian political concepts to the un-Indianized[30] states of South Sulawesi[31] where the Indic concept of *Cakravartin* or world-ruler never flourished, the cosmic polity models demonstrate that the idea of a state consisting of outlying communities linked to a center is not uncommon in Southeast Asian historiography. A number of other studies document this phenomenon on the basis of empirical data rather than Indian-based models. Thongchai points out that Siamese boundaries were determined at the local level and that they may or may not adjoin another boundary or segment of the Siamese state.[32] Similarly, parts of other Southeast Asian states were located at a distance from their centers. Leonard Y. Andaya's work on Maluku has shown that Ternate included Buton of the southeast coast of Sulawesi, Loloda on the northeastern coast of Halmahera and Bacan off the southeastern coast of Halmahera, among other areas.[33] Elsewhere in the world there are other examples of widely dispersed states. In western Polynesia, for example, the outliers of Niuatoputapu and Niuafo'ou are located 375 miles (600 kilometers) north of Tongatapu; yet academic discussions still refer to these distant areas as part of Tonga.[34] Thus it appears that in some cases a state's peripheral constituents are still considered part of the state regardless as to whether they are located close at hand or far away from the center.

Concepts of Diaspora

The concept of diaspora has become increasingly popular in academic, governmental and popular circles over the past few decades.[35] Innumerable studies have noted the shift from the specific usage of the term "diaspora" with reference to the Jews as the paradigmatic case to a broader application of the concept. Recent research, however, has revealed that the term has been more widely applied to more groups for longer than is commonly acknowledged.[36] For example, at the end of the nineteenth century, American encyclopedias used the word "diaspora" in reference to the Moravian church without mentioning the Jews. Explicit comparisons to the Jews were also made early on. Not only was the term "diaspora" used during the early twentieth century with reference to the descendants of Africans living on other continents but also were parallels drawn between Jewish history and black history.[37] The term "diaspora" was also used in reference to the Chinese at least as early as 1937.[38]

Despite these documented earlier usages, Abner Cohen's coinage of the term "trading diaspora"[39] in 1971 opened the floodgates for the use of the term "diaspora" in reference to an even wider variety of groups. Latching onto Cohen's concept of a trading diaspora, Philip Curtin's 1984 study *Cross-cultural Trade in World History* applied the term to an unprecedented number of groups. Chronologically he extends the argument from ancient Mesopotamia to the nineteenth century in which he locates the end of "the long era in history when trade diaspora had been the dominant institutional form in cross-cultural trade."[40] Geographically he includes North and Central America, Europe, Africa, and Asia as far as Japan. He even has a section on the Bugis. Aside from the wide-ranging application of the term, Curtin's work is also significant for its refinement of the concept. He defines a trading diaspora as "an interrelated net of commercial communities forming a trade network."[41] Significantly he sees diaspora as apolitical and argues for a clear distinction between the host societies and the foreign merchants. The former, he argues, are complete societies, and the latter not.[42]

Another important contribution of Curtin's work is that it started a trend towards recognizing the role of migrant groups in economic development and globalization. For example, Jonathan Israel's *European Jewry in the Age of Mercantilism 1550–1750*[43] details the manner in which Jewish commercial and financial networks facilitated economic development from the New World, across Europe and into the Ottoman Empire. He further argues that nationalist history has masked these contributions. This scenario resonates with the Wajorese case. While Wajorese contributions were made on a regional rather than global scale, Wajorese commercial networks helped to maintain the indigenous economy in the face of Dutch encroachment.

Despite the influence of Curtin's work, his sharp delineation between trading diasporas and host societies has not withstood the test of time. More recent scholarship has provided numerous examples of diasporas contributing not only economically but also politically to their host societies. While the emphasis has been on the contemporary situation, several important works have also treated the early modern period. An early example is Sanjay Subrahmanyam's article "Iranians Abroad," which documented Iranian political participation in state building in Golconda, Thailand, and the Deccan.[44] Ina Baghdiantz McCabe's more recent work on the Armenians in Julfa has revealed at least two cases of Armenian political participation in Safavid Iran.[45] Although not always described in terms of a diaspora, Bugis political participation in state building in the Malay world has also been considered so important as to merit the appellation of 'the Bugis period' of Malay history.[46]

Increasingly, diasporas are being considered as something contributing to, rather than distinct from, the mainstream. Yet the bounded nation-state's conceptual hold is so tight that a group or an individual's simultaneous participation in two societies is often considered paradoxical. Robin Cohen sees the desire of diasporas "to reach in and to reach out, to be ethnic and transnational, to be local and cosmopolitan" as a paradox.[47] Similarly, Stathis Gourgouris sees the manner in which diasporic communities simultaneously both confirm and exceed boundaries as not only "paradoxical" but also "bizarre."[48]

Using the Greek diaspora as his primary basis for comparison, Gourgouris also points out the conceptual difficulty that diaspora has existing independently from the nation-form.[49] Yet the juxtapositioning of diaspora against the nation-state is being challenged on several levels. One is in postcolonial studies of the non-Western world. Another is in a reevaluation of how the bounded nation-state works.

Increasingly post-colonial scholars have called for studying migration and diaspora in indigenous terms. Compelling examples come from Oceania where migration has always played an important role in society. In his visionary essay "Our Sea of Islands,"[50] Epeli Hau'ofa advocates an expanded view of Oceania by including Pacific diaspora.[51] Linking modern practices of jet travel across the Pacific to traditional practices of long-distance voyaging, he writes of thousands of Pacific Islanders "flying back and forth across national boundaries . . . far above and completely undaunted by the deadly serious discourses below . . . cultivating their universe in their own ways . . ."[52] Hau'ofa's insights have inspired numerous scholars to consider the sum of the total relationships and to focus on ordinary people's experiences with kinship and interconnected exchange networks instead of the isolations and dependency inherent in a Western colonial perspective. One example is Ilana Gershon who sees family as the basis of diaspora.[53] Another is Subramani who identifies diaspora's other as "rooted indigenous culture."[54]

From this body of work, much of which has insisted upon viewing migration in local contexts, it would appear that the dichotomy between diaspora and nation-form is culturally specific; that it depends upon Western ideas of bounded nation-states. Joel Bonnemaison eloquently asserts an alternative:

> Can the tree, symbol of rootedness and stability, be reconciled with the canoe, symbol of journeying and unrestricted wandering? At first sight, apparently not. Nevertheless, Melanesian civilization uses this dual metaphor, this apparent contradiction, to define traditional identity. On the island of Tanna in Vanuatu, they say that man is a tree that must take root and stay fixed in its place. The local group, on the other hand, is a canoe that follows 'roads' and explores the wide world. For traditional society, this metaphor would not present a paradox.[55]

A second front on which the juxtapositioning of diaspora against the nation-state is being challenged is in the study of the dialectic between cosmopolitanism and nationalism. As it has been redefined, "cosmopolitanism" is not Kantian unattachment, but rather plural and particular (re-) attachments that are not necessarily geographically restricted.[56] This redefinition has helped to inspire post-ethnic perspectives, which recognize the plurality of individuals' attachments and denies the paramountcy of history and biology in these attachments.[57] Espousing a postethnic perspective, David Hollinger has postulated that the nation does not have to be antithetical to cosmopolitan engagements. On the contrary, he argues, a "civic nation with democratic-egalitarian principles [can be] an instrument for transnational goals that can mediate between the ethos and the species."[58] Theoretically this implies that nations can be catalysts for transnational projects. Empirically it accounts for the possibility that an individual can be a soldier, a husband, a Muslim, a merchant, a judge, a member of a Sumatran royal house, and a Wajorese all at the same time.

Despite these and other challenges that have been made to the analytical value of the term "diaspora," this study uses the concept of diaspora as a means of understanding Wajorese society so as to transcend the borders to which historians are so frequently confined. These borders are both geographic and conceptual. Geographically it accounts for activity both inside and outside the homeland of Wajoq. This allows for a more realistic representation of a society deeply marked by migration. Conceptually, diaspora discourse's highly varied nature and its affinity with cultural studies invites the examination of not only politics and commerce but also identity. While identity is a daunting field for the early modern historian, a sense of reasons why people across the archipelago continued to invoke a Wajorese identity after migrating is essential to understanding how the Wajorese diaspora functioned. In turn, this provides insights into the nature of Southeast Asian statecraft and commerce.

Sources as a Windowframe

As the value of this book lies in its presentation of a detailed case study of a geographically dispersed society from a time and place that has been largely excluded from diaspora discourse, it is worthwhile to say a few words about the fortuitous confluence of circumstances that makes the study of South Sulawesi especially interesting for comparative early modern history. Located roughly in the longitudinal center of the Austronesian world, South Sulawesi was sufficiently involved in the commercial and cultural networks spanning the Southeast Asian archipelago and beyond to have adopted and adapted an Indic-based syllabary for the writing of indigenous languages.[59] Near the eastern extremity of these Indic influences, however, it maintained a higher level of cultural autonomy than its more Indianized neighbors. Thus for two centuries from the advent of writing around 1400[60] to the advent of Islam after 1600, people in South Sulawesi were writing about themselves independently of significant foreign influence. As a result, South Sulawesi's literary canon[61] is very reflective of indigenous concerns, and the texts provide an unusual window into the nature of Austronesian societies.

Without digressing too far into the field of Bugis historiography,[62] it is also worthwhile to mention several characteristics of Wajorese historiography. Wajoq is among the states for which not only a chronicle,[63] but also numerous versions of chronicles exist. J. Noorduyn carefully studied diverse texts and translated a representative text into Dutch which he then published in 1955.[64] Unfortunately these texts provide precious little information about the main period covered by this study. Most *lontaraq*,[65] as these texts are commonly known, provide little more than lists of *arung matoa* (paramount rulers of Wajoq) and some of their accomplishments, and there is little difference between the various versions. A notable exception is the *Lontaraq Sukkuqna Wajoq* (*Complete Chronicle of Wajoq*, hereafter LSW), which provides far more information concerning the late seventeenth and early eighteenth centuries than any other Wajorese source.[66] The LSW is apparently an attempt at all-inclusive history.[67] In contrast to typical Bugis lontaraq, which are generally quite short,[68] the LSW is extremely lengthy: 698 pages long.[69] An exceptional work, the LSW was ostensibly written by Ranreng Béttémpola La Sangaji Puanna La Sengngeng based on all the available lontaraq during the reign of Arung Matoa La Mappayung Puanna Salowang (r. 1764–1767),[70] but there are reasons to suspect that it was written later.[71]

Aside from these indigenous sources, there are also enviable European sources available for South Sulawesi.[72] The most substantial of these are the extensive archives of the Dutch United East India Company (*Vereenigde Oostindische Compagnie*, hereafter VOC),which developed a remarkable information network for its operations.[73] They are noteworthy for the detailed, albeit fragmented, information that they provide about the aspects of Southeast Asian society that were tangential to their concerns. Although primarily concerned with the VOC's own affairs, they also contain contemporary records of the letters, speeches, and comments of local rulers and nobles. The vast majority of the indigenous documents were translated from Bugis or Malay into Dutch, yet even in translation, they constitute a valuable source of information. Together the indigenous literary canon, the records of the VOC provide a historiographical treasure trove unparalleled in the early modern Austronesian world. That being said, it must also be mentioned that VOC archives pertaining to Wajoq from 1680 until 1730 are very limited. Fortunately there are records about the Wajorese in other places such as Makassar where they were under Dutch purview and western Sumatra where the English East India Company (hereafter EIC) employed members of a Wajorese family for several generations.

The Study

As described in the following study, Wajorese history shows that many processes governing Wajorese lives functioned similarly at both the local and translocal levels. When this is considered alongside the nature of Wajorese political systems, the division between state and diaspora is blurred. This introductory chapter argues that much of the discourse about diaspora presents a dichotomy between state and diaspora, and it describes a fortuitous confluence of historiographical circumstances that allow for a study of the Wajorese to reexamine this dichotomy. The next chapter describes Bugis political structure in general and Wajorese political structure in particular. It examines the geography of Wajoq, the general characteristics of Bugis states, and various unifying features of the Wajorese state. Thereafter it briefly traces Wajorese political history up to 1670 when intolerable conditions in the homeland added a new sense of urgency to Wajorese emigration.

The manner in which Wajorese political mechanisms transferred into a translocal environment is the subject of chapter 3. Here it is argued that institutions such as representative councils could be used to unify geographically disparate communities. A number of political arrangements with host communities are also discussed at length. Chapter 4 then looks at the lifeblood of Wajorese diaspora: commerce. The Wajorese were especially successful at overseas trade because they had a specialized legal framework that expanded their commercial potential and because the government in Wajoq explicitly encouraged commerce and undertook a number of concrete measures to facilitate it. In some instances the Wajorese also were able to fulfill the sort of intermediary roles that are common among ethnic trading communities. Given the overlap between politics and commerce as well as that between politics and family relations, the thematic division between chapters 3 and 4 may appear arbitrary, but it is hoped that the thematic division will assist readers who are interested in the workings of diaspora in general. Undeniably commerce and politics were inextricably intertwined in Southeast Asian statecraft,[74] but the heuristic division between the two fields is mirrored in Wajorese texts: laws of an explicitly political nature are contained in the Wajorese chronicles whereas Wajorese commercial laws are codified in a separate document.

Having looked at both commerce and politics, the study turns in chapter 5 to one of the mechanisms that the Wajorese used to solidify their networks: marriage and family networks. These were used to establish and maintain political alliances across the diaspora. The division between chapters on politics and family relations does not mean to imply that the two spheres were distinct from each other; rather, it is intended for the convenience of readers interested in families. Another essential element to the maintenance of the diaspora was a common identity which is given detailed consideration in chapter 6. This discussion touches upon many aspects of Wajorese culture, such as literature and ceremonies, which were used to forge and maintain social ties, but it focuses on the practical implications of identity for commerce and politics and for the maintenance of the diaspora over time. Once again, the treatment of one sphere of diasporic life in a separate chapter is not intended to imply that it was somehow separate from the other spheres of activity. On the contrary, the dedication of a separate chapter to identity is intended to signify that it is an absolutely fundamental aspect of maintaining a diaspora and therefore worthy of special consideration.

The question of what links the Wajorese to one another is further examined in chapter 7. This chapter looks in detail at the Wajorese leader La Maddukelleng, who returns from overseas exile and assumes rule in Wajoq. His attempt to oust the Dutch from South Sulawesi can be seen as an example of the involvement of diasporic communities in the affairs of the homeland. Finally, chapter 8 concludes the study by briefly examining the Wajorese diaspora in a comparative perspective.

CHAPTER TWO

Wajorese History and Migration

Wajoq is located in the Cenrana River Valley on the southwestern peninsula of the island of Sulawesi, also known as Celebes, situated between
Kalimantan (Borneo) and Maluku (the Moluccas) in eastern Indonesia.
The southwestern peninsula, now referred to as South Sulawesi, consists
of a mountainous area in the north and agricultural plains in the south that
are bisected by a cordillera of two mountain ranges running from north to
south. South Sulawesi's most important river is the Walennaé River, which
runs from south to north through the center of the peninsula almost to Lake
Témpé where its name changes to the Cenrana River and sharply turns
towards the southeast before finally emptying into the Gulf of Boné. The
Cenrana River, the only river in South Sulawesi navigable by ocean-going
vessels along its entire course, has long been an essential transportation
route.[1] Since at least 1300 CE, it has served as an important link between
the interior of the peninsula and the coastal trading networks criss-crossing
the Indonesian archipelago.[2]

Wajoq is bordered on the east by the Gulf of Boné, on the north by the
foothills of the Latimojong Mountains, on the west by Lake Témpé and
Lake Sidénréng, and on the south by the Cenrana River. Its immediate political neighbors are the Bugis lands of Boné to the south, Soppéng to the
west, Sidénréng to the northwest and Luwuq to the north. The importance
of Wajoq's location as well as that of the Cenrana River cannot be overem-
phasized. These factors made Wajoq ideal for both maritime commerce and
agriculture. The seventeenth-century Dutch Governor of Makassar, Adriaan
Smout, observed how the fresh-water Lake Témpé, the clean and deep Cen-

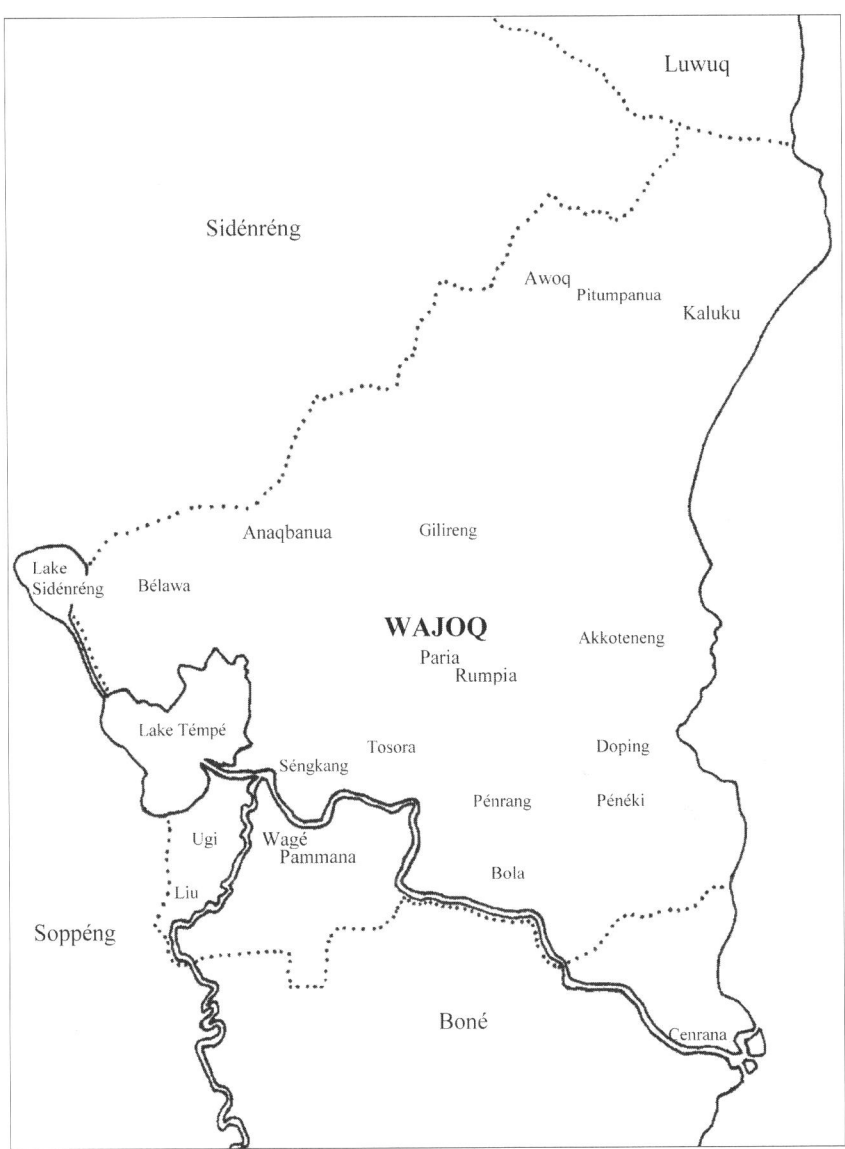

Map 1: Wajoq

Map 2: South Sulawesi

rana River, and the proximity of the sea provided the Wajorese with various opportunities for existence and encouraged them to go into commerce,[3] an opinion echoed by modern anthropologists.[4] Although the lower part of the Cenrana River valley is especially prone to flooding, the upper part is bordered by exceptionally fertile raised lands, eminently suitable for wet-rice cultivation. Indeed, some of the peninsula's most fertile agricultural lands are located in this area.

The peninsula possesses a variety of natural resources. Oral tradition tells of vast virgin forest, but extensive deforestation has occurred since the fourteenth century. In the late twentieth century, forest covered about 38 percent of the province of South Sulawesi with more of it concentrated in the mountainous north than in the south.[5] Aside from the resources of these forests, such as beeswax, honey, resins, rattan, and sandalwood, South Sulawesi also produces maritime products such as mother-of-pearl, giant clams, and tortoiseshell, as well as valuable metals such as gold dust, iron, and copper ore.[6] It should be noted, however, that these natural resources are not available in particularly large quantities. During the period under study, South Sulawesi's main export was apparently rice.

The ethnic complexity of South Sulawesi is commonly divided into four major ethnic groups.[7] Having long occupied the most fertile regions of the peninsula, the Bugis are the most populous. Second largest in population is the Makassarese, who live in the southwestern and southern parts of the peninsula, and the third most populous is the Toraja living in the mountainous areas to the north. Finally, the Mandarese inhabit both the coastal and mountainous areas in the northwest of the peninsula. In addition to these four, there are numerous smaller ethnic groups.

Recent archaeological work suggests that the Bugis were settled in the southern peninsula and organized into numerous independent, small chiefdoms by about 1200 CE. In the thirteenth century the Bugis polities on the shore of Lake Témpé then developed trading relations with Java via the Makassarese polities on the southern coast. The Lake Témpé Bugis apparently established trading settlements in the valleys of the Walennaé and Cenrana rivers by the mid-thirteenth century. They had commercial contacts with Javanese traders en route to Maluku with whom they traded rice, iron, and forest products for Southeast Asian and Chinese ceramics and Indian textiles. They also probably sailed themselves to the western parts of the archipelago and to the southern Philippines in search of such exotic goods. Rice came from Cina, a polity south of Séngkang, and other areas nearby; iron was probably obtainable from small non-Bugis polities along the northern and western coastline of the Gulf of Boné. The Lake Témpé

Bugis went to these areas to acquire iron which was plentiful throughout Central Sulawesi and which was important to international trade, the manufacture of *krisses* (daggers or short swords) and deforestation. By the late thirteenth century, some Lake Témpé Bugis settled at Malangké on the northeast coast of the Gulf of Boné. There they maintained mutually advantageous trading relations with the indigenous populations farther upstream and eventually united the various ethnic groups of the Luwuq region. As the Bugis assumed a position of commercial and presumably social leadership, Luwuq emerged as a Bugis polity and gained a widespread reputation for the production of iron.[8]

As the manufacture of iron farming implements facilitated agricultural intensification, it became increasingly important for rulers to control land, people and water for the production of rice to be exchanged for trade goods for redistribution. New political systems developed consequently. According to Bugis historical traditions, these were generally based on a social contract between the ruler and the ruled in which both parties had rights and responsibilities towards the other. While this system of organization was based on chains of loyalty, these new political systems were also accorded recognition. Bugis texts clearly refer to states that existed above and beyond the rulers and their systems of personal loyalties. One poignant example from Wajorese sources is the story of when the Wajorese appointed their first paramount ruler Arung Matoa Petta La Paléwo To Palippu. He was originally unwilling to lead and asked to be excused on the grounds that he was dumb, poor and weak. He was eventually convinced, however, by the statement that "Wajoq is smart, Wajoq is rich, Wajoq is brave and strong!"[9] While it may have been an interpretive element inserted well after it was purportedly said, this statement about Wajoq's qualities clearly exemplifies how traditional Bugis states existed independently of any one ruler. It is to a more detailed discussion of Bugis and specifically Wajorese statecraft that this study now turns.

Bugis Statecraft

At their most fundamental level, traditional Bugis states consisted of chains of loyalty between individuals.[10] Locals acknowledged a local ruler as their controlling superior and, in turn, local rulers acknowledged a supra-local ruler as their controlling superior. In some cases these rulers or supra-rulers were hereditary and in other instances rulers were selected from a pool of high-status individuals. In all cases, status preceded political authority. Political overlords were theoretically born to a higher status and said to have white blood. In instances when an exceptionally capable individual achieves something extraordinary, he is said to have forgotten white blood; and such an individual is almost always a man because status in more rigidly ascribed for women.[11] These chains of loyalty were then formalized by governmental structures which varied from place to place and which could exist at both the local and the state levels. These varied governmental structures could and did continue to exist even in the events of an office being unfilled or a particularly strong ruler exerting dispro-portionate influence.

Reflecting the absolute centrality of status in the societies of South Su-lawesi, the chains of loyalty were pyramidal in nature with communities of commoners and slaves at the base and the paramount ruler of each state at the top. In some states the middle section of the pyramid was occupied by progressively more influential leaders of multiple communities who some-times occupied formal positions within various community councils. This was the case with Wajoq as will be discussed below. In other states, such as Boné, there were more direct bonds between the general populace and the prestigious rulers, as is exemplified by the sharp distinction between the *tomanurung,* "people descendant [from heavens]' and the *tomaéga,* or "many people."[12] In all cases, and at all levels, there were reciprocal rights and duties between the rulers and the ruled. At the lowest levels, these were essentially patron-client ties and could be expressed by working in a noble's field or protecting commoners from poverty. At the state level, these obli-gations could include the public participating in the military and the rulers protecting the public from foreign threats.

This system of political control by status is a fundamental Austronesian concept. In South Sulawesi it dates back to prehistoric times, even if the scope of the system during the first millennium BCE was limited to a couple villages, or even a single village.[13] Therefore it predates the coalescence of states during the thirteenth and fourteenth centuries. Furthermore it sur-vived the increase of foreign influences during the early modern era includ-ing the Islamicization of the peninsula during the seventeenth century.

The hierarchical nature of this system is reflected in the nomenclature. In South Sulawesi the titles of the various rulers, both local and supralocal, are generally linked to the places.[14] The most common form is simply the name of the place preceded by the word *arung* meaning "ruler," such as arung Bila. Thus, a statement that a place—such as Lamuru, for example—belonged to Soppéng meant that the local arung at Lamuru acknowledged the datu Sop-péng (as the paramount ruler in Soppéng is known) as his or her controlling superior. When enough communities join together under a common ruler, they formed a state or, technically speaking, a complex chiefdom.[15]

Within each state were smaller polities known as *limpo.* "Limpo" literally means "surround" and it is also used to mean "people" or "village."[16] These smaller polities joined together for mutual advantage or for the prestige of being associated with a certain ruler or lineage, but they preserved a fundamental level of independence. Thus, even when participating in the political life of a state and recognizing its paramount ruler, the constituent polities maintained their own customs. They did not generally conduct foreign policy with other kingdoms as equals, but they could and did switch their allegiance from one kingdom to another according to their own self-perceived best interests.

When a community switched alliances, the population did not generally move into the territory of their new overlord. Instead the population remained and continued to farm their lands and fish their waters. Thus the boundaries of Bugis kingdoms were fixed according to the groups that were loyal to a specific state at a given time and were, consequently, in a constant state of flux. However, border disputes did not threaten the state; rather, they were an innate part of the hierarchical political system in South Sulawesi. Furthermore, despite the fluctuation of borders, there was an overall continuity to the states' territory. This is reflected in the fact that the main states of South Sulawesi occupied roughly the same area in the sixteenth century as the modern *kabupaten* (regencies) that now bear the same names.[17]

Bugis states were also characterized by the existence of a paramount ruler. The titles of paramount rulers varied from state to state. Although the paramount rulers in Boné and Luwuq held essentially the same office, their titles, *arumponé* and *payung riLuwuq* respectively, were specific to their countries. The role of the paramount ruler also differed. For example, the arumponé was generally more authoritarian than the Wajorese arung matoa. Such variations, however, were subject to the desire and capacity of particular rulers to enforce their authority.[18] Despite such variations and a few notable exceptions, autocracy was generally not permitted among paramount rulers in South Sulawesi. There were numerous obstacles to despotism, not the least of which was *adat* or customary law. A ruler would lose his or her authority if he or she did not rule according to adat that stipulated that the autonomy of local communities be respected.[19] A Wajorese example of this is Arung Matoa La Samaléwa (r. 1612–1616) who was deposed because of his arbitrary actions.[20] The state and the adat existed independently of the ruler, and he or she was expected to serve the state's interest, not vice versa.[21]

Wajorese Political Structure

Wajoq is now a kabupaten or regency of the Indonesian province of South Sulawesi. Politically independent until 1906, it was effectively a federative ethno-nation consisting of three main limpo, namely Talotenreng, Tua and Béttémpola. The paramount ruler, or arung matoa, was elected and was assisted by thirty-nine other officials. Whereas other Bugis kingdoms also had ruling councils, Wajoq's was particularly extensive. The *Petta Ennengngé* (the "Six Lords") consisted of six offices, two each for Béttémpola, Talotenréng and Tua. Each of these three limpo had its own regent known as a *ranreng* and its own army chief called *Pabbaté Lompo* or *Baté Lompo*[22] or simply *Baté*, which literally means banner. Their titles originate from the color of the banner that they carry: *Pilla* (scarlet), *Patola* (multi-colored) and *Cakkoridi* (yellow).[23] Although the Wajorese chronicles state that the rulers of the three divisions had the same rank, it appears that in practice the *Petta Pilla* was the chief commander during war, and the *Petta Béttémpola* was the highest ranking during peace time.[24] These six lords were at least as powerful as the arung matoa[25] and together with him they constituted Wajoq's highest ruling council, the *Petta Wajoq*. The Petta Wajoq is described in the folktale commonly referred to as *Pau Pau Rikadong,* the most widely known of Wajorese origin stories, as being sufficient for purposes of government, yet in practice there were still more officials. Each limpo had a courier for conveying messages; four *arung mabbicara* or deliberating judges, charged with solving problems relating to adat; and six *arung paddokki-rokki*, or deliberators. Ideally, this made for a total of forty lords known as the *Arung Patampulu*.[26] The representative nature of this council facilitated cohesion within the Wajorese state while the system of messengers allowed for cooperation among its constituent polities. It did not, however, provide for equal representation of each division within Wajoq. The lands to the north, known as Pitumpanua ("The Seven Lands") were not formally represented in the Arung Patampulu. Other constituents were only indirectly represented, such as Paria, which had its own government and own arung underneath the jurisdiction of the ranreng Béttémpola.[27] Furthermore, the various positions within the Arung Patampulu could be left vacant. Indeed, in the nineteenth century James Brooke recorded that the office of arung matoa was vacant and that there was little haste to fill it.[28]

The various constituent polities of Wajoq were also joined to the center by bilateral agreements as established by treaties concluded at various times throughout its history. Common throughout South Sulawesi, such treaties outlined the rights and responsibilities of both ruler and ruled, or determined the status of a polity in regard to another polity. These relationships were generally expressed in terms such as mother and child, or in even more metaphorical ones such as wind and leaves; the metaphor being that the people's direction is dictated by the ruler as leaves are blown by the wind. In this manner, treaties established a hierarchy of polities both within Wajoq and among the states of South Sulawesi that allowed each to maintain its sovereignty.[29] One such treaty was the Majauleng Treaty that was concluded between the population of Wajoq and their ruler La Tenribali. La Tenribali's reign can be dated to the early fifteenth century[30] and it is around this time that the early polity Cinnotabiq changed its name to Wajoq. The Majauleng Treaty stipulated that all polities within Wajoq respect each other's sovereignty, adat, judicial processes, and property, and that they help each other to remember and to do the right thing if confused.[31] An example of a treaty concluded between kingdoms is the Treaty of Timurung (1582), which stipulated that the three participating kingdoms were "brothers," albeit unequal brothers, and that they would support and respect each other. It compared the three lands to a rope in which a single string did not break but rather reinforced the others.[32]

The traditional Wajorese political system was extremely flexible. Not only did the constituent polities of Wajoq have their own adat, but also some of them had their own regalia and origin myths.[33] Indeed, the 17th century Dutch Admiral Cornelis Janszoon Speelman referred to Wajoq as "a number of small kingdoms or lands, bound to each other . . . but with their own freedoms since time immemorial."[34] Despite the existence of a paramount ruler, obeisance to the will of the people as voiced by their representatives was crucial to Wajorese kingship. Whereas other Bugis kingdoms had councils of nobles, they were not generally as powerful nor as numerous as the Wajorese Forty Lords who represented the various constituents of Wajoq. Other kingdoms also had a hierarchy leading to the top, but the Wajorese community was looser and less stable. Thus, despite the minute gradations of status in the Wajorese hierarchy,[35] there was greater opportunity for achievement-based advancement in Wajoq than in other Bugis kingdoms.[36] Social flexibility and freedom for the constituent polities therefore appear as hallmarks of traditional Wajorese society.

A number of systems served to promote unity within Wajoq. Among the most important of these were kin networks, which are discussed at length in chapter 5. Because family relations were pivotal to a state's foreign and domestic relations, marriage was a key mechanism for consolidating the state. One Wajorese example of this practice is found in the strategic marriages of Arung Matoa La Galigo To Suni (r. 1703–1711) and his children. La Galigo

To Suni himself married Petta Wé Maddanaca, the daughter of Arung Bét-témpola. She then became the ruler of Bila. They had two children named La Sangaji Dongkongé and Wé Tenrilawa Bessé. The former became ruler of Pénéki and the latter became ruler of Bila.[37] Such family relations fostered cohesion within the state and may have facilitated La Galigo To Suni's plans to strengthen Wajoq during the early eighteenth century.

A second means of promoting unity within the state was requiring constituent polities to provide contributions to state projects. One such project was the construction of a *baruga* (meeting hall) during the reign of Arung Matoa La Matoneq To Sakkeq (r. ca. 1702–1703). Like the central mosque, the baruga itself had the potential to promote unity within Wajoq. It served both as a location for state assemblies and as a hall for the recital of sacred texts. However, the requirement that constituent polities of Wajoq contribute to its construction was also key because the contributions functioned as a sort of tribute to the over-arching Wajorese state. Sanctions were imposed upon those who refused to formally recognize the center in this manner. More common than the construction of edifices was the expectation that the people contribute to state ceremonies or feasts in celebration of high-ranking individuals' marriages, ear-piercings or the like.

There were also cultural and psychological elements to Wajorese cohesion. Like other ethnic groups, the Wajorese have a distinct myth-symbol complex including their landscape, their origin myths, their culture and their history that serves as a *mythomoteur*.[38] At the heart of this myth-symbol complex are the Wajorese origin stories. While these are discussed in chapter 6, it is noteworthy to mention now that they all present Wajoq as a land of settlement and accord high status to the founding figures. Origin myths according different, higher origins to rulers than to commoners exemplify what Peter Bellwood calls a "founder-focused ideology" in which kin-group founders are revered and sometimes deified.[39] Their very nobility is a source of pride for the community. Furthermore, family linkages legitimized by such origin myths and loyalty to this lineage are important cohesive forces within the state.

Also worthy of mention, especially in an introduction to Wajoq, is the landscape that also forms an important element of any ethnic group's myth-symbol complex. Among the Wajorese, two features of the landscape are particularly important. The first of these is the trees after which Wajoq and a number of its constituent polities were named. Trees, especially those with more than forty branches, are revered among the Bugis.[40] Wajoq was purportedly established near a *bajoq* tree which bequeathed its name to the state. A number of Wajoq's constituent polities are named after trees as well, specifically Awoq, Bélawa, Kaluku, Pénrang, Paria, and Rumpia.[41] Another feature of the landscape that spiritually unifies Wajoq is the hill known as Pattiro Sompe on the edge of Séngkang. Lucie van Mens describes how elderly people climb this hill on the edge of Séngkang from the top of which one can see out over Wajoq. According to legend, the founders of Wajoq are buried there and they still help the Wajorese population. People who are sick, cannot resolve personal disputes, or cannot conceive a child climb up the hill and leave an offering, such as sticky rice in banana leaves, and after they are helped, do this repeatedly throughout their lives.[42] While this tradition may be a recent invention, it shows a consciousness of Wajoq as a unit.

The community's spiritual unity was also enhanced by pre-Islamic priests known as *bissu.*[43] Considered to contain both male and female elements, bissu served as intermediaries between the mundane and spiritual worlds and, in some instances, as keepers of the regalia. Extrinsically linked to the traditions of the Bugis cosmogonic myth *I La Galigo,*[44] they read and guarded these and other texts, thereby promoting these texts' sanctity. Their participation was vital to certain cyclical rituals intended to assure the prosperity of the land and the perpetuation of ruling house.[45] The bissu also served as spiritual advisors to the rulers and in this manner could wield considerable influence.[46] They promoted tradition, respect for the spiritual realm, and reverence for the rulers, thereby serving as a cohesive force within the state.

Among the peoples of South Sulawesi, notions of community are also linked to the indigenous concepts of *siriq* and *pessé.* The concept of siriq incorporates the ideas of both shame and self-worth. The combination of the two does not pose an inherent contradiction because it is believed that one cannot feel shame without possessing a sense of self-worth. So valuable is this sense of self-worth that people will risk their lives to restore it. The term "pessé" literally means "spicy," but has come to mean both pain and commiseration with one's community. Pessé is linked to siriq because the feelings of shame create the pain.[47] The concepts have the potential to unify a community in several ways. First of all, the idea that a community can feel pain as a whole reinforces its spiritual unity. Secondly, both siriq and pessé can be relieved through action that can be undertaken by the community as a whole. Finally, the concepts serve to remind individuals of their place within the community because an individual's self-worth is closely linked to his or her position within the community, particularly in the status-conscious societies of South Sulawesi. Thus the linked concepts of siriq and pessé can generate a particularly strong sense of community. Pessé can also be felt outside of the homeland. The homesickness that the soldiers in western Sumatra felt, and the sense of community that inspired the Wajorese residing in Makassar to repay the debts of a merchants whose house had burned down, both described in the following chapters, are examples of pessé.

From the above examination of the Wajorese political system and its cultural bases, it appears that the idea of Wajoqness is conceptually linked to the land, to the founders, to the governing council, to specific adat requirements, and to certain South Sulawesi-wide concepts such as siriq and pessé. The system was complex yet flexible and it allowed for essentially autonomous communities to participate in the greater unity despite being located at a distance from the center. As this study will show, this participation was not limited to the three main constituent polities and their subdivisions. Overseas communities participated in Wajorese statecraft as well. Indeed, the links between the polity and the overseas Wajorese communities resemble the links within the polity among its numerous individual parts. Particularly during the eighteenth century, Wajoq depended heavily on its overseas communities to advance political goals of the homeland. Family relations, leaders, money and weapons all crossed Wajoq's boundaries to such an extent that the overseas communities resembled constituent polities of the state. Physically separated from Wajoq by vast expanses of sea, Wajorese migrants had the option of severing all ties with Wajoq and adopting a new identity. Undoubtedly a number of Wajorese chose this and their identities and histories have been absorbed by their host communities. Yet numerous other communities opted to maintain their ties with Wajoq and their Wajorese identity. Their history remained entwined with that of Wajoq. This involvement did not preclude acting in their own best interest as dictated by local circumstances, but in some circumstances it did entail participating in Wajorese networks and contributing to Wajoq.

Early Wajorese History

The earliest histories of Wajoq, of which there are numerous versions, are stories of exile and settlement. The *Lontaraq Sukkuqna Wajoq,* for example, recounts how a noble named La Paukkeq out on a hunting expedition found and decided to settle in an area with wide fields, thick forests with wild boars, deer, and buffalo, and numerous lakes replete with fish.[48] Although the establishment of a settlement by roaming pioneers is a common feature of Bugis chronicles,[49] it is particularly conspicuous in the Wajorese case. There exists a multiplicity of origin stories that depict various arrivals, suggesting that there were numerous early settlements. A pervasive feature of these varied myths is that the Wajorese ruler never comes from Wajoq itself. While the concept of a stranger-king portrayed in these tales is common among Austronesian societies, what is striking about the Wajorese origin myths is that the land itself is portrayed as a frontier.

Wajorese legal texts also indicate that migration was important to early political history. The Cinnotabiq Treaty[50] explicitly guaranteed the people the freedom to enter and leave as they please for their livelihood and welfare. A later treaty, the Lappadeppaq Treaty,[51] does not specifically mention the right to migrate yet at the ceremony in which it was concluded, the right to migrate was reiterated. After burying a stone to solemnize the treaty, La Tiringeng To Taba spoke to all of the people attending, promising them freedom to leave, enter and reside in Wajoq at will. As mentioned in the introduction, he is recorded as saying "the door of Wajoq shall be open when they enter; the door of Wajoq shall be open when they leave; they enter on their own feet and they leave on their own feet."[52] When asked why he did not promise that before burying the rock, he replied that this freedom was simply Wajorese customary law. So engrained was this right that La Tiringeng To Taba found it unnecessary to mention it.

In the early modern era shifts in power within South Sulawesi created a situation that gave new meaning and urgency to Wajorese migration. As Luwuq, the peninsula's mightiest state during the fifteenth century, declined during the sixteenth century, agricultural kingdoms emerged farther south in the peninsula. Wajoq emerged as one of the major Bugis polities around the turn of the sixteenth century during the reign of the energetic Arung Matoa La Tanampareq Puang ri Maqgalatung, who is remembered for being a just, ambitious, clever, wise, and patient ruler.[53] As Wajoq's influence grew, Luwuq's relationship with Wajoq became more egalitarian. The balance of power further shifted after Luwuq launched an unsuccessful attack on Boné during which the royal standard of Luwuq was captured, and Boné eclipsed Luwuq as the paramount power on the eastern half of the peninsula.[54] Meanwhile, the twin kingdoms of Gowa and Talloq expanded into one of the most powerful states in eastern Indonesia.[55] After Gowa and Boné launched a combined attack on Luwuq and forced it to sign a treaty with Gowa, Wajoq became a vassal of Gowa.[56]

Wajoq proved to be exceptionally loyal to its new overlord. When asked to join an alliance with Boné and Soppéng in 1582, Arung Matoa La Mangkaceq To Udama (c. 1567–c. 1607) specified that Wajoq was a slave of Gowa and that this would not change, even if they concluded a treaty of brotherhood among the three of them. The three Bugis kingdoms then agreed to the previously mentioned Treaty of Timurung or *Lamumpatué ri Timurung* ("the burying of stones in Timurung") and its member states became known as the Tellumpocco, or "The Three Peaks." Essentially a defensive alliance against Gowa, it served its purpose temporarily and Gowa's attacks on Wajoq in 1582 and 1590, and on Boné in 1585 and 1588, were all repulsed or otherwise foiled.[57]

Gowa nevertheless succeeded in assuming a paramount position in the peninsula. Together with its twin-kingdom Talloq, Gowa expanded its sphere of influence by trading internationally and championing Islam.[58] The Tellumpocco even surrendered control of its external affairs to Gowa, an arrangement which was an acknowledgement of Gowa's overlordship but allowed the Tellumpocco to preserve its pride.[59] Then, during the second quarter of the seventeenth century, the ruler of Boné challenged Gowa's new role as effective overlord of the entire peninsula and champion of the Islamic faith. Arumponé La Maddaremmeng (1626–1643) forced a new, stricter version of Islam onto his people. When he tried to export this version of Islam to neighboring kingdoms, Gowa viewed his attempt as not just a religious issue, but also a question of sovereignty. Thus, when La Maddaremmeng's emancipation of all non-hereditary slaves provoked his own mother, Datu Pattiro Wé Tenrisoloreng, to lead a rebellion against him, Gowa was prepared to assist the rebels.[60]

Meanwhile, as tensions between Boné and Gowa intensified, a conflict developed between Boné and Wajoq. Whether for religious or political reasons, La Maddaremmeng attacked Pénéki in Wajoq. When the arung matoa demanded restitution of the goods seized in Pénéki, La Maddaremmeng refused, and war broke out between Boné and Wajoq.[61] In this conflict, Gowa sided with Wajoq and criticized Boné. Sultan Malikussaid (r. 1639–1653) asked La Maddaremmeng if his actions were based on Islam, adat or just on his own whim. When he did not respond, Gowa, Wajoq, and Soppéng attacked Boné at Passémpe in October 1643. Boné was soundly defeated and punished with unusually harsh and humiliating conditions for peace. While normal procedure would have been to demand the payment of a war tribute and the signing of a treaty placing Boné in a subordinate position, Gowa insisted that the new regent To Balaq be made accountable to the Makassarese lord Karaéng Sumannaq. Boné then revolted, and was soundly defeated at Passémpe. Thereafter, Boné was again harshly punished. With the exception of To Balaq, who had remained neutral and was allowed to keep his position, all of the Bonéan nobles were exiled to Gowa to prevent further rebellion, and Boné was reduced to the status of Gowa's slave.[62] Boné also lost a number of "disputed" territories to Wajoq, and many Bonéans were forced into corvée labor for Wajoq.[63] Boné was humiliated like never before and its resentment towards both Gowa and Wajoq grew. Eventually animosity between Bonéan and Wajorese migrants in the diaspora would be keenly felt.

Gowa emerged from this period as the region's most formidable political and economic power. In an attempt to check Gowa's power, Boné and Soppéng sought to revive the moribund Tellumpocco, but the third peak, Wajoq, declined. Although Wajoq had previously suffered Gowa's overlordship in a master-slave relationship, in the mid-seventeenth century Wajoq's recent experiences with Gowa were much more positive than those with Boné. Furthermore, the Wajorese still remembered La Maddaremmeng's brutal attack on Pénéki, and feared the extreme version of Islam that he advocated. Especially because Wajoq enjoyed the status of Gowa's ally, it is not surprising that Wajoq wished to align itself with Gowa. Wajoq's fierce loyalty to Gowa was to have far reaching consequences during and after the Makassar War.

The Makassar War

The Makassar War was the culmination of the long-standing conflict between the VOC which sought to monopolize the world spice trade, and Gowa, who wanted to maintain its position of paramountcy in eastern Indonesia. Gowa steadfastly refused to enter restrictive trading agreements with the VOC and Gowa's own aggressive open-door commercial policy threatened the VOC's monopolistic aims.[64] Eventually, the VOC and Gowa reached an impasse. In April 1660 the Dutch proposed yet another commercial treaty, which Sultan Hasanuddin (r. 1653-1669) eloquently rejected.[65] His refusal prompted the Dutch to attack Makassar. Although the attack was successful it was a Pyrrhic victory and the Dutch ended up withdrawing from their base at Fort Paqnakkukang.[66] Anticipating further conflict, Gowa tried to extract corvée labor from its Bugis vassals to build fortifications, which eventually resulted in the rebellion of Boné and Soppéng. Gowa was able to quell this rebellion within half a year and harshly treated the resultant prisoners of war, further sowing seeds of resentment. From this contemptuous situation there emerged an extremely charismatic Bonéan leader who vowed to liberate his people from Gowa's overlordship. Most commonly known as Arung Palakka (ca. 1635–1696), he is also known as Malampéqé Gemmeqna meaning "the long-haired one" because he vowed not to cut his hair until Boné was liberated.

Arung Palakka fled in late 1660 or early 1661 to the island of Butung of the southeast coast of Sulawesi and from there, with Dutch help, to Batavia. The Dutch themselves evacuated Makassar in 1662 when the lives of 15 Dutchmen came into question.[67] Having been vaguely promised a war against Gowa in exchange for their help, Arung Palakka and his followers assisted the Dutch in their campaign against the Minangkabau in western Sumatra. Arung Palakka distinguished himself in this military campaign and succeeded in convincing the Dutch that he and other Bugis exiles would be a valuable ally in any campaign against Gowa. When the VOC returned to Makassar in late 1666 under the leadership of Admiral Cornelis Janszoon Speelman, Arung Palakka accompanied them wearing the uniform of a Dutch officer complete with military decorations. While the official intent of this mission was to show the strength of the VOC and its readiness to wage war against Gowa, Speelman exceeded his authority and essentially conquered Gowa in what became known as the Makassar War.[68] Given the tremendous anti-Gowa sentiment in Boné and elsewhere, people were quick to rally around Arung Palakka and he became the linchpin of the campaign.

Unable or unwilling to conclude peace with the Makassarese, Speelman and Arung Palakka attacked. The Makassarese offered stiff resistance, but Dutch naval capabilities provided the VOC with a critical edge.[69] After Gowa's situation grew desperate, the two sides began negotiations which eventually resulted in the signing of the Treaty of Bungaya on November 18, 1667. Highly disadvantageous for Gowa, and unusually harsh within the indigenous political context, it demanded that Gowa make 26 concessions. Among these were payment of a war indemnity; destruction of fortifications; renunciation of overlordship over the VOC's Bugis allies; expulsion of non-Dutch Europeans from Makassar; the surrender of control over the port of Makassar and the northern fort of Ujung Pandang; and abandonment of Gowa's loyal vassals who had fought against the VOC, namely Wajoq, Bulo-Bulo, and Mandar.[70] Dutch sources record that shortly after the signing of this treaty, refugees started leaving South Sulawesi.[71] Yet the Bungaya Treaty did not put an end to the war and fighting recommenced in April 1668.[72] When the royal citadel Sombaopu finally fell on June 24, 1669, this symbolized the complete economic and political demise of Gowa.[73] The *Gowa Chronicle* also ends with the death of Sultan Hasanuddin as if the Makassarese no longer found it appropriate to record their history in the same manner.[74]

During its long struggle to resist Dutch encroachment, Gowa lost most of its allies. As it became apparent that the balance of power in the peninsula had shifted, most of Gowa's vassals gradually deserted. Wajoq was among the few vassals that remained loyal to Gowa throughout the war.[75]

Wajorese Impressions of the War

The intense loyalty that the Wajorese people felt to Gowa was a matter of siriq for the Wajorese. Wajorese historical sources present the Makassar War in a manner that glorifies Wajoq's faithfulness and bravery. This is especially apparent in episodes about Arung Matoa To Sengngeng's refusal to surrender and his unwillingness to abide by the Bungaya Treaty.

After the Bungaya Treaty had been signed, Arumponé La Maddaremmeng had tried to get the Arung Matoa La Tenrilai To Sengngeng (1658–1670) to abide by their mutual treaty, but the latter rejected these overtures in favor of Gowa's (Sultan Hasanuddin's) pleas for support.[76] The Wajorese residing in Makassar appear to have joined the conflict and fought on the side of Gowa. According to the LSW, when To Sengngeng himself arrived in Makassar, they fought all the more courageously.[77] At one point, the Wajorese were attacked and "2370 heads were made to dance in front of Arung Matoa To Sengngeng's face, 1300 heads of Soppéngers were hacked off by Wajorese. 504 Wajorese died."[78] Yet Wajoq still refused to give up. As late as May 1669 Wajoq and Cenrana sent 2,000 to 3,000 men to Gowa as reinforcements.[79]

The story of Arung Matoa La Tenrilai To Sengngeng's refusal to admit defeat is an exceptionally poignant episode in Wajorese historiography. The LSW relates how, when Arung Matoa To Sengngeng learned of the fall of Sombaopu and the need for Wajoq to attend now to its own welfare, " . . . tears came into La Tenrilai's eyes, his upper arm became tense as he pressed down upon the handle of his keris and said: 'Ten thousand men from Wajoq accompanied me here [to Makassar]. Let them all die before Gowa is taken.'"[80] This exchange is related similarly in other lontaraq yet the version quoted here is the most picturesque; no other version portrays the Wajorese leader as being so emotional. In this episode, To Sengngeng is portrayed as so exceptionally loyal that it is almost as if the episode was included to help Wajoq maintain its dignity.

After the war, Boné and the Dutch both sought reconciliation with Wajoq through their own channels. One lontaraq goes into particular detail about Boné's attempts to sway Wajoq. Arung Palakka went to Lamuru where he met with Bonéans and Soppéngers and they decided to remind Wajoq of the Treaty of Timurung. They went to Solo where they instructed To Sawa to go to the arung matoa. To Sawa told the arung matoa and the Wajorese, "I bring a message from your family Malampéqé Gemmeqna. Boné, Wajoq and Soppéng can only prosper if we adhere to the Tellumpocco, with each of us administering our own laws and each of us minding our own business." Wajoq replied:

> You are exactly right, but you Boné, are the one who strays, to the point of going together with Soppéng and calling the Dutch here. Wajoq greatly fears God. Wajoq is very ashamed to abandon its agreement with the Karaéng, ashamed to turn its back on its agreement with Karaéng Gowa. The death of Gowa is my death, the life of Gowa is the life of Wajoq.

To Sawa replied:

> Your family holds fast without slipping, as is witnessed by God and known by God, the death of Gowa is your death, Gowa's life is your life. Your family is only trying to guide you to goodness and brightness, but you do not want [to listen], because Gowa's death is your death. Go then to your death and we will go to our life.

To Sawa then concluded by reminding Wajoq about various aspects of the treaty, such as reminding each other in case of forgetfulness, not coveting each other's gold, and not abandoning the treaty.[81]

Such accounts foster pessé and promote unity within the Wajorese community. While they may have been recorded years after the events they describe, they exemplify distinctly Wajorese sentiments about the Makassar War. Furthermore, they offer dignity in consolation for the torment that Wajoq endured at the hands of the Bonéans during the aftermath of the Makassar War.

Attack on Wajoq

For its steadfast loyalty to Gowa, Wajoq paid a particularly high price. In August 1670, Arung Palakka set out to subdue Wajoq. First he attacked Lamuru, which surrendered voluntarily. A force of 3,000 men from (presumably repentant) Lamuru then joined in the punitive expedition against Wajoq.[82] Upon hearing of the impending attack, Pammana and Pénéki both deserted Wajoq and joined Arung Palakka; and so when the contingent finally invaded Wajoq, it consisted of some 40,000 men. The invasion itself presented no problem, because much of the population had fled to the walled city of Tosora, the seizure of which proved to be the real challenge.

In spite of the fact that Tosora had only recently been founded sometime between 1660 and 1666,[83] and had recently been damaged in a fire,[84] it nevertheless was well defended. Both sides fought earnestly without defeating the other. The fighting was intense and so many Wajorese people died that they were not able to recover and assemble the corpses. After four days and nights, the Wajorese asked for a cease-fire to bury their dead. An estimated 1,300 Wajorese died in this siege, including the Arung Matoa himself. La Tenrilai To Sengngeng was given the posthumous names *Mpélaié ngngi musuqna* ("he who left the war") and *Jammenga ri lao-laona* ("he who died by his cannon.")[85] Apparently he misloaded a cannon, having forgotten to close the place for the fuse. He was replaced by La Paliliq To Malu Puanna Gellaq (1670–1679).[86]

After To Sengngeng's untimely death, a number of Wajorese vassals switched loyalty and sided with Boné. One lontaraq describes a meeting of Wajorese politicians to discuss this.[87] *Limpoé seWajoq* (the Wajorese people) pointed out to Arung Matoa Puanna La Gellaq that all of the Wajorese vassals to the north of the Cenrana River, as well as those on the eastern extreme of the land, had become Bonéan vassals; that Limampanuaé as well as half of both Gilireng and Bélawa had become Boné's slaves. Wagé and Totinco were also made slaves, and only Sompeq remained free. After the death of To Sengngeng even more vassals had switched sides, including Pammana and Tua, because the ranreng Tua was related to the Bonéans. Puanna La Gellaq then pointed out that the people of Tua could indeed not be trusted, and even accused them of having intentionally let the enemy into Tosora. He asked Limpoé seWajoq what Wajoq should do. They replied that there were at least 10,000 men who could still bear arms, and that there remained a number of loyal vassals. Furthermore, there were still Wajorese slave-polities who could be ordered to run amok. Arung Matoa Puanna La Gellaq agreed, but pointed out a number of things that he thought could result in the defeat of the Wajorese. First was their lack of ammunition. He pointed out that the Bonéans were much better supplied because of the Dutch. Second was the infidelity of the many vassals who had deserted Wajoq. He suggested that eventually all of Wajoq's vassals might follow suit. Finally, he mourned the loss of To Sengngeng. According to Puanna La Gellaq, no one in Wajoq matched the bravery of their former leader.[88]

The situation was indeed desperate. So many Wajorese perished that they were not even able to bury them all.[89] The Wajorese were forced to abandon Tosora's outer fortifications, but the city itself continued to hold out. The siege of Tosora actually lasted four months, but numerous sources claim that it lasted longer.[90] Over-estimations of Wajorese tenacity reflect the siriq attached to this resistance. Tosora actually fell on December 1, 1670.[91] Arung Palakka and his forces continuously received reinforcements from the Dutch, and were eventually able to subdue the Wajorese.

According to Dutch reports, the Wajorese had shown great bravery.[92] Several reasons have been suggested as to why they held out for so long. First, Mandar and Gowa had pledged their continued support. Secondly, the Wajorese likely feared that, given their prior refusal to reaffirm the Tellumpocco, Boné's retribution would be excessively harsh.[93] This indeed turned out to be the case.

The entire government of Wajoq, consisting of the signatories Puanna Gellaq, *Cakkuridi Wajoq* La Pedapi, *Patola Wajoq* La Pangngambong, and *Pillaq Wajoq* La Lakkiqbaja,[94] as well as lesser officials, went to Fort Rotterdam in Makassar to "humiliate themselves"[95] and formally surrender to the Dutch. The majority of Wajorese chronicles make no mention of it, but this surrender still entered Wajorese historical consciousness. It is recorded separately as a treaty,[96] and it appears in the LSW. This even provides the dates of the fall of Tosora, the conclusion of the agreement and its signing, as well as name of the Dutch Governor Maximilian de Jong.[97] It describes how they swore upon the Qur'an, surrendered their weapons and drank "weapon water"[98] and signed a written treaty that was to apply to their grandchildren as well as themselves. These ceremonies are also described in Dutch accounts.[99]

The articles of the treaty as they appear in the LSW are the same as they appear in Dutch records. They state that 1) Wajoq was now a vassal of the VOC and that the Wajorese were permitted to reside in Wajoq, but must accept Dutch mediation in their external political affairs; 2) after the death of an arung matoa, the Wajorese were not to appoint another ruler independently according to their custom but instead to have their choice approved by the VOC; 3) all fortifications in Wajoq were to be destroyed and new ones could be built only with the approval of the VOC; 4) the Wajorese were not permitted to admit any Europeans or Indians (including Malays, Javanese, and Moors) into their land; 5) the Wajorese were forbidden to trade anywhere besides Bali, along the Javanese coast to Batavia, and on Borneo without first obtaining passes from the VOC; 6) any European seeking refuge in Wajoq must be returned to the company; 7) the Wajorese were to uphold the Treaty of Bungaya in so far as it applied to them; 8) the Wajorese were to pay a war indemnity of 52,000 *rijksdaalders* (Dutch silver coins) over a period of four monsoons in gold, silver or jewels; and 9) the conditions of this agreement were solemnly sworn on the Koran and by the drinking of kris or weapon water, and were to apply to all the people of Wajoq.[100]

Harsh as this treaty was, the actual treatment of the Wajorese following their surrender was much harsher. The new effective overlord of South Sulawesi, Arung Palakka, carried a grudge against both Wajoq and Gowa. He employed his best soldiers to attack Wajoq[101] and induced a state of misery previously unknown in Wajoq. The animosity between the Wajorese and the Bonéans was also carried overseas, as will be discussed in chapters 3 (politics) and 5 (identity).

One aspect of his campaign against Wajoq was kidnapping. Countless slaves were seized from the Wajorese. Women, children, and lower-ranking men were also kidnapped and presumably enslaved. Although the nobles suffered less, they were also affected.[102] Another aspect of this campaign was Bonéan harassment of the Wajorese, which carried on to such an extent that the population in Wajorese areas bordering Boné declined. If a Bonéan wanted something belonging to a Wajorese, he would simply seize it without asking. Fishermen were forced to transport Bonéans across Lake Témpé. If a Wajorese tried to resist the demands of the Bonéans, he would be slapped or even killed. In the face of such continuous torment, there were incidents of Wajorese people running amok, in spite of the known severity of the punishment.[103]

The territory of Wajoq was also dismembered. After To Sengngeng's untimely death, all of the Wajorese vassals north of the Cenrana River switched loyalty and sided with Boné, as did half of both Bélawa and Gilireng.[104] Technically, Pammana remained under Wajoq but its devotion to Boné was greater.[105] Among the vassals that in theory were left to Wajoq were Sompeq, Kalola, Bila, Ugiq Beruku, Boto and Otting.[106] After the war, however, these were under Bonéan control, and Arung Palakka further diminished Wajoq's territory by seizing Timurung and Pitampanua. The loss of these last two territories was particularly significant because it entailed the loss of Wajoq's access to the sea via the Cenrana River. In Wajoq's greatly reduced territory, the people were forced to undergo the further humiliation and trials of prohibitions against the use of metal farm implements.

Already in 1671, the Wajorese were forced to turn to the Dutch for help. The Dutch admonished the Bonéans to cease their oppressive practices but this had little effect. Finally, they asked Arung Palakka, who wielded tremendous influence among his people, to prevent the Bonéans from harassing the Wajorese.[107] The Dutch, however, were well aware of Arung Palakka's animosity toward the Wajorese, and so the sincerity of their request is suspect. Indeed, some Dutch records say that the Wajorese should have expected nothing less than their punishment and that they actually deserved Arung Palakka's harsh treatment.[108]

The war indemnity was a substantial burden. According to the contract of January 1671, the Wajorese were required to pay 52,000 rijksdaalder*s* within four monsoons. They paid 7,800 *mas* of it promptly in gold and slaves. In June, the Dutch sent an envoy to collect more, but he received only 700 rijksdaalders. The Wajorese government said that they could not obtain more than that from their impoverished people.[109] By the end of 1671, the Wajorese had only paid 8,800 mas, or about a third of the indemnity. They again complained about their inability to pay, and requested that this debt be pardoned. There was some Dutch recognition of Wajorese poverty, and some officials thought that the Wajorese should not be taxed beyond their means. Yet it did not appear to the Dutch that the Wajorese had lost all their money and gold, and thus the request was denied.[110] In 1675 the debt was still not settled and the Wajorese promised to pay 1,500 rijksdaalders by the end of October.[111]

In 1678, Wajorese again sought the assistance of the Dutch. The arung matoa went to Makassar and appealed to the VOC for the restoration of the Wajorese lands of Pammana, Timurung, Wagé, Totinco, Wugiq, and Séngkang that Boné had seized, ostensibly according to the treaty of 1670. The Dutch president, Jacob Cops, verified that the treaty did not stipulate any cession of lands to Boné and assured Wajoq that he would seek some sort of resolution to the problem. A year later, when the arung matoa came to Fort Rotterdam again, Cops asked him about the state of affairs in Wajoq. The arung matoa replied by covering his mouth with one hand and sliding the other across his throat, thereby indicating that he would lose his life if he said anything. He then said that since the VOC and Arung Palakka were one, and Wajoq was defeated by the VOC, that the Wajorese were considered Arung Palakka's slaves. Cops responded by explaining to the Arung Matoa that Arung Palakka and the VOC were not one and the same; that according to the treaty Wajoq was not a slave of Boné but rather a subject of the company; and that as such Wajoq should report to the VOC any abuses suffered at the hands of Boné. A few days later, a Wajorese delegation presented the Dutch with a list of grievances, among which were the seizure of 3,000 Wajorese people together with their buffaloes and possessions; the kidnapping of many Wajorese who were in Luwuq at the time of the Luwuq-Boné War in 1676; and the forced relocation of many skilled Wajorese and their families to Boné.[112] Cops was sympathetic but did not act because the Dutch were counting upon the support of Arung Palakka and his troops in an expedition against Java. When the expedition left, the Arung Matoa demanded restitution of the seized goods and people, but the Bonéan leaders argued that they could not do anything while Arung Palakka was absent.[113] As the Dutch were too dependent upon Arung Palakka to risk alienating him, they left the Wajorese at his mercy. What the Dutch did not imagine is that Wajoq would effectively harness the power of its emigrants, that the balance of power would shift, and that Wajoq would become a force with which to be reckoned.

Wajorese Migration in Historical Perspective

An examination of Wajoq's earliest history reveals that migration has always played a role in the lives of its people. All of the Wajorese origin myths attribute foreign origins to the first Wajorese leaders, and the chronicles present Wajoq itself as a land of colonization. Furthermore, the right to migrate is encoded in the Wajorese system of government. These factors reflect the centrality of migration in the constructed reality of the Wajorese people. Furthermore, recent archaeological research suggests that the foundation of Luwuq, once believed to be the cradle of Bugis civilization, was likely influenced by migrants from the Cenrana valley. Clearly, then, migration played a central role in Wajoq's pre- and early history. These early emigrants may have been in search of iron for use in the agricultural development of their homeland.

Wajorese emigration during the early modern era did not constitute a radical break from the past, but it became much more intense following the Makassar War. The intensely difficult conditions in Wajoq after the Makassar War and the inability to obtain Dutch protection forced many Wajorese to emigrate. The LSW specifically states that it was after the fall of Tosora and the signing of the treaty with the Dutch that many Wajorese emigrated.[114] While the Wajorese were not alone in emigrating,[115] their feelings of siriq and pessé were intensified during the Makassar War and its aftermath, as is clearly reflected in Wajorese lontaraq. In Smithian terms, the Makassar War is a classic example of the manner in which warfare can strengthen a community's identity.[116] Given the state of affairs in South Sulawesi, migration was virtually the only way of redeeming themselves. Indeed, while individual migrants may not have realized it at the time, their contributions were to become essential in Wajoq's plans for refortification in the early eighteenth century.

CHAPTER THREE

Overseas Politics

Located strategically at the crossroads of major trading routes, Southeast Asia's history is one of continuous interaction with the outside world. This interaction intensified between the fifteenth and eighteenth centuries with the rise of Chinese and European interest and commerce in the region. Whereas Southeast Asian politics had long incorporated foreign influences, during the early modern era mobility, fluidity, and cosmopolitanism became hallmarks of Southeast Asian politics, especially but not exclusively in the port cities. Migrants were valued for their international contacts, their goods and wealth, and their knowledge and skills. Thus, in contrast to other regions, migrants in early modern Southeast Asia generally did not form pariah communities sequestered from the mainstream. Rather, they played an important role in shaping the histories of their host societies, politically, commercially and culturally. There were, of course, more receptive and less receptive societies within Southeast Asia, but overall there was a tendency to absorb, personalize, and domesticate desirable foreign influences.

Such an environment was favorable to the Wajorese migrants. Nevertheless, like all diaspora, they still had to adapt to local circumstances. Each of the four areas covered in this study, Makassar, eastern Kalimantan, the Malay world and western Sumatra, offered unique opportunities and challenges to Wajorese migrants. Moreover each of these areas had their own ways of dealing with migrants. In all of these areas, the Wajorese integrated into, superimposed themselves upon, contributed to, or competed with local power structures.

In the interests of the majority of readers who, it is presumed, are either more interested in diaspora than Southeast Asia or who are already

knowledgeable about Southeast Asia, the background information about local political conditions is limited to the absolute essentials. Readers requiring more information are requested to consult the bibliography. Nevertheless, because the Wajorese invariably had to contend with local systems of
power, some context is absolutely essential to understanding the variety of
Wajorese experiences.

Makassar

While South Sulawesi enjoys a central position in the archipelago and
there is plenty of evidence of early trading with other places in the region,
the commercial vessels bringing spices from Maluku to Java and Sumatra
seem to have sailed farther south along the islands of Nusa Tenggara. This
began to change, however, after 1511 when Melaka fell to the Portuguese
and Malay refugees established themselves on the coast of Gowa.[1] This was
one of several elements in the expanding power of Gowa and the development of a coastal settlement which became Makassar. Their presence was
formalized by treaties, which are a common aspect of statecraft in South
Sulawesi, and set a precedent for accommodating foreign traders in mutually beneficial relationships. Then during the last quarter of the sixteenth
century, Makassar experienced a dramatic rise to pre-eminence among the
port cities of Indonesia. This resulted through a combination of talented
and unusually inquisitive leaders, a staunch open-door policy, pluralistic
political institutions, an effective, albeit extremely hierarchical labor system including the use of slaves.[2] When the Dutch attempted to control the
spice trade in the archipelago from the early seventeenth century, Makassar
became a haven for those wishing to escape its restrictions, including the
English, Danes, Dutch, Portuguese, Malays, and South Asians. The Wajorese also settled in Makassar which enabled them to expand their trade.

After the Makassar War, Makassar's emporium declined but still remained an important port in eastern Indonesia. However, it assumed a different character under Dutch influence, albeit not exactly what the VOC
had in mind. In his memorandum written immediately after the Makassar War,
Admiral Speelman outlined his vision for Makassar as a company town. He
envisioned "a merchant town with the houses of foreigners and strangers" and
advocated organizing settlements according to ethnic lines, with "each nation
under its own headman."[3] There were significant discrepancies between what
Speelman envisioned and the realities of late seventeenth- and eighteenth-
century Makassar.[4] Instead of being hermetically sealed from each other and

Figure 1: Early twentieth-century map showing Kampong Wajoq in Makassar. Source: KITLV Image Library

Figure 2: Photo of Fort Rotterdam taken ca. 1900. Source: C. Schulze Collection, KITLV Image Library

therefore easy for the Dutch to control, the various ethnic communities in Makassar interacted extensively.[5] The city's largely immigrant population and the considerable commercial cooperation between the different ethnic groups created attractive commercial opportunities for the Wajorese.

Many of the Wajorese who resided in Makassar prior to the Makassar War departed during the war and kept away thereafter for fear of persecution. Only in 1671, after "peace" had been concluded between Wajoq and the Dutch and Bonéans, did they return to Makassar in any numbers. The existence of Wajorese records of their community in Makassar starting in 1671, discussed below, suggests a formalization in their presence in Makassar at this time.

East Kalimantan

Located just across the Straits of Makassar from South Sulawesi, East Kalimantan is another area where the Wajorese settled. It is distinguished by its rivers and the mountainous terrain through which they flow, lands

Map 3: The Makassar Strait

containing numerous products that were highly valued on the international marketplace. The region's agricultural base was extremely limited, thus the power of rulers of coastal states lay not in the control of the population for agrarian enterprises, but in the revenues generated by international commerce.[6] These revenues were linked to both the interior populations and the mobile seafarers, between which the state and its ruler served a mediating role. Given that trade travelled up and down rivers such as the

Mahakam, it would seem that controlling the mouth of a river would suffice for establishing a state. However, this type of statecraft was actually precarious because the coastal rulers had to depend on two different mobile populations to maintain their position as a trade intermediary: the interior populations who collected forest products and the mobile seafarers who exchanged these for imported goods, including cloth, brass, and salt. Were they not pleased with the ruler of a given coastal polity, either population could relocate easily. Both groups, the tribes of the interior and the seafarers along the coast, naturally wanted to trade their goods in the manner that was most commercially advantageous for their own party. Furthermore, both groups differed from a more reliable, sedentary urban population because they could easily shift their commercial interests and activities according to market conditions.[7] Thus state interests, such as security and continuity, were subordinated to the commercial interests of the individual factions.[8]

The precariousness of the relations between the hosts and migrants communities must be kept in mind when considering the actions of the Wajorese immigrants and Malay host societies in eastern Kalimantan such as Kutai, Pasir, and Berau. It was this unstable situation, as well as the use of violence, that enabled the Wajorese to gain considerable power in the societies of eastern Kalimantan.

Wajorese enterprises in Pasir and Kutai occurred against the backdrop of Makassarese migrants who made claims to the Malay thrones. After the Makassar War, a large community of Makassarese settled near Pasir.[9] Karaéng Karunrung, the first minister of Gowa (1654–1687), was among them and he married into the royal family of Pasir during his exile.[10] Around the turn of the century his daughter Bontoramba, a.k.a. Daéng Matene, who may have been quite young, lay claim to the throne of Pasir.[11] Gowa naturally supported this claim. Complicating the situation further, Bontoramba also married the ruler of Kutai, thus bringing that kingdom into the conflict.[12] The Dutch offered to mediate in the dispute in order to avoid a disruption to their profitable trade in wax, resin, tortoise shells, and birds' nests.[13] Their attempts failed, and about 1711 the ruler of Pasir Sultan Dipatti Anom reported to the Dutch that Bontoramba's forces had attacked him and the inhabitants of several local communities, taking 300 hundred captives. He sought help from the Dutch to reclaim these people and insure the safety of traders from Pasir in Makassar.[14] Bontoramba also complained to the Dutch that it was the Wajorese who opposed her.[15] Thus it appears likely that the Wajorese established good relations with the local population and that Pasir looked to the Wajorese for help defending itself from the Makassarese. In this case the strong loyalty that the Wajorese held towards the Makassarese does not appear to have transferred overseas.

The Malay World

In the Malay world, delineated roughly here as the Malay peninsula, eastern Sumatra and western Borneo, the Wajorese competed with the Malays, the Minangkabau, the Dutch, and other Bugis groups in the region for political and commercial control. As in eastern Kalimantan, statecraft in the Malay world was closely related to the control of trade in the region's specialized produce and to the maintenance of a balance of power between those who could harvest forest and sea products and foreign merchants. However, in the Malay world there was an essential genealogical component, specifically the ruler and his mythological lineage.[16] Through intermarriage the Wajorese were able to compete in this world; yet other Bugis in the area offered fierce competition.

Operating in the Malay world at the same time were the five sons of Opu Daéng Rilaga: Opu Daéng Parani, Opu Daéng Menambun, Opu Daéng Maréwa, Opu Daéng Cellak, and Opu Daéng Kamisi. These brothers and their followers are commonly referred to as the Riau Bugis because of the stronghold they established on Riau. Their use of the Bugis title *opu*, which is given to the sons of reigning rulers in Luwuq, suggests that this family came from there; and indeed the *Tuhfat al-Nafis* claims that Opu Daéng Rilaga was a son of the ruler of Luwuq. However, conclusive evidence as to their precise origins is lacking. The royal genealogies of Gowa, Talloq, Boné, Wajoq, Luwuq, Pammana, and Lamuru do not reveal a clear connection with the genealogies contained in the *Tuhfat al-Nafis* and the *Salasilah Melayu dan Bugis*.[17] An examination of both Bugis court documents and Dutch records suggests that Opu Daéng Rilaga was more likely a cousin or nephew of the ruler of Boné and that he held Pammana in Wajoq and Lamuru in Soppéng as appanages, or that he originated from a royal family in one of these small kingdoms. It also appears that Opu Daéng Rilaga was in the service of the Bonéan ruler.[18]

Despite their uncertain lineage, the Riau Bugis dealt magnificently with the long-standing political traditions of the Malay world. The Riau Bugis shaped them according to their own institutions and then wrote elaborate histories to justify their own presence. Compounded by Bonéan-Wajorese animosity that was felt even overseas, their tremendous success somewhat

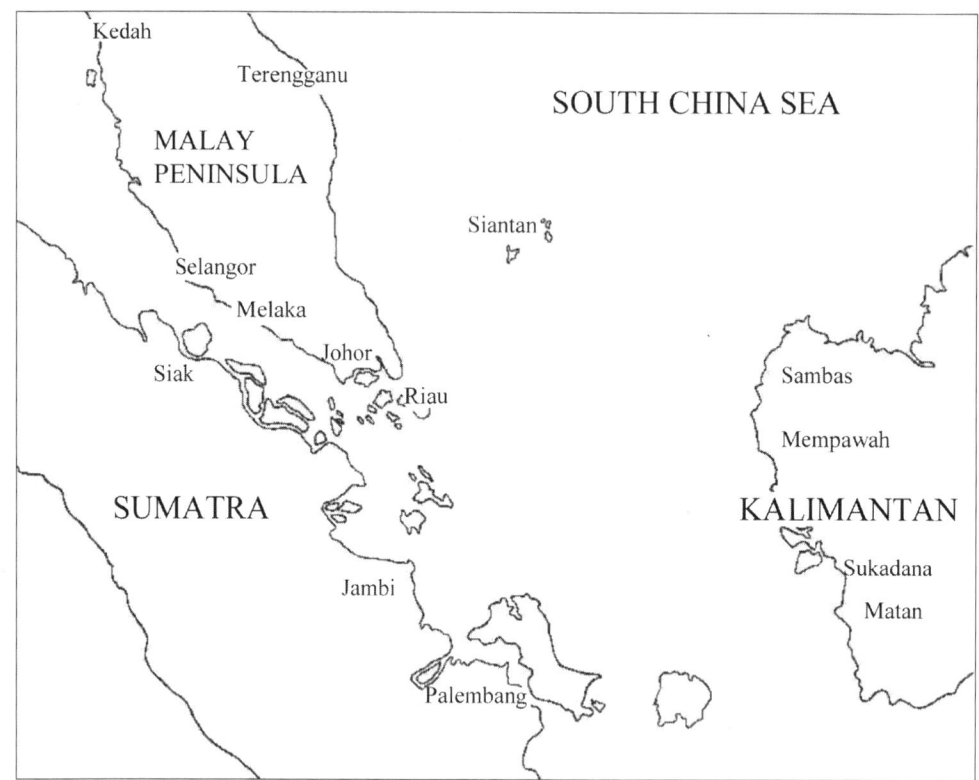

Map 4: The Malay World

overwhelmed their Wajorese rival Daéng Matekko, whose career is discussed in chapters 5 and 6. Fueled by memories of the animosity between
Boné and Wajoq in Sulawesi, the rivalry the two camps endured for generations.

Whereas there exists more information about the Bugis migrant communities in the Malay world than in any other part of the archipelago except Makassar, the rivalry between different Bugis factions is only subtly
portrayed in the sources. Both Malay and Dutch language sources tend to
portray the Bugis as a monolithic group. Even the works of the eminent
historian Raja Ali Haji Ibn Ahmad, such as the *Salasilah Melayu dan Bugis* and its sister text the *Tuhfat al-Nafis,* exaggerate Bugis cohesion in the
Malay world. Raja Ali Haji Ibn Ahmad has been praised for his historical
accuracy, but he had a definite aim in justifying Bugis presence in the Malay world. To this end he overemphasizes the role of the Bugis and of Opu
Daéng Rilaga's son Daéng Maréwa in particular, while minimizing the ten-

sion between the Malay and Bugis elements in Johor's court. Only a few passing references in these and other texts such as the *Hikayat Siak* divulge the animosity between the different Bugis groups and the strength of their respective identities.

The ability of both the Riau Bugis and the Wajorese to function in the Malay world was also greatly influenced by timing. They made their presence felt after the regicide of Sultan Mahmud of Johor (r. 1685–1699) in 1699, which marked the end of Johor's commercial zenith. In the resultant political vacuum there was room for new political influences. There was also room for an alleged descendant of last of the prestigious rulers of the Melakan line.

Western Sumatra

In contrast to the Malay world, where the Wajorese were overshadowed by other Bugis groups, the Wajorese enjoyed tremendous prestige in western Sumatra. Located along a notoriously inhospitable coastline replete with jungles, cliffs, narrow rivers, and dangerous surf, the coastal plain of western Sumatra is never wider than twenty miles (32 kilometers) and is nonexistent along numerous stretches of noteworthy length. Whereas the eastern coast has been at the heart of the Malay world from the days of Srivijaya, the western coast has been comparatively isolated. In part because of this comparative isolation and in part because of the nature of the indigenous political structures, western Sumatra provided unique opportunities to immigrants.

The Minangkabau have long exerted influence in western Sumatra. The *Alam Minangkabau,* or Minangkabau world, consists of both the inland region, which is known as the *darat,* and the outer regions and the coast, which are known together as the *rantau.* As Jane Drakard has shown, the rulers expressed their authority from the darat through language and royal signs. Although these means were dismissed by the Europeans as being mere verbiage, in actuality the Minangkabau rulers exerted considerable influence by their use. The darat received taxes and homage from rantau and exerted ritual and symbolic authority that was more important than coercive power. Although the mobile and scattered communities of the Alam Minangkabau did not allow for a centralizing ruler, courts in the rantau still publicized their connections with the darat.[19] While it appeared to seventeenth-century European observers that there was no clearly defined authority in southwestern Sumatra, in fact, authority was just expressed in

Map 5: Western Sumatra

terms that were difficult for Europeans to understand. Thus it was that two European companies, the Dutch VOC and the English EIC, competed with each other and intervened in local affairs without a good idea of how indigenous politics worked.

As the Dutch and the English competed for the same resources in this region, especially pepper, the English imposed a system of forced pepper cultivation and sought to establish alternative local authority to effectuate it. It is within this context that the descendants of the Wajorese migrant

Daéng Maruppa came to exert considerable influence serving the EIC as soldiers, intermediaries, surveyors, and adjudicators. According to one of two available accounts,[20] Daéng Maruppa's arrival in western Sumatra was facilitated by the gratitude which the ruler of Inderapura felt towards Bugis traders already settled there.[21] While there is no clear indication when the Wajorese or other Bugis arrived in Inderapura, it appears that Daéng Maruppa arrived in western Sumatra during the 1670s.[22] Five generations of his family played a leading role in the Bugis community in Bengkulu and the surrounding areas. Although this community consisted of both Wajorese and non-Wajorese elements, its leaders were of Wajorese origin.

Having briefly examined the areas into which the Wajorese settled, the rest of this chapter looks at the various ways in which they integrated themselves into, superimposed themselves upon, contributed to, or competed with the local political structures. These include establishing formal agreements with the host societies; creating their own government; and serving in military of European companies. Often these strategies were combined with marriage which, while of undeniable political importance, is discussed a later chapter.

Formal Agreements with Host Societies

As discussed in chapter 1, treaties were an essential part of statecraft in South Sulawesi. Bugis and Makassarese polities were accustomed to regulating their affairs by contracts outlining the rights and responsibilities of both parties. The ceremonies through which treaties were concluded and the treaties themselves were considered sacrosanct in nature,[23] and they were often accorded more importance than the ruler.[24] An adage from Wajoq makes this exceptionally clear:

> Although one may contest the decision of the ruler, one may not contest the decision of the council; Although one may contest the decision of the council, one may not contest the decision of the elders; although one may contest the decision of the elders, one may not contest the decision of a mutual agreement.[25]

This distribution of authority accords the most importance to contractual arrangements. Furthermore it places the authority of the ruler two steps beneath such agreements. Given the importance of mutual agreements to Wajorese politics, it is not surprising that the Wajorese used them overseas.

Formal agreements between Bugis migrants and Malay hosts were common. According to the *Tuhfat al-Nafis*, which records the history of Bugis involvement in the Malay world, "the oath of loyalty between the Malays and Bugis"[26] originated with Opu Daéng Marewa. The oath was part of the political arrangement through which Opu Daéng Marewa became the *Yang Dipertuan Muda* in Johor. Despite its Malay language name, this very position is based on the Bonéan political division between *Tomarilaleng Matoa* and *Tomarilaleng Malolo.*[27] While in theory the Yang Dipertuan Muda was subordinate to the *Yang Dipertuan Besar*, in actuality the Yang Dipertuan Besar was ceremonial and the Yang Dipertuan Muda wielded the real political power.[28] Such agreements were the basis of numerous Malay polities and the *Sejarah Raja-Raja Riau II* (von de Wall 62 [4]) lists no fewer than ten such oaths of loyalty.[29] However, the specific contents of these agreements are generally not recorded in contemporary Malay sources.

The surviving documentation about Wajorese agreements with their hosts, or other groups within the host societies, is very uneven. At least seven agreements are known to have existed: four are mentioned in passing; one is described in detail in a Malay history; one is referred to in a dialogue in a Bugis diary; and one is described in European sources. There appears to have been significant variation in the levels of control that they established, with some being very wide-ranging and establishing a detailed framework for co-existence and others perhaps being limited to a particular issue.

Two examples are agreements made in 1698 by Amanna Gappa, the leader of the Wajorese in Makassar from 1697 until 1723. Unfortunately available sources do not describe them in any detail. The first was made with the captain of the Chinese, I Wak Ko. It was agreed that if a Wajorese conducted trade in *Kampong Cina*, the Chinese village, and came into conflict with Chinese traders there, then the problem would be resolved by the Chinese captain with the help of the Wajorese *matoa* or leader. Similarly, a dispute arising between Wajorese and Chinese merchants in *Kampong Wajoq*, the Wajorese village, would be resolved by the Wajorese matoa with the help of the Chinese captain. The second was a similar agreement that Amanna Gappa made with the captain of the Malays Encik Cuka.[30] These jurisdictional agreements helped facilitate commercial cooperation between the Wajorese and the Chinese and Malays which expanded during Amanna Gappa's regime. Furthermore, they were consistent with the Wajorese saying: "Wherever there is fire, near or far, there is also the extinguisher."[31]

A third and fourth example come from eastern Kalimantan. They provide two different perspectives on how these agreements work. In the third instance, that of Kutai, the actual text of the agreement is available. In the fourth instance, that of Berau, a dialogue between the Berauan sultan and a Wajorese leader is recorded in a contemporary text. This provides insight into how such agreements were used to achieve a particular political aim. There also appears to have been a fifth formal agreement between the Wajorese and a host society. This was made with Sultan Sulaiman's court in Pasir to maintain friendly trade relations but the details are lost.[32] Therefore, among the agreements made with hosts in East Kalimantan, only those with Kutai and Berau can be discussed in any detail.

Kutai

The early history of the Wajorese in Kutai on the Mahakam River in eastern Kalimantan is described the so-called *Salasilah Bugis*, which is a Malay-language history of an agreement between the Malay rulers of Kutai and the Wajorese settlers. The Dutch assistant resident of Kutai, S. W. Tromp, published a copy of it with a Dutch translation and a commentary in 1887,[33] but he provided nothing about the provenance and date of the document, nor any information on its whereabouts. The same document appears in translation in another journal, but again without references or other pertinent data.[34] The original document appears to have been lost.

While the *Salasilah Bugis* does not contain any dates, it does contain a number of chronological clues. First is its mention of when the Kutai seat of government moved to Pemarang Jembayan, which is presumably named after the twelfth ruler of Kutai Pemarangan Jembayan, a.k.a. Pengeran Dipati Tua Jembayan (r. 1700–1710.) Second is its mention of the thirteenth ruler of Kutai, Ratu Pemarangan, a.k.a. Pengeran Anom Panji Pemarangan (r. 1710–1735). Yet these names are mentioned only halfway through the text, after the events surrounding the establishment, withdrawal and re-establishment of the Wajorese in Kutai. There are only vague indications of how much time all of these events took; so it is difficult to determine how long before the reign of Pengeran Anom Panji Pemarangan the Wajorese arrived in Kutai. Unfortunately, the events recorded in the *Salasilah Kutai*, which might have been able to resolve the question of chronology, end sometime during the first half of the seventeenth century.[35] External evidence, however, strongly suggests that the Wajorese must have arrived in Kutai no later than the second half of the seventeenth century. Wajorese lontaraq specifically mention emigration to Borneo after the Makassar War,[36] the rulers of Kutai and Pasir are known to have visited Sulawesi in 1686,[37] and there is known to have been a Wajorese leader in Kutai during the administration of

Amanna Gappa.[38] Furthermore, VOC archival sources state that the ruler of Kutai in 1693 was the son of a Bugis prince. If this ruler was born in Kutai, then his age at the time, fourteen years, would seem to indicate that the Bugis had been in Kutai since at least 1679.[39]

The *Salasilah Bugis* describes the arrival of the first Wajorese[40] migrants in Kutai and the development of their political relations with their hosts. It relates how a few boats of Wajorese arrived at first, followed by more and more until they established a *kampong* or village. The chronicle specifically mentions how the Wajorese went home[41] leaving their village unattended and then later returned. When it appeared that they might stay indefinitely, Kutai asked the Wajorese about their intentions. The Wajorese replied that they wished to remain in Kutai, during both prosperous and difficult times. Kutai then asked them to establish a permanent place of residence, which they did, and Kutai offered customary assistance. Furthermore, Kutai asked the Wajorese to choose a leader. This position became known as *pua adu.*

The position of pua adu attests to the tremendous degree of independence that the Wajorese originally enjoyed in Kutai. The Wajorese community leaders elected the pua adu in their own village without the interference of Kutai. The ruler of Kutai could nullify the Wajorese community's choice of pua adu, but he could not appoint one himself. The pua adu had tremendous influence on the socio-political, commercial and even legal affairs of the Wajorese in Kutai.[42]

The chronicle further relates how, as a result of a perceived insult to his honor, a certain pua adu fled from Kutai to Sulu in the southern Philippines with his entire family and presumably much of the Wajorese population. When the Suluans inquired about their unexpected arrival, the Wajorese described the shameful events in Kutai in minute detail. They further promised to remain in Sulu indefinitely if Sulu would assist them in eradicating their shame. Sulu agreed and together they launched an attacked on Kutai. While the inhabitants of Kutai were surprised they were still able to repel the attackers within a few days. The Wajorese and Suluan attackers fled, taking prisoners of war with them from Kutai who remained in Sulu for generations.

After this attack, the government of Kutai moved upstream from Kutai Lama to Pemarangan Jembayan. Thereafter the Wajorese returned and established a trading center that came to be known as Samarinda. Eventually, they were summoned before the ruler of Kutai, Ratu Pemarangan. Just as had happened previously, he required the Wajorese to appoint a leader, and the Wajorese did so in their own village. They appointed a certain Anakoda Latuji to the position of pua adu. Ratu Pemarangan then asked Anakoda

Latuji if he had the same intentions as his predecessor, to which Anakoda Latuji replied that he, his children, his grandchildren, and further descendants would all be loyal to his majesty. Ratu Pemarangan was pleased by the reply, and said that the Kutaians would be like the right hand of the *kerajaan* or kingdom and the Wajorese like the left hand. The ruler of Kutai further stipulated that if the Wajorese did not wish to follow local adat, they were free to leave. The remainder of the text provides the details of the agreement, which are given in the very allegorical style characteristic of the Bugis. It emphasizes the mutual benefits of co-existence, such as one helping the other in times of need. It also explicitly specifies that they will not interfere in each other's affairs. As a whole, the agreement creates a somewhat tenuous alliance between the Wajorese settlers, who essentially constituted an independent republic, and the government of Kutai that extended hospitality to them.[43]

Berau

The alliances the Wajorese struck with their hosts in Berau were as tenuous as those with their hosts in Kutai, if not more so. This may have partially been influenced by the multi-ethnic nature of the Berauan polity. Strategically located on the east coast of Borneo between Sulu and Sulawesi, Berau developed as an entrepôt during the eighteenth century. Catering to traders from Magindanao, Sulu, Sulawesi, Kaili, Java, and other areas, it had a highly diverse population.[44] The Bajau, who had also established communities in eastern Kalimantan, are known to have plundered Berau in 1715,[45] and Taosug traders from the Sulu archipelago in the southern Philippines also frequented this area, occasionally competing with the Bugis for political influence.[46] While the establishment of the Wajorese in Berau is not outlined in as detailed a document as the *Salasilah Bugis* does for Kutai, there are references to the establishment of Wajorese communities in various modern histories from East Kalimantan. Furthermore, Amanna Gappa's code specifically mentions Berau, thereby establishing that there were already Wajorese connections with Berau during the late seventeenth century or early eighteenth century. Berauan histories also date the arrival of the Wajorese in Berau in the early eighteenth century and indicates that they resided at Sambaliung and Talisayan.[47]

The most interesting text about the Wajorese in Berau comes from Wajoq itself. This is the diary of a Wajorese man who visited eastern Kalimantan.[48] While the keeping of Bugis diaries has been viewed as exclusive to the Bonéan court,[49] at least two Wajorese diaries are also known to exist.[50] Although catalogued under the dates 1711–1732, the diary actually records events from during the reign of Sultan Sulaiman of Pasir, probably during the very early nineteenth century.[51] If, as one local tradition states,[52] La Maddukelleng's son had indeed established the Wajorese community in Berau, then this would concur with evidence from the diary suggesting that the Wajorese community there was already well established. Owned (at the time of microfilming) by Petta Ballasari and copied into a modern notebook, presumably by her mother, the diary was written by a Wajorese man whose identity unfortunately is not known. That he was an official within the Wajorese government, perhaps one of the Forty Lords, is suggested by the fact that he participated in Wajorese governmental meetings.

The diary is especially rich in detail about the relations between the Wajorese community residing in Berau and their hosts. It describes how the diarist proceeded from Pasir to Berau and two weeks after his arrival he fought a battle with a Bugis noble named La Kamsa and sank his boat(s).[53] Although the diary does not reveal the reason for this conflict, in context it appears that it was a punitive action in response to some act or acts of piracy or pillage by La Kamsa and his forces that resulted in many people being killed. Following the encounter with La Kamsa, the diarist had an important meeting with the Sultan of Berau,[54] and shortly thereafter married Wé Isa, the daughter of a *pengeran*[55] in Berau.[56] Both the marriage to the Bugis woman Wé Isa and the position held by her father not only indicate that the Bugis were established in Berau, but also suggest that they had already assumed a role in its government. The exchange between the Wajorese diarist and the Sultan of Berau over the wrongdoings of the Bugis La Kamsa, and their effect on the relations between Berau and the Bugis, is further evidence of the influence of the Wajorese in Berau affairs.

Presumably a year and a half after the diarist arrived in Berau,[57] he recorded detailed information about the relations between the Wajorese in Berau and their hosts. He referred to a previous agreement between the Berau and the Bugis in which it was agreed that the people of Berau were Bugis and that they would strive for mutual benefit. The text does not provide extensive information about this agreement, but it does detail the way the communities interacted during times of conflict. This information is presented in the form of a dialogue between the diarist and the Sultan of Berau, both of whom struggled with the manner in which the relationship went awry.

The dialogue begins with the diarist mentioning the previous agreement and questioning how such a conflict could arise in which Bugis were burned and hacked to death. Had this been the work of the Berau government or of an individual? The Sultan of Berau's reply confirmed that the people of Berau are like Bugis, and he explicitly stated his desire that they mutually agree to banish wrongdoers. He confessed ignorance of the situation's specific details, but said that La Kamsa is reputed to be an evil person. He offered to banish La Kamsa and thereby distance himself from the evil that the latter had perpetrated. The Wajorese diarist replied by stating that La Kamsa's guilt had not yet been established and that therefore he should be given an opportunity to defend himself. The diarist mentioned a number of other issues, such as the murder of certain individuals and retaliation without sufficient examination. He also expressed his own desire to cooperate with Berau in banishing wrongdoers and capturing thieves.

The Sultan of Berau, however, was not as confident that the problem posed by La Kamsa and other wrongdoers could be resolved. He said that he was deeply ashamed of the whole situation and suggested that it might even ruin him. He hoped that one day all of the stars will align so that debtors can repay their creditors and wrongdoers will be brought to justice, but added that he is disappointed that the Bugis did not appear to wish the same. The diarist then questioned to what extent the Sultan wanted him to acquiesce, which was tantamount to questioning the Sultan's authority. The Sultan replied that the Wajorese can retreat to Kutai and Pasir and that the only thing he wants is to assist the good and distance the bad.[58] The Wajorese diarist answered that the Bugis would willingly do so as long as the Sultan of Berau granted them their rights, presumably referring to their right to collect debts from Berauans; but he threatened to wage war against Berau if the Wajorese were to withdraw and then those rights were not granted. The Sultan of Berau replied that peaceful conditions had to be reestablished before the debtors would feel safe to come forward and pay, and asked for an extension of the deadline for repayment. He also reminded the statesman of their agreement to help each other. The desire of the Sultan to placate the Wajorese is clear at this point in the dialogue and the Wajorese diarist agreed to extend the deadline as long as no more Bugis blood was spilt. If more Wajorese die, however, they will come from Kutai specifically to wage war upon Berau. This exemplifies the manner in which one community within the Wajorese diaspora could come to the aid of another. Furthermore it is indicative of the importance of Wajorese settlements in eastern Kalimantan. The Sultan mentions the Bugis retreating to Kutai or Pasir, not Wajoq, and the diarist mentions coming from Kutai, not Wajoq, to wage war. Apparently the settlements in Kutai and Pasir functioned as bases for Wajorese extending their sphere of influence into other parts of eastern Kalimantan.

From this dialogue it is clear that, even when there was a previous agreement between the Wajorese and their hosts and explicit statements of goodwill from both sides, relations could be extremely difficult. More than just experiencing tense relations, the two parties were threatening to wage war. What is significant is that both sides continued to wish to cooperate with each other for mutual benefit, albeit with different ideas of fairness. The Wajorese and Berauan communities had close relations with each other, but these relations were frail. Furthermore, both communities maintained their distinct identities as is evidenced by the manner in which their respective leaders referred to the two communities. Despite these distinct identities, there appears to have been a mutual recognition of mutual dependence. The Wajorese needed a place of residence and business contacts. The Berauans needed imported goods. The agreement was designed to provide them with their respective needs.

Western Sumatra

A sixth example of agreements with host societies comes from western Sumatra. In this case the Wajorese established agreements both with the indigenous host societies and with the European companies present in western Sumatra. Information about these agreements appears in both local traditions and European sources.

According to one tradition, the Wajorese pioneer in western Sumatra Daéng Maruppa was the brother of a ruler in Wajoq.[59] He fled out of shame after an attack on Tosora, siriq being a common motive for migration among the Bugis. He sailed without a particular destination, until his ship came by chance to Inderapura, where it was wrecked.[60] Many of his followers drowned and the rest were imprisoned. Their goods were confiscated and they themselves were brought to the ruler of Inderapura to be his slaves. Then negotiations began. When Daéng Maruppa explained to the ruler who he was and what he had endured, the ruler gave him a position in his court and returned his people and possessions to him, purportedly out of gratitude to the Bugis traders who were already settled in his land. After Daéng Maruppa had served the ruler of Inderapura for some time, the latter adopted him and married him to his sister. With the ruler's sister Daéng Maruppa had a son named Daéng Mabéla who was raised alongside the Sultan of Inderapura's own son, presumably Raja Mansur a.k.a. Sultan Mansur Syah (1691–1696). When Daéng Mabéla was still young, Daéng Maruppa returned briefly to Wajoq, leaving his wife and children behind.

While he was away, the Sultan of Inderapura died. In consideration of the fact that Daéng Mabéla was raised alongside the sultan's son, the two were appointed as joint rulers of Inderapura. While not a contract per se, this joint appointment constituted a formal agreement with the government of In- derapura for the participation of Daéng Mabéla in local government. While difficult to corroborate with other sources, especially since Raja Mansur did not rule Inderapura until after Daéng Mabéla began serving the English, their joint reign is remembered as a prosperous period for Inderapura during which they were reputed for their fairness and wisdom.[61]

In addition to their arrangements with local rulers, the Wajorese made for- mal agreements with the EIC. Having been expelled from Banten in 1682, the English were in search of an alternative settlement from which to main- tain their participation in the Southeast Asian pepper trade. In 1685 they accepted an invitation to establish an outpost from the chiefs of Bengkulu, who were anxious to safeguard their realm from Dutch encroachment. That same year they also signed an agreement with Sultan Muhammad Syah of Inderapura who sought their help to reestablish his authority in Menjuto.[62] Almost immediately, the English encountered difficulties because the lo- cal chiefs lacked strong leadership to prevent the numerous rebellions that arose from the unstable political situation in western Sumatra. The English therefore sought a mediator to reside at Bengkulu and help them establish an alternative authority. English archives relate how they extended an in- vitation to an influential individual in Inderapura known only by his title, Orangkaya Lela, but that Daéng Maruppa arrived instead. Accompanied by a force of Bugis and Ambonese troops, he restored order to the area.

Thereafter Daéng Maruppa's family gained influence in Bengkulu. In 1688, Daéng Mabéla's brother Sultan Endey agreed to enter the service of the EIC as "Chief Captain" of the Bugis Corps.[63] This specially constituted body of Bugis troops served the EIC as guards, soldiers, and explorers, and eventually came to play a very important role. Sultan Endey then went to Menjuto to persuade Daéng Mabéla to join him in this enterprise.[64] In time Daéng Mabéla replaced his brother as Captain of the Bugis and assumed the title Sultan Selan.[65] This arrangement is mentioned in Daéng Mabéla's family history. According to this account there was a formal contract, but the details of the contract are not specified. There was also an agreement that the Bugis contingent serve as the first line of defense in the event of an attack by an inland enemy. However, if an enemy attacked from the sea, the Bugis were to serve as the rear guard.[66]

While the formal agreement established the basis for cooperation, the services that Sultan Endey and Daéng Mabéla, a.k.a. Sultan Selan, provided to the EIC presumably extended beyond their official role as captains of the Bugis Corps. Sultan Endey sold a house to the company[67] and provided passage to the Deputy Governor on his boat.[68] The EIC held him in great esteem and in at least one instance requested his testimony when determining the guilt or innocence of a European.[69] This esteem contrasts sharply with the negative view that VOC courts in Makassar had of the Wajorese.[70] By 1696, the EIC had grown extremely dependent on Sultan Endey and found it "almost impossible to carry on our affairs here and more especially att Trijamong without him."[71] Like his brother, Daéng Mabéla served the company in a variety of important positions. Sultan Selan was referred to as "the King of the Buggesses,"[72] and appears to have commanded considerable loyalty from his Bugis followers. He was also accepted as the EIC's representative by local rulers.[73] He was asked both to call upon local leaders for a public discussion (*bicara*)[74] and to encourage pepper cultivation among the Sumatrans.[75] These functions constituted an intermediary role between the English and the Sumatrans.

Unable to coerce the locals through their own rulers, the EIC employed Bugis soldiers to supervise cultivation in the pepper-producing areas. This practice dated from at least the second quarter of the eighteenth century.[76] The English thought that the Bugis were "disinterested people among the Mallays, & will not offer nore dare they to impose any false [account] . . . upon us, because we are able to detect them, if they do, & then they know the consequences will be their ruin, which they will infallibly take care to avoid . . ."[77] Of course, the Bugis were not completely disinterested; on the contrary, they sought to use their supervisory role for their own benefit. As a result, the Sumatran pepper planters grew suspicious of the Bugis. Yet when the British themselves became increasingly involved, by dictating cultivation methods and more stringently applying the harsh requirements of the enforced cultivation system, their interference was strongly resented,[78] and it was the Bugis Captain who eventually became the sympathetic ear to whom the Sumatrans turned.[79] These changes took place over a period of several generations.

Daéng Mabéla's son Daéng Makkullé and his son Daéng Maruppa (II) eventually replaced his father as Chief of the Bugis Corps and as head of foreigners in Bengkulu.[80] As such, Daéng Maruppa served the EIC in both military and mediating capacities. In 1763, he led an expedition to Manna to help quell the rebellion of Mass Panjee. They chased the rebels into the hills, but could not apprehend them.[81] The following year Daéng Maruppa was sent with a certain Lt. Cook to Pasummo "in order to adjust matters with the inhabitants."[82] Daéng Maruppa also continued his father's legacy of participation in the judicial system. As the Bugis chief, he had an important voice in the pengeran court at Fort Marlborough. In part because of his sympathetic mediation, these courts gradually gained the confidence of the Sumatrans who regularly appealed the decisions of their local pengeran to the higher authority at Fort Marlborough. When they were displeased with their chiefs for enforcing the stringent regulations of the EIC's enforced cultivation system, pepper cultivators would appeal to Daéng Maruppa to help them escape its burdens. This eventually began to undermine the very authority that the British had established to assist in the enforcement of stringent cultivation regulations. In fact, the resident at Seluma, John Hay, attributed the defiance of the pepper cultivators to their ability to gain access to Daéng Maruppa, and tried to disband the local court and settle all disputes himself.[83] Viewing this attempt as a violation of the local chiefs' rights, the Council at Fort Marlborough condemned it and reinforced the existing hierarchy of appeals. Thus the Bugis captain retained an influential position in the judicial system; likely an even more influential position that the British had intended.

When Daéng Maruppa died in 1792, his son Unus a.k.a. Raja Bangsawan and Daéng Mabéla (II) succeeded him as Captain of the Bugis[84] and head of all non-European foreigners. Daéng Mabéla also controlled the Malay bazaars in Fort Marlborough[85] and like his father and grandfather before him, Daéng Mabéla participated in the judicial system. The influence of Daéng Mabéla was tremendous. He received an eighth of all of the revenues collected by the court and was responsible for distributing another eighth among the *datuks* of Pondok Tuadah, Pasar Malintang, Pasar Baru, and Pasar Marlbro.'[86] Although Daéng Mabéla was officially third in rank after the pengeran of Sungai Lemau and Sungai Itam, in practice he was the most important member of the court.[87] The long-standing influence of his family was important to the Sumatrans and the EIC alike.[88]

Undeniably Daéng Mabéla was an extremely prestigious and powerful figure. Yet the formal arrangement established between the British and the Wajorese so many years before did not guarantee his position. In 1807 the British resident Thomas Parr found Daéng Mabéla guilty of embezzlement from money that he had been commissioned to transport to an out-lying district. Daéng Mabéla was discharged from both his position as Captain of the Bugis Corps and adjudicator in the Fort Marlborough pengeran court. Feeling tremendous siriq or humiliation, he seemingly withdrew from the public sphere[89] until the British recalled him to help deal with a rebellion. When the British conducted investigations into the causes of the uprising, Daéng Mabéla was implicated.[90] There was not, however, sufficient evidence to convict Daéng Mabéla, so he was given the benefit of the doubt and re-employed. When the British surrendered their possessions in western Sumatra to the Dutch in 1825, Daéng Mabéla was still recognized as chief of non-European foreigners in Bengkulu.[91] Thus the arrangement made between the EIC and the Wajorese outlasted the British presence in western Sumatra.

Diaspora Government

While formal agreements with host societies were an important means of social organization across the archipelago, the Wajorese also had their own systems of political organization. One of these was the establishment of a Wajorese administration in the locations where they settled. Not only does this appear to be a widespread construction, but also are these leaders known to have sometimes worked in concert on the codification of commercial laws. The following section looks in detail at the position of Wajorese leaders in Kutai and Makassar.

Kutai

As previously mentioned, the Wajorese and their hosts in Kutai agreed that the Wajorese would be governed by their own leader known as pua adu. Surrounding the pua adu in Samarinda was an entire Wajorese government. Just as with the arung matoa in Wajoq, the paramount ruler of the Wajorese in Kutai did not have absolute power. He was assisted by two other officials known as the *tau abeyo* and *tau atau,* literally the "people on the left" and "people on the right." All three were elected by community leaders known as *kapala maneng,* literally "head of all." Defined by Tromp as "chiefs of prominent extensive families under whose protection new immigrants placed themselves,"[92] the kapala maneng resembled the *tau matoa* described by Millar. (See chapter 5.) The kapala maneng elected the pua adu as well as the tau abeyo and tau atau. Furthermore, in the event that the pua adu and his two assistants could not agree on any given issue, the kapala maneng would convene as a council and resolve the matter. They might also convene if they were not in agreement with the decision of the pua adu and his advisors. The existence of a paramount ruler assisted by numerous officials and a council mirrored political culture in Wajoq, albeit presumably on a smaller scale.[93]

Despite these limits on his authority, the position of pua adu was a prestigious one with concomitant obligations and benefits. One of the pua adu's main responsibilities was the administration of justice. His authority curbed only by his assistants and the council, he could mete out the death penalty for crimes such as theft, adultery, and slave revolt. These sentences were carried out through drowning in the Mahakam or trampling by a buffalo.

Occupying a powerful and influential position, the pua adu had various sources of income, including taxes upon ships docked in Samarinda and gifts from the *anréguru,* or head, of entering ships. Taxes were also levied upon the construction of houses of a certain size. The pua adu also had two caretakers, whose salaries were paid by the kapala maneng. Known as *pernu,* these attendants would collect betelnut and its accompaniments for him on a weekly basis. The collection of betelnut for the pua adu's use reflects the community's concern for his well-being.

With a powerful leader heading an independent community in the midst of a different state, it is easy to imagine tensions arising between the Wajorese and their Malay hosts. Indeed, there were numerous disputes between the Wajorese and their Malay hosts in Kutai, most frequently over trade. The Wajorese could and did blockade the Mahakam River thereby undermining the position of the sultan as trading intermediary. They also revolted repeatedly and on several occasions even besieged the royal palace, forcing the Malay ruler to flee. Despite these difficulties, the ruler of Kutai was dependent upon the Wajorese. Their trading contacts were important. Furthermore, the military assistance provided by the Wajorese in the event of armed conflict with Dayaks or hostile seaborne groups was absolutely essential to the government of Kutai.

Given his dependence upon the Wajorese, the ruler of Kutai tried to maintain their loyalty. To the mightiest Wajorese individuals who were most capable of helping him, the ruler of Kutai awarded titles which were considered to be a great honor. In descending order of rank these were the *kapitan*, the anréguru, and the *panglima.* Individuals holding these titles were required to pledge their loyalty to the sultan in the mosque and they constituted part of the Kutai nobility.

Thus there were two main groups exercising influence within the Wajorese community in Kutai. The first consisted of the Wajorese who had pledged their loyalty to the ruler of Kutai and received orders from him. The second consisted of the council of kapala maneng and the officials they elected. While it is unclear exactly when these two factions formed, it appears that tensions between these two groups eventually led to the loss of the Wajorese community's effective independence.

Writing during the nineteenth century, S. W. Tromp describes the prevailing conditions during the reign of Sultan Muhammad Sulaiman (r. 1845–1899.) Because of the strength of the various community leaders and their willingness to use violence, it was impossible to enforce law. Furthermore, the Wajorese increasingly meddled in the affairs of their host community. The Wajorese leader was unwilling to cooperate with the officials appointed by the sultan. Eventually the government of Kutai found it necessary to limit the authority of the pua adu in formal agreement. Containing seven articles, this agreement forbade the pua adu from enforcing the death penalty, hearing complaints from the Kutai Malays, admitting refugees, providing shelter to dissidents, authorizing cultivation of lands, collecting debts, and meddling in the affairs of non-Bugis. The Wajorese leader in Kutai refused to accept these terms and resigned.

Shortly thereafter a prominent Bugis known as Daéng Mattiro attempted to settle the affairs of a deceased passenger of a recently arrived ship in consultation of the resigned pua adu, thus without knowledge or consent of the authorities of Kutai. Bitter conflict ensued. In accordance with the original treaty, Kutai invited the Wajorese to leave. Not wanting to depart, the Wajorese went to the royal capital at Tenggarong and pledged their loyalty to the sultan. They also agreed to abolish the position of pua adu. Thereafter the leader of the Wajorese community was known by the title pangeran and he was chosen by the ruler of Kutai rather than elected by the Wajorese. Furthermore, the pangeran's authority was much more circumscribed than that of the pua adu had been. Thereafter the sultan went even further and abolished the kapala maneng, and appointed his own representative as leader of the Wajorese thereby undermining Wajorese power structures and thus the independence of the Wajorese community in Kutai.

Makassar

Similar to the manner in which the Wajorese in Samarinda lived under a leader known as the pua adu, the Wajorese in Makassar lived under a leader known as the matoa. This office appears to have been created in 1671, when many Wajorese returned to Makassar after the war. As with the pua adu in Kutai and the arung matoa in Wajoq, this office was not hereditary. The matoa were chosen for their personal qualities such as fairness, sociability, eloquence and wisdom. Nevertheless, ancestry may have played a role.[94] The Wajorese matoa in Makassar originated from various limpo in Wajoq, but none of them is recorded in the lontaraq as originating in Makassar. It is possible, however, that a matoa's family's origins is meant and not his birth-place. If this were the case, then it testifies to the strength of the Wajorese affiliations with a particular limpo or village of their ancestors.

The Wajorese matoa in Makassar was invested in a ceremony very similar to that of the arung matoa in Wajoq, which reflected the ruler's fundamental dependence on the population.[95] Just as the first paramount ruler of Wajoq Petta La Paléwo To Palippu originally declined his appointment, so did the most famous matoa in Makassar, Amanna Gappa. He denied the compliments paid him by the community when they tried to persuade him to act as their leader, but eventually he was persuaded to accept the appointment.[96]

At the inaugural ceremony, the community pledged its loyalty to the new matoa[97] and outlined the matoa's privileges as well as the community's responsibilities towards the leader.[98] These were that the matoa could not be outbid; that the matoa may participate in other peoples' purchases;[99] that the matoa might commission the captain of a ship[100] to sell goods worth up to 100 *reals* (Spanish silver coins) for him; that the community would provide for the matoa's housing; that the matoa would receive a portion of the meat and food from the *kenduri* (ritual meal) held for a deceased Wajorese trader; that the matoa would have priority in chartering; and that the matoa would receive a duty of one real for each Wajorese ship arriving in Makassar from overseas. Although the ceremony did not specifically outline the duties of the matoa, other descriptions of the various matoa and their administrations indicate that the matoas' primary functions were to settle trading disputes, and to represent the Wajorese community *vis à vis* higher authorities, such as VOC governors and the arumponé.[101]

Although the Wajorese matoa in Makassar was not limited in his powers by thirty-nine other lords as was the arung matoa in Wajoq, or by the kapala maneng as in Kutai, he was subject to the influence and demands of the Bonéans. This stemmed in part from the influential position that Arung Palakka had secured with the Dutch[102] and in part from family relations between Boné and Wajoq.[103] After the appointment of Arung Palakka's successor and nephew La Patauq (1696–1714), there came into existence a dual function of arumponé and ranreng Tua. Within the official structure of the Wajorese government, the ranreng Tua's jurisdiction was limited, as s/he was just one of the seven most powerful lords. However, this interdependence did not hamper the dual function arumponé/ranreng Tua, who resided far from the other Wajorese lords yet close by the Wajorese in Makassar.[104] In Makassar, the arumponé/ranreng Tua exerted considerable influence on the Wajorese community. The Bonéans exacted corvée labor from the Wajorese; influenced the election of a new matoa; demanded that it be they who confirmed a new matoa's appointment and that he formally swear his loyalty to adat and to his inaugural pledges in front of Bontualaq; required the Wajorese to live within Kampong Wajoq; and restricted Wajorese navigation by refusing to allow them to set sail before a new matoa had been appointed.[105] The control that the arumponé/ranreng Tua had over the Wajorese was also reflected in the hierarchy for settling disputes. If there were a problem that could not be resolved by the individuals involved, it would be referred to a *taroanang,* a meeting of prominent (rich and wise) members of the community who were to discuss the case impartially and try to interject reason. If this failed, they would go to the matoa. If their own matoa proved unable to resolve the dispute, it would then be sent to the ruler of Boné as ranreng Tua.[106] Thus even the matoa was subject to the Bonéan leader. While Bonéan interference in Wajoq itself was also strong during the last decades of the seventeenth century, nowhere else in the diaspora were the Wajorese subject to such rigid controls as in Makassar.

It is interesting to note that, even within Makassar, the Wajorese resided according to the same divisions as they did in Wajoq. This is to say that each of the three Wajorese limpo, Talotenréng, Tua, and Béttémpola, had their own community in Kampong Wajoq. There also appear to have been smaller sub-communities within the limpo communities.[107] In essence this constitutes a transfer of intra-Wajorese loyalties to the diaspora. The loyalties which individuals felt to their local community leaders remained significant enough to serve as a basis of social organization. This attests to the strength of the bonds that people felt to their leaders and their communities.

At times, the Wajorese matoa in Makassar participated in a council of Wajorese matoa from other overseas communities. The exact nature of this council is unclear but, given the ease with which these leaders could have travelled on Wajorese boats, it is likely to have convened on more than one occasion. Furthermore the mention of different domiciles of these leaders in different chapters of Amanna Gappa's law code (Makassar, Pasir, Sumbawa, Kutai, and Pontianak in one instance; and Makassar, Pasir, and Sumbawa in another instance) suggests that they convened repeatedly. Interestingly, no mention is made of a representative from western Sumatra in this council. This may have been because of the distance or because the basis of the authority of the Wajorese community leaders in western Sumatra differed radically. In Makassar and Kutai, the leader was elected whereas in western Sumatra position of Captain of the Bugis was hereditary and reinforced by proto-colonial authority.

The existence of this council suggests that the matoa within the various Wajorese communities played an active role in regulating the affairs of overseas Wajorese.[108] The council is known to have held a conference at which they agreed upon the code of commercial laws that is discussed at length in chapter 5. The frequency with which this council met is uncertain, as is the scope of its influence. Perhaps its sphere of influence was limited to commerce but it is easy to imagine that other issues, such as marriage strategies, employment opportunities and the state of affairs in the homeland, were discussed. Such a council is tantamount to a formal diaspora government, however broad the council's scope.

In addition to the practical implications in the legal sphere, the style of the law code agreed upon by this council suggests that Wajorese overseas politics, or at the very least Wajorese commercial shipping, was regulated in a manner similar to the general affairs of Bugis states. In some ways, the code resembles a conventional Bugis treaty. For example, it contains similar, albeit much less metaphorical, language about warning each other and helping each other remember.

The Politics of Diaspora

Far from being apolitical, the Wajorese had a variety of political mechanisms to ensure their success overseas. These included appointing officials to govern their overseas communities and concluding formal agreements with their host societies. The specifics of the political arrangements differed from place to place. For example, in western Sumatra the EIC lent the Wajorese considerable political authority whereas the autonomy of the Wajorese community in Makassar was curtailed by the Bonéans, at least during the late seventeenth century. The ways in which the Wajorese governed themselves also differed. In Samarinda, the pua adu was assisted by two individuals whereas the arung matoa in Wajoq was assisted by a large representative council. The variety of political arrangements made by Wajorese across the archipelago points to tremendous political flexibility. This stems in part from the nature of Wajorese statecraft. The same sort of chains of loyalty that held Wajoq together could be recreated elsewhere, like Samarinda where a new hierarchy was created; or transposed to another location, such as Makassar where the Wajorese resided according to their limpo of origin. New links were also established to facilitate relations between the communities. This is exemplified by the council of matoa who agreed upon a code of laws for the regulation of commerce which is discussed at length in the next chapter.

Given that the Wajorese had a separate law code specifically to regulate commerce, it is possible that they saw politics and commerce as distinct spheres. Undeniably, however, there was considerable overlap between the two. Numerous Wajorese statesmen such as Sultan Endey and even the arung matoa[109] participated in both commerce and politics. In western Sumatra in particular the combination appears to have been particularly empowering. Here the Wajorese fulfilled a semi-administrative, semi-commercial role for both the British and the Dutch and played a significant role in indigenous politics as well. Comparable to Iranian migrants in South and Southeast Asia,[110] the ability of the Wajorese to balance these roles made them attractive immigrants and facilitated their assumption of a prominent position in west Sumatran society. It is to Wajorese commerce that this study now turns.

CHAPTER FOUR

Commerce

Numerous observers have noted the success and extent of Wajorese commercial networks. The nineteenth century observer John Crawfurd described the people of Wajoq as "by far the most industrious and enterprising people, not only of that island [Sulawesi] but of the whole Malay archipelago." Crawfurd continues by mentioning their voyages "from one end of the Archipelago to the other" and their independent settlements in places like Borneo and Flores.[1] Indeed, Wajorese networks spread from Aceh on Sumatra's northwestern tip to the bird's head of West Papua and beyond. To ensure the financial and commercial success of these wide-ranging networks, the Wajorese deliberately designed laws, taxes, and institutions that benefitted trade both in Wajoq and in the diaspora. The breadth and scope of their network that so impressed observers like Crawfurd flowed in large part from these innovations.

Another key element in Wajorese commercial success was solidarity which, as discussed in chapter 2, is known among the Bugis as pessé. Statistical studies of commerce in early modern Makassar have shown two ways in which pessé influenced Wajorese commercial shipping. First of all, Wajorese ship owners had a strong preference for hiring Wajorese skippers. They did so 90 percent of the time, as opposed to Malay and *burgher* (Dutch residing in Asia) shipowners who did so 78 percent and 63 percent of the time respectively.[2] The Wajorese also appear to have worked together to ensure that their cargos were both differentiated and stable. In comparison to other ethnicities, there were more instances among the Wajorese of groups of traders cooperating for commercial success than of individual traders with large-scale endeavours.[3] The variety and number of people involved resulted in a greater number of commercial contacts and thus in a smaller chance of sailing with an undifferentiated cargo or with no cargo at all.

Pessé is also evident in the manner in which the Wajorese also worked together as a group to preserve their communal reputation for fair commercial and financial practices. This is clearly illustrated by the following description of Wajorese solidarity written by the Dutch Governor of Makassar Smout for his successor Loten:

> Indeed, it has even happened that a single Wajorese owed more than 20,000 rijksdaalders to a person who is still known in these parts, that the entire Wajorese village burned down and that this man lost all of his goods. But just a few days after the fire, all of the Wajorese went together to the creditor and stood up for the unlucky (debtor) so that his credit would not be diminished. The creditor did not lose a single penny of the capital or the interest, and he told me this repeatedly in person.[4]

Obviously relations among Wajorese merchants were not always harmonious, but they did look out for each other's trade and finances in a systematized, institutionalized manner. The care that they took for the reputation of the group helped to facilitate the success of both individuals and the community as a whole. Giving particular emphasis to the underlying financial and legal systems and to a microanalysis of several Wajorese traders' affairs, this chapter explores Wajorese commerce.

The Commercial Worlds of the Wajorese

Early modern Southeast Asian commerce is marked by political changes occurring across Asia. Port cities became an increasingly popular model of commercial and political organization after the 13th century. This was followed by the rise of large territorial states during the 16th century. These new states offered opportunities for foreigners not only to trade but also to contribute to their development. Foreigners became partners in the creation of new economies, polities, and societies.[5] The Wajorese were one of numerous groups to take advantage of these opportunities.

After the Makassar War, South Sulawesi's main emporium Makassar declined under the Dutch, yet the city still maintained an important position in regional trade with numerous networks converging at Makassar. Especially given the affordability of rice,[6] the price of which can be considered as a barometer of the economic climate, Makassar remained an important port in eastern Indonesia, to the Wajorese as well as to other trading groups. It was almost impossible, however, for the Dutch to exert effective control over this trade. Dutch officials, such as the harbormaster and the prosecutor, were charged with combating evasions of the VOC's monopolies, but their attempts were futile.[7] Furthermore, if Dutch control over Makassar was limited, Dutch trading restrictions elsewhere in the peninsula were even less effective. This left plenty of opportunities for alternative commercial networks and "illegal" trade, which were both endemic and highly profitable. In fact, neither the VOC nor the burghers were able to compete effectively with Asian traders.[8]

The balance of power in South Sulawesi also influenced Wajorese commerce in Makassar. Immediately following the Makassar War, the resentful Bonéan leader Arung Palakka was the effective overlord over the peninsula. After his death, however, his successors were unable to exert the same level of control. With Boné in decline, Wajorese commerce could flourish with fewer restrictions during the eighteenth century. This appears to have been the case even despite the combined roles of arumponé and ranreng Tua which technically limited Wajorese autonomy.

Commerce in the Straits of Melaka depended very much upon the balance of power between different specialized groups and the Malay rulers who maintained trade emporia. The *orang asli*[9] could locate aromatic woods, camphor, beeswax, birds' nests, dragons' blood and the like, and *orang laut*[10] could maneuver the dangerous waters and reefs to obtain such products as pearls, edible seaweeds, tortoise shell, and mother of pearl. The orang laut also formed the most important component of the ruler's fleets. Equally important was the enticement of foreign merchants by providing them with favorable and safe trading conditions. Given the importance of trade, Malay polities were typically located in commercially strategic locations along rivers and at river mouths and the rulers were very dependent upon the interior populations for the collection of such as wood, resins, bezoar stones, and in some places gold.

The Straits of Makassar was another commercially important area, especially for the Wajorese. Ports on the east coast of Kalimantan, such as Pasir, Kutai, and Pulau Laut were important sources of rattan while ports like Kaili, Mandar, and Soreang on the west coast of Sulawesi were important sources of coconuts and Bugis textiles. Banjarmasin in southeastern Kalimantan also emerged as a transit port for Chinese goods, especially earthenware; indeed Dutch reports from 1727 suggest that Banjarmasin's trade was equal to Makassar's. Much of this trade bypassed Makassar, especially trade in bulky, low-value goods, and the VOC found it impossible to moni-tor or restrict the subregion's trade. This was especially so during the 1720s and 1730s when Makassar's trade to Pasir was all but closed as a result of the unrest caused by La Maddukelleng.[11] Significant trade to and from Sulu also passed through the Straits of Makassar.

Western Sumatra exported a number of valuable commodities, including gold, camphor and pepper. Gold was of primary importance in the long term development of the coast's commerce[12] and the Minangkabau in the highlands deliberately encouraged a fear and awe of the darat in order to protect their mines.[13] Camphor was also an important export from western Sumatra, most notably from Barus. Because of the high-quality camphor exported from this kingdom, this resin is associated with its name and is known in Indonesia as *kapur Barus*.[14] The cultivation of pepper, an im-ported crop, probably began when navigation along Sumatra's west coast increased during the mid-sixteenth century following Portuguese attacks in the Straits of Melaka. Until the seventeenth century, it was apparently confined to Inderapura where it facilitated that polity's emergence as an independent sultanate.

Wajorese Commercial and Legal Frameworks

Wajorese commercial activities spanned the entire archipelago. Destina-tions on or near Sulawesi included Makassar, Mandar, Kaili, Selayar, Buton, Muna, Wowoni, Tombuku, Lohiya (east coast of the island Muna), Bing-koka, Benongko (island to the southeast of Buton), and Mandonu (island on the east coast near Tombungku). Destinations elsewhere in the archi-pelago were Pasir, Sukadana, Mempawa, Sambas, Brunei, Banjarmassin, and Berau on Borneo; Aceh, and Palembang on Sumatra; Banda, Ambon, Seram, Kei, and Aru islands in Maluku; Selangor, Melaka, Kedah, Johor, and Terengganu on the Malay peninsula; Bima (in eastern Sumbawa) and Manggarai (in western Flores) in the Lesser Sundas; as well as Batavia and Lombok. Outside of the archipelago, Cambodia is known to have been a destination of the Wajorese and other Bugis.

Commodities traded across this vast network included rice, cloth, spices, diamonds, gold, Buton boxes, slaves, gambir, salt, and tobacco. A full chap-ter (22) of Amanna Gappa's law code (discussed below) devoted entirely to the fares for transporting slaves suggests that traffic in humans was also an important dimension of Wajorese trade. For the eighteenth century there is also evidence of livestock being transferred from Sulawesi across the

Straits of Makassar to East Kalimantan, a practice which was likely to have been established earlier.

Formal frameworks for establishing and regulating business relationships were a key element in Wajorese success. The Wajorese established various systems both in Wajoq and elsewhere to promote and regulate trade. The most significant of these are the set of laws codified by Amanna Gappa and the fund established for the common good by Arung Matoa La Saléwangeng (r 1715–1736). Nothing short of institutional innovations in their own right, these systems expanded the commercial potential of the Wajorese and gave them advantages over their counterparts. Furthermore, the law code in particular created an element of unity in dispersion among the Wajorese who upheld it.

Wajorese customary laws pertaining to commerce and navigation were codified by Amanna Gappa, the matoa of the Wajorese in Makassar from 1697 until 1723.[15] While there are various versions, they share an underlying structure.[16] The laws were designed to prevent strife/disharmony among merchants, be they on land or at sea, debtors or creditors, peddlers or wholesalers. The precise date when these laws were first committed to writing is uncertain but it was most likely during the early eighteenth century.[17] The law code was agreed to by the Wajorese matoa in Sumbawa, Pasir, Kutai, and Pontianak. This clearly shows that the various Wajorese communities cooperated for mutual benefit. It also shows the importance of the trading connections between these places in particular.

The law code consists of 25 chapters, each dealing with a different aspect of commerce and navigation. If not unique, such a law code is highly unusual for early modern insular Southeast Asia. Outlining matters from how to treat castaways to the settlement of a deceased trader's debts, the law code is extremely comprehensive. It was also very effective. A lontaraq detailing the administrations of the Wajorese matoa in Makassar says "it ended badly for violators [of Amanna Gappa's regulations]," implying that the code was actively upheld, at least during the administration of Matoa To Tangngaq (1730–1732).[18] While Wajorese sources do point disapprovingly to instances of Wajorese in Makassar seeking arbitration from the king of Boné,[19] the Wajorese generally succeeded in settling their own commercial disputes and no Dutch court records of cases contested between two Wajorese parties survive.

Intended to prevent conflict among merchants, the laws are primarily concerned with fair business practices. Eight chapters (3, 7, 8, 13, 14, 18, 19, 21) relate to borrowing and lending money and goods; whereas three (2, 7, 12) pertain to the sharing of profits and losses. One chapter (9) concerns inheritance, and another chapter (15) sets forth to who exactly was to be held responsible for goods that are mishandled or damaged.

The regulations surrounding borrowing and lending are extensive. Chapter 7 defines five different types of loans. *Bagilaba pada* (equal sharing of profits) refers to a loan where the borrower and the lender share the profits or losses. If the principal is repaid and only the profits are shared, the loan is called *bagilaba samatula* (sharing profits with an agreement). The third type of loan, where there is no interest or loss, is called *inreng pettu* (loan without interest or loss). Fourth, *inreng réweq* (loan of goods) refers to a loan of merchandise in which the unsold portion is returned. The fifth type of loan, called *laloang* (commissioned goods), refers to when people sell goods on behalf of the Wajorese matoa, in Makassar or elsewhere, and do not profit from the sale themselves. The law code also lists circumstances in which the transporter or borrower must take complete responsibility for loss of the goods. These are if he loses them through betting; if he lends them; or if he spends them in order to commit adultery, buy opium or pay for a wedding. In addition, less formal loans were made with the understanding that the money or goods lent would be returned after a commercial voyage. Loans were also made for non-commercial purposes, often with collateral.

The law code also offers continuity in the event of a merchant's death. Chapter 15 provides guidelines for what was to be done with the goods of a trader who died on a voyage. The main goal was to ensure that his or her heirs did not suffer damage. The prescribed policy was to sell the deceased person's wares, record the profits, and place the receipt in the coffin with the deceased. If someone then used the deceased's money for further business ventures that failed, that person was then bound to recompense the deceased's family for the money lost. If the ventures were profitable, on the other hand, the gains were to be divided with the heirs. Amanna Gappa's law code also provided guidelines for the division of property and debts in the event of a merchant's death. Chapter 12 states that in such an event, the merchant's family could only be held responsible for half of his debts.

Chapter 10 then stipulates exactly what happens when commercial cooperation goes awry. If disputing parties take their case to a judge, they must both swear to the veracity of their testimonies. Thereafter the plaintiff speaks first and then the defendant. If they both so desire they can continue the process and respond to each other's statements. Then the judge applies the "roots" of justice to the situation. The most important of these fundamental principles are that the judge listens to both sides, that the judge hears testimonies from both parties' witnesses, that the defendant's behavior and social rank be considered. Less important are the practices of calling upon God's help so that debtors will acknowledge their debts and so that the innocent can confirm their innocence, listening to the defendant in his or her own residence, and hearing testimony from the defendant's confidants so as to uncover any secrets. Chapter 10 also explicitly states that rulers must never behave unjustly towards merchants, thereby protecting them from despotism. Furthermore, it explicitly forbids debtors from denying their debts. This legal insistence upon acknowledging debts helped to maintain their communal reputation and to ensure the availability of loans to Wajorese entrepreneurs.

Related to the explicit prohibition against denying debts are numerous other regulations promoting transparency at various point in the law code. One example states that creditors have the right to make debts publicly known so that part of any money that the debtor earns will go to the creditor. A second example is that passengers carrying more than 110 reals of worth of gold or 330 reals worth of diamonds on board a ship were required to disclose this and pay appropriate freighting charges. In the event of non-disclosure, they could be fined. In these regulations promoting transparency, one can see the emphasis on fair business practices and mutually beneficial arrangements. Clearly the code was designed to benefit the Wajorese community as a whole.

Containing advice to merchants, chapters 21 and 25 of Amanna Gappa's code provide insight into what the Wajorese considered wise business practices. Chapter 21 consists of Amanna Gappa's personal advice regarding lending money and goods, profit sharing and debt collecting. This advice includes his suggestions that careful consideration be given to both who is borrowing and who is lending; that it is inadvisable to go into business with influential people because they may try to bend the rules; and that it is better to let someone work or trade in order to pay off his debt than to enslave him. He further advises that merchants should assist each other through loans and look out for each other's well-being. Chapter 25 provides advice for maintaining a capital and fortune. It compares the capital involved in bagilaba loans to a tree with four roots. If one fails to take care of the tree's roots, then the tree will die and there will be nothing for one's children and grandchildren to inherit. Thus one should not use the capital involved in bagilaba loans to purchase opium lest it go up in smoke, nor to gamble lest it sink to the bottom of the sea, nor to buy excessive presents for friends. It also encourages merchants to take as good care of the capital of a bagilaba loan as they would of their own. Chapter 25 then offers four suggestions for maintaining a fortune: One should be prudent and honest, one should not talk too much, one should not take on too much business at once, and one should not make too much commotion.

Also included in the code are various regulations protecting private property. For example, captains must assume responsibility for any mishandled goods that they confiscate from slaves, unless they have received prior authorization from the owners. The theme of respecting the goods of others appears repeatedly and doubtlessly served to foster pessé or communal solidarity.

Given that so much of Wajorese enterprise was seaborne, Amanna Gappa's code also deals extensively with affairs on board ships. The captain was naturally the supreme authority on board, but there were limits on his authority, as was typical of all Wajorese leaders. For example, chapter 4 describes how the captain might change the destination of a vessel at the last minute without the consent of the *sawi* (unsalaried maritime traders, discussed below), even though they had paid in advance for passage to another port. In such a case, however, the captain was required to provide the sawi with passage aboard a comparable vessel to make the agreed upon voyage. Showing once again that the authority of the captain was not absolute, chapter 11 describes the procedures for settling disputes on board. It stresses the desirability of the captain settling all shipboard disputes immediately, or at least before the ship arrived in port. If this proves impossible for him, however, then the issue must be adjudicated by the leaders of the land where the ship calls. While at sea the decisions of the captain cannot be challenged unless all of the sailors, including the sawi, agree to oppose him. This regulation underlines the importance of consensus among the Wajorese.

The law code also reflects a high degree of awareness of market conditions. Chapter 3 specifies that if transported goods were not sold, then only half of the freight costs could be charged. Clearly, then, those involved in transportation were involved in negotiation and decision-making processes. Although there were ship owners and capitalists who did not make voyages themselves, there was no clear distinction between the businesses of transportation and selling. In the court proceedings of Abraham Franzson vs. Tombo (discussed below), it is clear that while not traveling on the same ship, shipowner Abraham Franzson was considered to have made the same voyage as his business associate Nakoda To Anko.

Amanna Gappa's code of laws also tells us something about the links between different Wajorese communities. Except for pure passengers (*to manumpang*), people were expected to make a round trip voyage on the same vessel; and unless prior arrangements were made, they were always required to pay the round trip fare. This shows that Wajorese traveled extensively to and from Sulawesi, perhaps even more so than they emigrated. Given the transsocietal nature of Wajorese business contacts (see the case of lo Anko below) it is possible that there were passengers of many different ethnicities on board Wajorese ships. There is, however, no indication of this in Amanna Gappa's code. The fact that the code of laws was agreed to by the Wajorese matoa in Sumbawa, Pasir, Kutai and Pontianak clearly shows that the various Wajorese communities cooperated for mutual benefit. It also shows the importance of the trading connections with these places in particular. The code also suggests that Wajorese commercial shipping was regulated in a manner similar to the regulation of general affairs of Bugis states. In some ways, the code resembles a conventional Bugis treaty. For example, it was agreed upon by various community leaders, and it contains similar, albeit much less metaphorical, language about warning each other and helping each other remember.

The codification of laws pertaining to loans was extremely significant because it provided a range of reliable options through which people could lend and borrow money. In early modern insular Southeast Asia, local traders were generally at a disadvantage when compared to Chinese, Indian, and European merchants because of the relative absence of investment capital and because of their enduring preference for personalized, kin-based trading relations.[20] While the range of relatives considered trustworthy included "milk relatives" and in-laws as discussed in chapter 5, it was nevertheless limited. The establishment of a framework for loans therefore not only expanded the commercial potential of the Wajorese, but also gave Wajorese traders an edge over their insular Southeast Asian competitors. Instead of preferring to trade with kin, the Wajorese exercised extra caution when conducting business with family, as discussed in chapter 5.

Aside from the laws codified in Makassar, there was an equally important institutional innovation established in Wajoq itself. That was the fund for the common good which La Saléwangeng started. It is best examined within the context of La Saléwangeng's financial and social reconstructive projects.

La Saléwangeng was one of several arung matoa in Wajoq who deliberately sought to revitalize Wajoq through the expansion of international commerce. His predecessor the twenty-ninth paramount ruler of Wajoq La Tenriwerrung Puanna Sangngaji (r. 1711–1713) tried to strengthen the Wajorese economy by advocating the philosophy that the Wajorese could not stand upright unless they sought riches.[21] While he is remembered for this standpoint, the short two-year length of his reign does not appear to have allowed him to initiate any real changes in commercial practices. La Saléwangeng, on the other hand, encouraged commerce in very real and practical terms.

La Saléwangeng specifically ordered people to trade overseas.[22] He facilitated their endeavors in a variety of ways, thereby seeking to harness the
power of overseas commerce for the benefit of Wajoq. He appointed La Tiringeng Daéng Mangngapasa to organize commerce and the lontaraq record
that there were many of these traders and captains in Wajoq during the reign
of La Saléwangeng.[23] La Saléwangeng also improved Wajoq's waterways
by dredging the river Topaceddo, thereby providing boats with easy access
to Tosora by way of Lake Seppangngé and Lake Talibolong. In addition, he
encouraged the organization of traders and fisherman and required that they
appoint representatives.[24]

La Saléwangeng's most famous accomplishment was the establishment
of a fund for the common good. Immediately after harvest, he or his representative would go from house to house, collecting rice for storage in a
granary, the rice then being used both to feed the poor and to guard against
hunger in the event of crop failure.[25] During prosperous times, he or his representative also went from house to house collecting money for a number of
different reasons. Some went to support the poor, and, in the event of their
death, to pay for their burials. Money collected in this manner was also used
for the advancement of agriculture and especially trade.

La Saléwangeng's fund was particularly important for trade because it allowed people without their own financial resources to engage in commerce.
The government lent money to entrepreneurs according to *bagilaba tematé
ponna,* a loan in which the capital does not die. The borrowers could use
the money to advance their own commerce and then they had to return the
principal along with one-third of the profits. The government's share of the
profits was then used to purchase of weapons, gunpowder, and ammunition as well as to construct an arsenal and to remodel the mosque.[26] In this
manner, La Saléwangeng not only facilitated the international merchants'
business, but also harvested their power for the betterment and security of
Wajorese society. Unique or extremely rare within early modern Southeast
Asian societies, the fund was nothing short of an institutional innovation.

Traders: Types and Individuals

Such institutional innovations for the advancement of Wajorese commerce do much to dispel the cliché of the Asian peddler incapable of ra-
tional organization. Indeed, among the Wajorese, even the peddlers were
organized. Peddlers were one group within a tripartite division of merchants
established to protect the rights and business of each group. Wholesalers

were the only ones who could purchase from the Dutch and the Chinese, but they could not participate in retail trade. Retailers had to purchase their goods from wholesalers, but could not act as peddlers. Peddlers were then required to buy from retailers, not wholesalers. Repeated violation of this division could result in being banned from trading, but repentant offenders could be pardoned.[27]

Aside from these three types of traders there existed unsalaried maritime trader-sailors known as sawi. The sawi system was highly significant because, like La Saléwangeng's fund, it gave people with limited financial resources a means of participating in international commerce. It was also key to the formation of capital. Sawi were traders who worked as sailors without receiving fixed wages.[28] While precise statistics are unavailable, it appears that sawi were the most numerous people on board any given ship. There were different categories of sawi based on the extent of their freedom and the amount of goods that they were permitted to bring on board. *Sawi puli* were essentially debt slaves.[29] They generally did not have enough capital to trade themselves, so they offered their services on board ships as a deposit for loans from the captain. They generally voyaged with the same captain at least once a year, hence the word *puli*, meaning "firm." They were permitted to bring as much compact wares on board as they wanted. To transport bulky goods they had to negotiate with the captain but were generally given preference over the other sawi out of recognition for their continuous and important services, including bailing.[30]

A second kind of sawi were the *sawi tungka*, also known as *sawi alé-alé*, whose very title means that they came on board without merchandise. Like the sawi puli they exchanged their labor for loans, but there were several differences in their position. First, their work was generally more closely related to trade than to sailing. For example, they might be responsible for cooking sea cucumbers. Second, they were only required to work until one in the afternoon as opposed to the sawi puli, who were required to work the entire day. Thirdly, the captain interfered less with the commerce of the sawi tungka, and since the captain was less invested in their success, their goods were also more likely to be thrown overboard. Their loans from the captain were limited to 25 reals and their only payment was their profit.[31]

Sawi maloga and *sawi menumpang* more closely resembled passengers than crew. Sawi maloga brought their own capital or merchandise with them. They were not as closely affiliated with the captain as the sawi puli and sawi tungka. They could only be required to help with work on board a ship in an emergency, and their wares were the first jettisoned in the event of a ship running aground. The last class of sawi were the *sawi menumpang*. Paying their own fare and free to disembark at any time, they were distinguished from *to menumpang* or normal passengers in that they were traders by definition and not, for example, religious pilgrims. Furthermore, sawi were expected to make a return voyage unless other arrangements were made whereas the to menumpang were not. Sawi manumpang also differed from the other sawi in that the captain furnished them with fire wood and water.

As an institution, sawi may have stimulated the economy by allowing people with very little money to get involved with trade. It also may have promoted solidarity or pessé within the community because the captain was once a sawi and he looked after their well-being, offered them advice, and lent them money. If modern relationships can be used as any sort of a guide for understanding the past, then this solidarity might have been felt on land as well. In contemporary South Sulawesi, the wives of the sawi have a close relationship with the wife of the captain, seek her advice on personal matters and borrow money and supplies from her.[32]

In addition to the sawi, there was another class of maritime trader known as *kalula* (lit. inseparables.) Kalula were akin to apprentices to the captain and as such were also known as *anaqguru* or students. The captain generally made them responsible for the safe keeping and trading of the goods belonging to the Wajorese matoa of any given overseas community or of the arung matoa in Wajoq. They also made use of a special sort of commission known as *inreng ripasa* in which a small quantity of goods or money are lent without a formal contract. While the captain does not profit from inreng ripasa, he does keep an eye on the trade and helps to prevent confusion between private and common goods.

The captain himself also engaged in trade. Chapter 6 of Amanna Gappa's code outlines the requirements for this position. A captain must be patient, alert, and willing and able to speak for the entire group. He was also required to possess weapons, ammunition, a sturdy ship, and capital. Furthermore, he was required to have money on hand to invest for the ship's maintenance, even though this money was later to be reimbursed later by the ship's owner. Amanna Gappa's code also required that the captain treat the sawi justly without threatening them, let them choose from the purchased goods, and share his own food before allowing them to go hungry. It is also interesting to note that the captain's authority on board was not as supreme as that of his European counterparts. In the event that everyone on board except the captain agreed to change course, the captain was obliged to acquiesce. In contrast, a Western captain's authority was supreme on board and conspiring to change course was punishable as mutiny. This difference may be indicative of the importance of consensus in Wajorese culture.

Whereas the law code of Amanna Gappa provides a Wajorese perspective on the affairs of captains in general, Dutch judicial records offer insight into the trade of one captain in particular. The affairs of the Wajorese captain To Anko were scrutinized in a court case between the shipowner Abraham Franzson and To Anko's Makassarese widow Tombo.[33] In 1728 Abraham Franzson sued Tombo for money that her deceased husband To Anko owed him. According to Abraham Franzson, To Anko mediated loans to the sawi amounting to 408 rijksdaalders. According to Tombo and a business associate of To Anko known as Karre Mangale, however, these loans amounted to 240 rijksdaalders. To Anko and the sawi traveled together to Batavia on Abraham Franzson's ship *Sulena*, which was then sold in Batavia for 30 rijksdaalders because it was old and unlikely to survive the return voyage. Another ship then was purchased for 170 rijksdaalders. This ship in turn required new sails and rigging, which cost an additional 50 rijksdaalders.[34] Also while in Batavia, To Anko bought goods that Abraham Franzson and To Anko agreed he would sell in Sumbawa and then return the capital to Abraham Franzson, but To Anko died on Sumbawa before completing this transaction.

Following To Anko's death on Sumbawa, Abraham Franzson approached Tombo about her husband's debt. She claimed that his papers were with his Wajorese associate To Koa and refused to settle the debt in a friendly manner. Abraham Franzson therefore brought the matter before the VOC court. His case against Tombo was based on his claim that she possessed money that he had lent her husband. Because the court did not believe the plaintiff's statement that the sawi loans amounted to 408 rijksdaalders, and because To Anko had accrued numerous expenses on Abraham Franzson's behalf, the plaintiff was unable to adequately substantiate a claim for more than 60 rijksdaalders. The court ruled that the defendant must reimburse him for that amount.

The image of To Anko that emerges in the court proceedings is multifaceted. Indeed, in today's terms, he might be called an "umbrella capitalist" because he was involved in a variety of business fields including transportation, sales, and finance. From Amanna Gappa's code it appears that this was typical of Wajorese captains. To Anko helped organize the business affairs of the sawi, collected money, and delegated authority. In the matter at hand he also served as the intermediary between the sawi, who made their own investments and took their own risks, and the boat owner Abraham Franzson. He also renovated the ship purchased in Batavia which involved purchasing beams, planks and nails from a certain Guastos. Furthermore, the fact that the ship was replaced to make a return voyage emphasizes the fact that round trips were generally expected, which is also indicated in Amanna Gappa's code.

Had Abraham Franzson and Tombo's case been settled according to Wajorese custom as outlined in Amanna Gappa's law code, the outcome might have been very different. Apparently, in To Anko's case, nobody followed the Wajorese custom selling the deceased person's wares, recording the profits, and placing the receipt in the coffin; or if they did it never reached Tombo. In any case, the VOC court did not believe Tombo that To Anko's papers were with To Koa. Amanna Gappa's law code also provided guidelines for the division of property and debts in the event of a merchant's death. Chapter 12 states that in such an event, the merchant's family could only be held responsible for half of his debts. If the spirit of this principle had been applied in the VOC court, then Tombo would only have been required to pay 30 rijksdaalders. Indeed, according to Wajorese practices, Tombo might not have been held liable for any of the money. Chapter 9 specifies that debts from a previous marriage may not be carried over into another marriage. Had the dispute been decided by the Wajorese matoa, Tombo might have been excused on these grounds, because when she was brought to trial she was already in a new relationship and residing with a certain Karre Mangewai.

While the case of Abraham Franzson versus Tombo sheds light on the affairs of the Wajorese captain To Anko, a different case sheds light on the affairs of the Wajorese trader To Uti. It thereby offers a rare, detailed glimpse into the affairs of an individual Wajorese trader. According to the court proceedings, To Uti, a Wajorese trader, lent 300 rijksdaalders to Diogo Towaris, a Makassarese burger, in the early 1710s in Batavia. No mention of interest was made, but it was agreed upon that To Uti would be able to transport goods back to Makassar on Towaris' ship. According to To Uti, the loan was to be repaid within five months, but Towaris maintained that no time limit was set. Then, for reasons that do not appear in the court transcripts, Towaris was imprisoned for five months and was unable to complete his side of the bargain. According to To Uti, he sought Towaris out, presumably visiting him in prison. Because Towaris was unable to return the money or fulfill his side of the bargain, he promised to repay the 300 rijksdaalders with appropriate interest in Makassar.

Several years after the loan was made, the two met again in Makassar. Towaris then gave To Uti 100 or 120 rijksdaalders worth of goods (*rasamala*, a type of fragrant wood) and transferred to To Uti a debt of 30 rijksdaalders owed him by the Bugis To Minta. Believing that he was entitled to interest, To Uti considered this payment as part of the interest, and the Wajorese

Amanna Tale and To Budaela supported this claim by testifying that they had seen Towaris pay To Uti 130 rijksdaalders 26–28 years before as part of the interest. Towaris, on the other hand, claimed that this payment was part of the principal. To Uti then further contended that the prosecutor[35] Van der Anker (deceased at the time of the trial) agreed with him that Towaris should pay 100% interest. Although Wajorese Puanna Budu testified as to the prosecutor's position, the court found that advocating such a high rate of interest was uncharacteristic of a prosecutor and dismissed the claim. Towaris then went to Ternate, returning in 1724. When To Uti was again in Makassar in 1725, he went to Towaris' house and met with his son Adriaan who, curiously enough, was not called on to testify. According to To Uti, he was offered nothing but excuses and pretexts to avoid payment of the debt and ended up being chased out of the house with a bamboo stick. According to Towaris, To Uti threatened Adriaan and asked that he tell his father to come to his house the next morning to settle the matter once and for all. Towaris testified that he was anxious to do this but that To Uti ran away, probably fearing that Towaris would complain about the bad way in which he had behaved. Towaris and To Uti then met again in 1741, but once again were unable to resolve their dispute. Following this, To Uti sued Towaris in 1742, arguing that since Towaris did not transport his goods from Batavia to Makassar as agreed, he no longer had the right to an interest-free loan. The court ruled in favor of the defendant. Although it ordered Towaris to repay the remaining 150 rijksdaalders of the original loan, he was not required to pay any interest, despite the length of the loan's term.

The court's attitude towards To Uti is also noteworthy, especially since it contrasts so sharply to the attitude of the EIC court towards Sultan Endey. The court found that To Uti had intentionally misled it and ordered him to pay court costs. Furthermore, the court concluded that nothing To Uti said could be believed because there was a discrepancy between To Uti and Towaris's recollections of when the loan was made. The testimonies of other Wajorese witnesses were similarly disbelieved on the basis that they were "vagrants and unbelieving enemies," which reflects Dutch attitudes towards the Wajorese in 1742 following the attempt of the Wajorese under La Maddukelleng to expel the Dutch from South Sulawesi, described in length in chapter 7. The court's repeated emphasis on the domicile of the litigants and its disparaging references to people without a fixed residence also implied that people without fixed residence not only were of lower status, but also had fewer legal rights. While this view would have complicated business for Wajorese migrants, their very mobility was in and of itself advantageous. It allowed them to use dispersion as a resource and to take advantage of distant opportunities as they arose without having to worry about such matters as a fixed home or place of business.

The case of Towaris vs. To Uti exemplifies the difficulty of determining the length of time in which a loan[36] was to be repaid, and this was one of the most problematic aspects of debt-credit relationships in Southeast Asia.[36] That being said it also highlights the geographic integrity of Wajorese commerce. Were it not generally expected that debts incurred in one part of the archipelago be repaid in another, then there never would have been a lawsuit. Presumably entrepreneurs regularly lent money to each other and only sought adjudication in the event of problems. It should also be noted that other ethnic groups collected debts across large distances as well.

The Flowering of Wajorese Commerce

Amanna Gappa's code and the specific Dutch legal records present an idealized view of Wajorese maritime traders and detailed, personal images of individual traders respectively. A third view of Wajorese commerce is presented in the VOC records concerned with the company's own trade and competition. Dutch records mainly describe "legal" trade, that is to say, commercial activities occurring under the purview of the Dutch which much of Wajorese trade was not. As the Wajorese increasingly out preformed the Dutch, however, there are references in Dutch records to "illegal" Wajorese trade from which a general overview can be gleamed.

As discussed in chapter 2 of this volume, both Dutch and indigenous records relate the devastation of Wajoq following the Makassar War and the ensuing exodus of Wajorese emigrants. Then they both describe the renaissance in Wajorese trade that occurred during the following half-century in very different ways. Wajorese records emphasize the initiatives of various matoa, such as the aforementioned Arung Matoa La Saléwangeng. Dutch records emphasize the difficulties that Wajorese success created for VOC trade.

An important element to this success was a shift in the balance of power in South Sulawesi during the first quarter of the eighteenth century. Both Dutch and Bugis records about this period attest to the manner in which political instability within Boné weakened that kingdom, and it no longer exerted the tremendous political influence over the rest of South Sulawesi that it had under Arung Palakka.[37] Instead, the Dutch refer to Wajoq as "a mighty realm."[38] The records of the Wajorese matoa in Makassar state that "The king of Boné also said to the governor that the Wajorese were not slaves and neither was their country."[39] Governor Cops had made a similar statement before, but this time it was true. By 1730 it appeared that the relative power of Wajoq and Boné had reversed. Wajoq had now regained a considerable amount of its strength whereas Boné, Wajoq's former tormentor, was suffering from political turmoil.[40]

In his Outgoing Report, Governor Sautijn explained how Boné's decline helped facilitate the rise of Wajorese trade. He wrote that:

> When the Bonéan government was in its prime and not bastardized, this sort of thing (clandestine trade) did not usually happen, because if any Bugis or Wajorese should attempt it, the king of Boné knew how to discover the transgression, and the transgressors or adventurers were stripped of everything they had in the world, even their wives, children and slaves, and the king of Boné became master of these, which served as an example.[41]

Yet as Sautijn lamented, those times were long since over, and he went on to point out that the VOC's cloth trade had declined each year during his presence in Makassar.[42] Dutch attempts to combat evasions of the VOC's monopolies were futile and they were unable to compete effectively with Asian traders.[43]

As frustrated as the VOC was with their own inability to compete, the success of the "illegal" Wajorese networks was partially its own fault because the Dutch made it difficult for the Wajorese to trade "legally." In order to participate in what the Dutch referred to as "legal" trade, Asian traders were required to pay outgoing and incoming tolls and to obtain passes. In the case of the Wajorese, the procurement of these passes was complicated by Dutch attitudes. Whereas Smout considered the Wajorese to be skilled and trustworthy merchants,[44] one of his predecessors had a very different opinion. Governor Gobius avoided giving passes to the Bugis in general and "especially to the Bugis and the Wajorese who were driven out of their homes by the Bonéans, I refuse to give them passes unless there is a citizen who will faithfully guarantee that they'll come back."[45]

As difficult as obtaining passes may have been, the Wajorese still conducted part of their trade within channels controlled by the VOC. Statistics from Makassar in 1722 reveal that Wajorese captains figured prominently in the trade recorded in the harbor master's log to both Java, 8 percent, and east and southeastern Kalimantan, 3.7 percent.[46] Although there was a sharp decline in official Wajorese trade in Makassar during the following half century,[47] this does not include the trade occurring outside Dutch purview.

While most of the Dutch records about "legal" Wajorese trade are statistical, certain documents also shed light on the trade of individual Wajorese merchants such as a certain To Palla and To Adang.[48] Suspected of trading in spices, To Palla and To Adang were interrogated in Makassar in 1716. While carrying a load of rice and slaves belonging to Arung Timurung, To Palla's pass was controlled by a Dutch gatekeeper whom he had known for several years and addressed as Toontje (Anthonij van Aldorp). After checking his pass and trying to purchase young boys, the gatekeeper asked To Palla if he had any spices, saying that he needed some for medicinal purposes. To Palla replied that his people did not have spices for their own use, much less any to sell, and suggested that he ask the other captains. Later, To Palla himself made inquiries and purchased 100 pieces of nutmeg from the captain of the Chinese Encik Bieouw which he then sold to the gatekeeper without making any profit for himself or Encik Bieouw.[49] A conflicting account of these events was offered in Van Aldorp's report. He stated that To Palla's companions delivered cloves and 10,000 pieces of nutmeg in Buton boxes, that these spices were from Ambon and Banda, and that they were bought by European burghers and Chinese in Makassar. Furthermore, Van Aldorp maintained that To Adang had refused to show his pass to him, and that To Adang had brought a quantity of spices to Johor and sold him a *gantang* (a unit of measure) of cloves for two Spanish dollars or 2 ½ Dutch dollars.[50] Because of the conflicting testimonies, and because of reports of company servants engaging in illegal private trade, To Palla and To Adang were not punished. However, it is entirely plausible, if not probable, that To Palla and To Adang traded in spices from Maluku and were simply careful to conceal this from the Dutch.

The inquiry also provides information about the empowerment of representatives and the handling of debts. When Van Aldorp was preparing to return to Melaka, he suggested that he collect debts there for To Palla. To Palla declined because Van Aldorp did not know the debtors, and so he sent one of his men named To Patti with Van Aldorp to Melaka to collect the debts. In this particular instance, however, Van Aldorp accused To Palla of using this trip to illegally deal in spices and imprisoned his agent To Patti.[51] While this case has no great significance in and of itself, it does show that the Wajorese captain tried, in this instance, to abide by Dutch restrictions. The Wajorese were not always antagonistic in their dealings with the Dutch. It also shows the manner in which a Wajorese captain empowered his servant to represent him on a trip that he could not make himself. Using a representative allowed the Wajorese captain to conduct business in more than one place at a time, thereby extending his trading network. Finally, the case also underlines the manner in which commercial debts were preserved despite geographical distances, a practice that is likewise illustrated by the case of To Uti. While not unheard of among other ethnic groups, these sorts of arrangements and a legal system for regulating them gave the Wajorese a commercial edge.

Aside from the trade which the Wajorese conducted under Dutch purview, the Wajorese had their own trading networks, referred to by the Dutch as "clandestine." In this trade they benefitted from the special opportunities afforded to them by their own networks through which information was exchanged and commercial partnerships were established. The imports of this trade presumably consisted mainly of goods, particularly textiles, from the Straits of Melaka and Kalimantan.[52] Weapons are also likely to have been extremely important. Exports included textiles and are likely to have included slaves and rice as well. Here again the paramount ruler appears to have participated. According to one lontaraq, Arung Matoa La Saléwangeng himself led an expedition to Java (or unspecified points west, as is sometimes intended by the use of the toponym Java in Bugis texts) in order to purchase firearms.[53] Wajorese trade was so successful that by 1715, the VOC's trade in textiles had declined as a result of Wajorese imports.[54]

By the mid-eighteenth century, the declining trend in the VOC's textile trade had reached such an alarming extent that an influential burgher, J. H. Voll, was assigned to investigate. His report provides a fascinating description of Wajorese trading networks. He describes how Wajorese traders transported local textiles to Riau where they exchanged them for Spanish reals. They then proceeded to Kedah and Selangor where they used the reals to pay for "English textiles," meaning Indian textiles purchased from the English. They made excellent profits because of a higher exchange rate for reals in these parts. They then brought these textiles to various places along the western coast of Sulawesi such as Mandar, Bacukiki, Soreang and Laboso or to any of a number of other places along the coast of Sulawesi that afforded them the opportunity to sail upstream. After reaching the furthest point inland possible, they then would transport the textiles overland to Wajoq. What they could not sell there they traded in other places eastwards, such as Ternate, all the time being careful to avoid Makassar and the Dutch.[55] Thus, despite the aforementioned decline in Wajorese participation in the "legal" trade of Makassar during the mid-eighteenth century, the Wajorese traders were still competing effectively.[56] Even in spite of Dutch efforts to curb their trade, the Wajorese were outperforming the VOC.

The reasons for Wajorese success are multiple. Wajorese trade was highly organized in terms of participation, shipping fees, loans, caring for goods, and cooperation. Amanna Gappa's law code and La Saléwangeng's initiatives exemplify this high level of organization perfectly. Another reason for

Wajorese success was their detailed knowledge of local conditions. British records testify to the exceptional understanding that the Wajorese had of local conditions in western Sumatra. There the Wajorese were regarded with "the greatest awe upon the natives as best acquainted with the country and [were] able to pierce [penetrate] it when Europeans cannot."[57]

In some situations, the extensive trading networks of the Wajorese and the middleman position that they often held also allowed them to collect duties or taxes. In eastern Kalimantan, for example, the sultan of Kutai appointed a shahbandar to represent his own interests and collect duties in the face of expanding Wajorese trade. This official was generally not very effective, however, because the Bugis had control over the mouth of the river and collected their own duties which constituted an important source of income for the pua adu. Elsewhere, in western Sumatra, the Wajorese were the enforcers for British pepper cultivation. This position would have presented numerous opportunities for income. Sultan Endey, for example, could afford to serve the EIC for years without being paid. Presumably his willingness to work without remuneration stemmed from other financial advantages that his position offered. The license to trade in opium that was issued to Daéng Maruppa[58] would also have presented enhanced opportunities for financial gain. Especially because opium was an important commodity within the Bugis community in western Sumatra,[59] this license can be considered as a mark of the EIC's favor.

The Wajorese Trading Diaspora

The strength of the Wajorese commercial community and its ability to adapt to changing circumstances enabled it to withstand VOC restrictions and compete successfully with what has been called "one of the most advanced capitalist institutions produced by seventeenth-century Europe." When conditions in one port declined, they switched to another. When favorable opportunities arose, they did not hesitate to expand their operations. In this manner they were essential to the maintenance of the indigenous economy in the face of Dutch encroachment. Furthermore, specifically because they were geographically dispersed, they were well poised to advance to the economic integration of the archipelago.

The Wajorese developed sophisticated systems to expand their commercial potential and safeguard their trade. Key elements of these systems were the codification of commercial laws; various mechanisms allowing individuals with limited means to trade and/or borrow money; and group solidarity.

While clearly influenced by prominent individuals such as Amanna Gappa and La Saléwangeng, these systems were part of a commercial cultural complex that was bigger than any one leader. It was a communal effort requiring the cooperation of peddlers and umbrella capitalists alike. That the framework existed above and beyond individuals is perhaps nowhere easier to perceive than in the system for regulating the affairs of dead merchants.

These systems enabled the Wajorese to expand. They spread their networks to the farthest reaches of the archipelago and to the innermost banks of rivers. Trading amongst themselves and with a wide variety of other groups, they became experts in certain commodities and routes such as the trade in cloth and reals spanning from Kedah to Ternate.

In turn, their commercial networks enabled them to refortify Wajoq. Successive arung matoa deliberately sought to expand international trade as a means of strengthening the state. Wajorese commercial goals clearly extended beyond individual profit. While group solidarity and commercial success are common characteristics for a diaspora, this use of the proceeds from trade to refortify the homeland appears unusual in the early modern world.

While not unheard of, the development of a commercial code of laws is also unusual among early modern trading diasporas. This gave the Wajorese an advantage over their competitors because it provided a framework for regulating commercial relationships outside the limited contacts of kin. Nevertheless, family was an important means of social organization among the Wajorese and it is the subject of the following chapter.

CHAPTER FIVE

Family Relations

Upon his departure from Wajoq, La Maddukelleng was asked what his provisions were. He replied "I am prepared, my lord. The good fortune of Wajoq is with me because its population wishes me well. My supplies are three: the gentleness of my tongue, the sharpness of my weapon's point, and the curve of my penis."[1] His references are to diplomacy, military prowess, and marriage. Common among the Bugis overseas, these three skills can be considered the arsenal of the migrant. Because a tongue, weapon, and penis all have a tip, they are known among the Bugis as the *tellu cappaq* or "three tips." The inclusion of marriage is indicative of the importance of marriage and other types of family relations to the Wajorese diaspora.

The importance of family ties to the Wajorese is not surprising. Family relationships have served as an important unifying factor for many diaspora in various times and places. For example, genealogies served as a basis for organizing the movements, exchanges, and identities across the Hadrami diaspora[2] and family firms figured prominently in the trade of the Indian diaspora in early modern Turan.[3] Furthermore, family was a very important element of statecraft in early modern Southeast Asia. In many Southeast Asian states, family networks constituted an important, state-like mechanism for power relations.[4] Thus the connections established by family relationships were valuable both at home and abroad.

Widely valued, family relations are also well documented. In some parts of Southeast Asia virtually the only indigenous historical sources are genealogies known, among other names, as *salasilah*. Generally documenting only descent and marriage, however, the salasilah can be deceptive because they do not reveal emotions, obligations, or communication. They can also omit certain branches of the family. Other aspects of family relations are depicted in sources like *hikayat,* a Malay genre of literature. These, too, can be misleading because while hikayat are based on historical fact, they are heavily romanticized.[5] Contemporary European observers also took an interest in family relations, particularly in family conflicts that affected, or risked to affect, succession. Yet the influence of European notions of bounded states prevented them from fully recognizing the important role of family in Southeast Asian statecraft.[6] Despite the abundance of references to marriage in the indigenous sources, however, and the manner in which they have attracted the attention of historians since the nineteenth century, very few secondary works have stressed the implications of marriage. This is regrettable because entire communities could be implicated in a marital relationship, especially when foreign trading groups, like the Wajorese, were involved.

As powerful an integrative force as family relations were, they were also complicated and ambiguous. Often serving as the arena for pride and politics, families could be wrought with tension and conflict. When family relationships went awry, they could result in enormous problems. The stakes were higher up the social ladder and at the elite level family conflicts could even bring societies into a war. Families could be complicated and ambiguous in economic terms as well, especially because business dealings frequently occurred within the framework of family relationships, be they real or putative. While kin often were considered to be reliable partners, jealousy and hatred were just as common as support and affection. Indeed there existed a whole wealth of unexplained emotions and relationships that this chapter can only begin to explore in a few cases.

Marriage and Family in Early Modern Southeast Asia

In the face of the unpredictable and precarious nature of life in early modern Southeast Asia, family offered a sense of security. A group of related persons upon whom an individual could rely was a very important asset, all the more so for migrants. This group could consist of a wide variety of relatives, related through blood, milk, sex, vows, birth, or marriage. Significantly, this group could be expanded at any time during an individual's life. Given the variety of ways in which relationships could be established, it is important to think of early modern Southeast Asian families in very broad terms.

It is also important to consider the unusual autonomy of women in the region. By world standards, women enjoyed significant economic, sexual, political, and legal autonomy as well as ritual importance. Indeed, it has become commonplace to regard the autonomous position of women as a defining characteristic of Southeast Asia.[7] Furthermore, the high position of women was arguably even more evident during the early modern era than during later periods. As world religions and Western imperialism increasingly made their impact felt, Southeast Asian women lost some of the autonomy that had been part of indigenous traditions. Whereas this trend was also felt in South Sulawesi, some of its manifestations were later than in other parts of the region. For example, in South Sulawesi female rulers continued to exert power into the nineteenth century when their counterparts in other Islamized parts of the world had largely disappeared.[8]

Generally speaking, marriages in early modern Southeast Asia reflected the region's pattern of female autonomy. Pre-marital sexual experience and divorce were widely accepted, whereas domestic violence was not.[9] At elite levels, however, women might enjoy less freedom than their commoner counterparts. High-ranking women could be expected to be virgins at the time of marriage and their movements might even be restricted. Moreover, at the elite level the stakes were higher. As described in the following sections, diplomacy often rested upon marriages between high-ranking families and any perceived mistreatment of women or perceived neglect of kinship obligations could result in a diplomatic crisis or even a war.[10]

Across Southeast Asia, marriage often served as an integrative force. Rulers frequently used marriage as a means of strengthening alliances with powerful families within their own society and beyond it.[11] Significantly, the resultant links sometimes proved more durable than alliances formed through treaties. A case in point is David Bulbeck's research on the marriage politics of Gowa, which has shown that such inter-state alliances were often longer lasting than those established through treaties.[12] Marriage served a similar purpose among migrants. Throughout the region migrants and overseas traders often used marriage as a way to gain access to local societies and their resources.[13] Similarly, local rulers used marriage as a means of affiliating themselves with powerful groups of migrants.

The marital career of the Makassarese noblewoman Karaenga ri Bontojeneq (1628–1669) provides a rich example of how marriages could be used to forge alliances. During her lifetime she married and divorced four times. Her first marriage was to the ruler of Bima I Ambela with whom she had numerous children, including a son who was slated to become the ruler of Bima. Two daughters resulting from this marriage went on to marry the sons of prominent Makassarese noblemen. Karaenga ri Bontojeneq's second and fourth marriage was to Karaeng ri Jarannika, a prominent noble in

Gowa. Her third marriage, lasting less than a year, was to the ruler of Sumbawa. Family relations to Gowa through Karaenga ri Bontojeneq would have been a source of pride among Biman royalty and, had her marriage to the ruler of Sumbawa endured, it might brought prestige to Sumbawan royalty as well.[14] In all likelihood her marriages to Biman and Sumbawan rulers were intended to extend the influence of Gowa overseas.

Another means through which ties were forged and consolidated was through adoption. Societies across Southeast Asia recognized adopted relatives and often accorded little importance to whether or not family ties were biological or not. This is clearly exemplified in the *Hikayat Hang Tuah*. In the classical Malay literary work, the protagonist appears willing to gloss over thorny questions of ethnicity and family and simply accept that he is related to his companions. Including attendance at a dancing party, the exchange of presents, and an exhortation not to harbor feelings of distrust, the process is referred to as "playing relatives."[15] It exemplifies considerable flexibility and a strong desire to create a community based on purported kinship ties.

By no means limited to the adoption of orphaned children, adoption also could consist of adopting an adult, often an outsider. This was such an important means of incorporating foreigners into society that it even existed in societies where the adoption of children was not practiced.[16] It was a particularly important strategy in the absence of appropriate female relatives for the forging of marital alliances, but could be used whenever securing an individual's loyalty was considered desirable. When adoptions were framed in terms of parent child, they established an intrinsically hierarchical relationship.

Another means through which one's family could be enlarged was through the adoption of siblings. People bound themselves to each other on the basis of common interest or shared experiences and ritualized this bond with an oath-taking ceremony. Taken very seriously, the adoption of siblings could also involve the exchange of blood, thereby establishing a blood brotherhood. Alternatively, the sharing of a female sexual partner could also establish an important bond between men.[17]

As powerful as ritualized, consensual bonds of brotherhood were, the relationships established by breast milk were just as significant. The sharing of a common milk mother created a bond between otherwise unrelated people. Tantamount to a consanguineous relationship, the bond between milk relatives precluded them from marrying each other according to Islamic law, with some interpretations extending this prohibition to the relatives of the wet nurse.[18] One was also obliged to protect a so-called milk relative (*saudara susuan*) and one could count upon a milk sibling for protection,[19] just as would be expected with a biological relative. The significance of milk relatives is indicated by the position of wet nurses in Southeast Asian society. In other parts of the world, wet nurses were hired as contract laborers, but there is no known example of a written contract for a wet nurse in early modern Southeast Asia. By contrast, wet nurses were accorded tremendous importance in Southeast Asia and even could have ceremonial functions in addition to their biological ones. The significance of their roles frequently resulted in wet nurses forming the nuclei of networks of interrelationships of milk relatives.[20]

In some circumstances the bond between milk siblings or half siblings could be even stronger than those between siblings with the same parents. Especially in monogamous situations, birth order established a culturally significant hierarchy. This hierarchy resulted from the age difference between siblings which, in areas of low fecundity, was commonly several years. Milk siblings, on the other hand, could be close in age and therefore grow up with each other as equals. Polygamy could afford the same sort of egalitarian relationship to siblings with different mothers. Less hierarchical than the relationships between children of the same parents, the bonds between such milk siblings or half siblings could be the most important relationship in their lives.

The importance of sibling relationships should not be underestimated. While it is commonplace to think of family in terms of women and men, relations between men and men were crucial. Southeast Asian historiography contains numerous bands of wandering brothers, like the sons of Opu Daéng Rilaga, who themselves claimed to be "five brothers with one father and one mother like one soul and one body. There is no separation in the event of good or evil."[21] There are also many instances of brothers defending each other's honor, such as when La Maddukelleng sought vengeance on behalf of his brother Daéng Matekko.[22]

In terms of kinship, South Sulawesi shared much in common with the rest of Southeast Asia but there were several distinguishing aspects. One such characteristic is the importance of status in marriage. Marriage patterns in South Sulawesi generally followed those of the larger region. They did not inordinately privilege men as might be expected of an Islamic society. However, in the status-conscious societies of South Sulawesi, there was a critical difference between the marriage options for men and women. Men could raise their status by way of achievement and marry up, but this opportunity was not generally available to women whose status was ascribed. This difference has long resulted in the preponderance of unmarried high-ranking women in South Sulawesi and in the use of women to mark the status of their husbands.[23] This use of women as status markers, deeply entrenched among the Bugis and Makassarese, was not shared by the inhabitants of some of the societies where the Wajorese settled and was a source of contention with the host societies.

Another area in which the Wajorese sometimes differed from their host societies was in the use of bilateral kinship. Because ancestry and kinship among the Bugis are traced along both the mother and the father's lines, Bugis kinship is said to be organized bilaterally.[24] According to this principle, both the mother's and father's families maintain relationships with a child, and both men and women maintain relations with their family of origin upon marriage. There are tendencies towards uxorilocal residence and endogamy but virilocal residence and exogamy are also practiced. The result is a society of overlapping groups of bilateral kindreds as opposed to sharply delineated descent groups.[25] Bilateral kinship has very far reaching ramifications. For example, bilateral kinship offers individuals a wider selection of kin and concomitantly the opportunity to choose their particular affiliation.

Among the Bugis, an individual's opportunities to choose his or her own affiliation are further enhanced by the possibility of kinship by alignment. Kinship by alignment refers to the practice of forming kindred-like groups through various types of formal or not-so-formal association. The anthropologist Susan Millar refers to these groups as "*tau matoa* networks." Whereas 'tau matoa' literally translates as 'elder,' it commonly refers to an unusually astute, eloquent and competent man or woman to whom others turn for guidance and leadership. These powerful individuals attract a following which then forms a "tau matoa network." While the members of such a group do not technically form a family, relationships are commonly expressed in terms of kinship metaphors.[26] Because Millar's focus is on marriage and thus on kinship, she deliberately avoids the term "coalition" because of its economic and political connotations. Given the importance of family to indigenous politics, however, these groups sometimes functioned as political coalitions, as will be described in the section on La Maddukelleng below.

Marriage and Family in the Wajorese Diaspora

Culturally specific ideas about marriage, family, women and status were deeply engrained among Wajorese emigrants before they even left Wajoq. When these differed from the ideas of their hosts, there were sometimes important and dramatic ramifications. In one instance such differences are known to have resulted in war.

The *Salasilah Bugis* describes how the Wajorese migrants' views on the ceremonial use of women generated conflict with their hosts in Kutai. When the Wajorese leader, the pua adu, was asked to choose a wife, he selected a woman of royal lineage, and thus presumed her to be of high status. This woman, however, came from a family descendant from war captives whose participation was needed in a ceremony to mark a successor to the throne of Kutai. When such an heir to the throne was born, he was not allowed to walk on bare ground until this ceremony was completed. The ceremony entailed dragging the prince over the head of a living person, a cropped human head, the head of a living buffalo, the head of a slaughtered buffalo, a piece of old iron and a rock so that the prince touched all of these objects with his feet. Only then was he allowed to walk freely on the ground. However, according to custom, the living human participant had to be selected from this family, which traced its origin back through the centuries to war captives. Until at least the late nineteenth century this family resided at the mouth of the Mahakam River, enjoying certain privileges in exchange for providing this service.[27]

When the Kutai leaders learned that the Wajorese leader wished to marry a woman from this family, they tried to persuade him to change his mind. The pua adu then said that he would not be bothered by his wife's participation in the ceremony and so they were permitted to marry. In the event, however, the pua adu was deeply shamed by his wife's role. Designed to exalt the prince, it was considered denigrating to the living participant and as a Bugis, the pua adu would have felt this particularly keenly. Among all Bugis, women are important status markers and the Wajorese are considered especially status-conscious. Thus the pua adu's wife's participation was an insult to his siriq. As a result he packed up and left Kutai with his wife, children and followers and went to Sulu. His grievances against Kutai clearly lingered, because he later joined forces with the Suluans in an attack against Kutai. They were defeated and withdrew, but took prisoners of war from Kutai.

Parallels exist between this example from Kutai and other histories of migrants from South Sulawesi. Following the Makassar War a group of Makassarese migrants led by Karaéng Bontomarannu established themselves in Banten. The relationship between the host society and the migrants began well but was irreparably damaged when the Sultan of Banten attempted to exercise his traditional prerogative to marry any woman in his kingdom. When the Sultan of Banten tried to marry the wife of a Makassarese noble, the Makassarese noble was deeply offended. The Sultan of Banten's attempt to marry this noble's wife this was perceived of as a rejection of Karaeng Bontomarannu's claim of being his equal. As a result the Makassarese fled Banten.[28]

Despite the potential for marriages to go awry, they were still an important strategy among the overseas Wajorese. The marriages of La Maddukelleng, Daéng Matteko and his daughter, Daéng Maruppa and his grandchild, and the anonymous diarist demonstrate the different ways in which family relations were used in attempts to achieve social and political goals. Less apparent in these examples is the use of family relations to achieve commercial goals, but the law code of Amanna Gappa suggests that kinship was also a factor in commerce.

Family as a Network: La Maddukelleng

Both contemporary Dutch and modern local sources attest to La Maddukelleng's use of marriage as a diplomatic tool. Dutch sources record a marriage between La Maddukelleng and a daughter of the Pasir ruler[29] Aji Patti. Dutch sources also records La Maddukelleng's forces having espoused the women and girls they captured on a punitive expedition to Kutai. (The men, by contrast, were sold.)[30] It is also possible that La Maddukelleng married into Sumbawan royalty.[31]

The situation in which La Maddukelleng ended up waging war against his wife's family in Pasir presumably was extremely complex. Full details are not revealed in Dutch sources, which were primarily concerned with the financial success of the VOC. Nevertheless, it is conceivable that he employed all three of his avowed strategies in Pasir. He may have first used the point of his tongue or verbal diplomatic skills to gain entry into important circles in Pasir. Then he used the tip of his penis and married the daughter of the ruler of Pasir. Almost certainly, the marriage was an attempt to secure concessions but he is likely not to have obtained all the concession he desired. Subsequently, La Maddukelleng turned to violence and used the tip of his sword. He ousted the ruler of Pasir in a formal war during the mid-1720s and then claimed the throne for himself.[32] The combination of tactics helped him rally support for his own political ambitions. Unfortunately, the fate of La Maddukelleng's wife is unknown, a lacuna illustrating the limitations of the sources for reconstructing family relationships.

Modern historiography from eastern Kalimantan provides a very different view of La Maddukelleng. Accounts vary but none of them ever portray him as the ruthless conqueror described in contemporary Dutch sources. Instead they portray him as a capable leader at the center of a large *tau matoa* network. The most detailed account, H. A. Demang Kedaton's typescript *Sedjarah Ringkas Kedatangan Suku Bugis di Samarinda Seberang* (*A Short History of the Arrival of the Bugis in Samarinda Seberang*) comes from Samarinda. It is a salasilah in the true sense of the word (lit. genealogy) in that it portrays La Maddukelleng as the progenitor of an extensive network of Wajorese dynasties. Although it contradicts the *Salasilah Melayu dan Bugis,* the *Tuhfat al-Nafis* and Dutch sources, it testifies to the magnitude of La Maddukelleng's legend in the Wajorese society in eastern Kalimantan, a legend that is still held dear by local aristocrats. Furthermore, this historiography, regardless of its factualness, illustrates the manner in which various Wajorese communities in eastern Kalimantan perceived of each other as kin.

A *Short History of the Arrival of the Bugis in Samarinda Seberang* portrays the establishment of a Wajorese diaspora as a conscious decision. According to this typescript, La Maddukelleng left Sulawesi with three of his children, eight devoted members of the nobility and two hundred other people in his entourage. They remained in Pasir for about a month after which thousands of refugees from Soppéng and Wajoq arrived with news of Boné conquering Wajoq and assuming control of its government. La Maddukelleng called a meeting to discuss this predicament and decided to send his followers to establish communities in different localities. The meeting exemplifies the use of the tip of his tongue for deliberation and diplomacy.

While La Maddukelleng's wives are curiously absent from the account, his offspring, the products of the tip of his penis, feature prominently. According to this salasilah, La Maddukelleng's biological children played an important role in the establishment of his network. One of the three sons who accompanied him, Petta To Sibengareng, married one of the daughters of the ruler of Pasir. The oldest daughter of this couple then married Sultan Muhammad Idris of Kutai, and her son Aji Imbut replaced his father as Sultan Kutai. Another son of La Maddukelleng, Petta To Siangka, went to Donggala where his descendants became incorporated into the royal families of Donggala, Banawa, Tawaeli, Biromaru (Palu) and Bulungan. The third, Petta To Rawé, went to Berau and Sulu, became friends with the ruler of Sambaliung, and developed the Bugis communities at Tanjung Redeb and Banjarmasin. His ability to function in more than one location is indicative of an exceptionally high level of mobility.

Aside from La Maddukelleng's biological sons, the salasilah also accords important roles to the members of La Maddukelleng's tau matoa networks. One of the eight accompanying nobles, La Mohang Daéng Mangkonaq, went to Kutai where he became the effective ruler of Samarinda. Another of the accompanying nobles, La Pallawa Daéng Marowaq, resided in Pasir where he intermarried with the local aristocracy. Yet another, Puanna Dekkeq, a nephew of the ruler of Soppéng, went to Bumbu. He was joined there by his own nephew, who in time became ruler of Pegatan and founded the La Paliweng dynasty.[33] A fourth companion, La Sirajeq Daéng Menambong, went to western Kalimantan where he supposedly married the sister of the King of Matan and founded Mempawa.[34] A fifth companion, La Manjaq Daéng Lebbiq, went to Penyengat (Riau) where he married the daughter of the *bendahara*, the principal official in Johor. Their son, Ahmad Daéng Kamboja, became Raja Muda.[35] Another of La Maddukelleng's companions, La Manripiq Daéng Punggawa, participated in Javanese commerce and called repeatedly at Pasir, Kutai and Tuban. The last two nobles, Puanna Tereng and La Sawedi Daéng Sagala, stayed with La Maddukelleng and accompanied him on his travels.

As portrayed in *A Short History of the Arrival of the Bugis in Samarinda Seberang*, both La Maddukelleng's children and the other nobles accompanying him were part of a larger, conscious strategy to establish a geographically dispersed tau matoa network. The text locates the origins of the more prominent Bugis families throughout the archipelago in La Maddukelleng's entourage and the flight of La Maddukelleng is thus seen as the sole catalyst for Wajorese, indeed for all Bugis, migration. While such an extravagant claim cannot be justified, it shows how important La Maddukelleng is in local historical consciousness. Furthermore, like the *Salasilah Bugis*, *A Short History of the Arrival of the Bugis in Samarinda Seberang* is a history intended to justify the prominence of the Bugis in an area of overseas settlement. Historically it appears to be less accurate, but socially it fulfills a similar purpose.

Published modern histories from eastern Kalimantan[36] also place tremendous emphasis on the role of family in the establishment of the Wajorese in eastern Kalimantan. While they vary in details, they generally they state that it was La Maddukelleng's son, rather than La Maddukelleng himself, who marries a princess from Pasir, and specify that Aji Imbut a.k.a. Sultan Muhammad Muslihuddin is a direct descendant of La Maddukelleng. That the ruler of Kutai during the nineteenth century was of Bugis descent is also recorded in contemporary records.[37] Furthermore, the prominent social position of Wajorese migrants described in modern histories from East Kalimantan matches the prominent economic and political position of the Bugis described by contemporary observers. Even if violence was the more persuasive tactic during the eighteenth century, in local historiography and in the minds of the descendant populations, marriage has prevailed as an important and long-lasting element in the arsenal of the migrant.

Daéng Matekko's Marriages as Political Initiatives

Whereas La Maddukelleng used a combination of tactics including marriage effectively to advance his goals in East Kalimantan, his brother Daéng Matekko did not enjoy the same success. Marital alliances, both failed and successful, colored the career of Daéng Matekko across the Malay world. He himself married twice, but these marriages do not appear to have been politically useful. His daughter, however, married Tengku Mahmud, a son of Raja Kecik of Siak. This marriage solidified Daéng Matekko's own relationship with Raja Kecik who was an important figure in the Straits of Melaka during the early eighteenth century.

Daéng Matekko's career, his marriages and his political affiliations all took place against the backdrop of conflict between different groups of Bugis within the Malay world. While Daéng Matekko's departure from Sulawesi is not recorded in Wajorese historical sources, legend has it that his older brother La Maddukelleng's departure resulted directly from a conflict with the ruler of Boné described in chapter 7. The two brothers would have carried vivid memories of the animosity between Boné and Wajoq with them into exile. This anti-Bonéan sentiment was particularly important in the career of Daéng Matekko because he settled in the Straits of Melaka. In this region the Riau Bugis were exceptionally powerful. Thus it is no coincidence that Daéng Matekko sided with anti-Bonéan elements in the Straits. He came into conflict both with the Riau Bugis and with To Passarai, the uncle of Arumponé Batari Toja.

During the early 1720s Daéng Matekko settled in Matan[38] in southwest Borneo where he married the daughter of the Pangeran Agung, the younger son of the ruler Sultan Muhammad Safi al-Din. Here he enjoyed the companionship of other Wajorese migrants, most notably Haji Hafiz. Haji Hafiz was married to a different daughter of the Pangeran Agung thus the family relations between the Wajorese and Pangeran Agung's branch of the royal family of Matan were well-established. When Sultan Muhammad Safi al-Din died, he was succeeded by his older son who then assumed the title Sultan Muhammad Zain al-Din. A succession dispute ensued and Pangeran Agung claimed the throne for himself. In this case brotherhood was insufficient to dampen political rivalry. Sultan Muhammad Zain al-Din's family fled to Banjar but he himself remained in a mosque in Matan. He sent a request to Siantan asking the Riau Bugis for help in regaining his throne. The opu obliged, came to Matan and tried to persuade Pangeran Agung to resolve the conflict with his brother peacefully. When this failed they went to Banjar to retrieve Sultan Muhammad Zain al-Din's family. Upon their return to Matan Sultan Muhammad Zain al-Din married his daughter Puteri Kesumba to Opu Daéng Menambun, thereby strengthening his alliance with the Riau Bugis.[39] Together they launched a campaign against Pangeran Agung. Apparently the campaign was so difficult that Opu Daéng Menambun suggested that Sultan Muhammad Zain al-Din either give up and establish himself in Sulawesi, or seek reinforcements there.[40] Eventually their campaign succeeded after which they reportedly imprisoned Pangeran Agung in a fort with thirty women. According to the *Tuhfat al-Nafis,* this imprisonment resulted in Pangeran Agung having an exceptionally large number of children but their fates are not known. What is significant is that by providing Pangeran Agung with access to many women, Sultan Muhammad Zain al-Din showed mercy upon his brother and afforded him with the opportunity to enlarge his family, a chance that would have been cherished in a land with an endemically low population.

His father-in-law defeated, and the family of his rivals in power, Daéng Matekko fled Matan. It is unclear whether Daéng Matekko took his wife with him. The *Tuhfat al-Nafis* mentions the cannon he took with him by name ('Kedah') but omits both the name and the fate of his wife.[41] As with the case of La Maddukelleng's wife from Pasir, this omission exemplifies the difficulty of reconstructing family relationships on the basis of available sources. In any event, Daéng Matekko's marriage to the daughter of Pangeran Agung failed to secure him a prominent position within Matan society. This was likely due to Pangeran Agung's overly ambitious political designs, the failure of which would have jeopardized the position of his supporters. Having sided with the less powerful element in Matan, Daéng Matekko then departed to pursue his fortune elsewhere.

After fleeing Matan, Daéng Matekko went to Siak on the eastern coast of Sumatra. There Daéng Matekko allied himself with the charismatic Raja Kecik. Although his origins are obscure, Raja Kecik was most likely a Minangkabau prince who was sent from Pagar Ruyung to lead migrant Minangkabau on the eastern coast of Sumatra. He differed from other such princes, however, in that he appealed to orang asli and Malay concepts of leadership. Claiming to be the son of Sultan Mahmud, the last ruler descendant from the prestigious Melaka-Johor line, Raja Kecik also claimed the *daulat* (sovereignty) and provided a means by which it could be perpetuated. Although the veracity of his claimed origins was easily disputed, he had wide-ranging appeal and he gained the loyalty of diverse groups in the Straits, especially the peoples of eastern and upstream Sumatra, as well as the orang laut. Eventually, he gained enough of a following to enable him to attack Johor, demote Sultan Abdul Jalil to his former position as bendahara, and, in March 1718, claim the throne for himself and his line.[42] Daéng Matekko probably opted to ally himself with Raja Kecik because of the pre-existing animosity between Raja Kecik and the Riau Bugis.

Especially for the purposes of this chapter, it is interesting to note that part of this animosity appears to stem from an engagement scandal that occurred while Raja Kecik ruled Johor.[43] In an effort to gain the support of Abdul Jalil, Raja Kecik had reappointed him as bendahara, and promised to marry his daughter Tengku Tengah. When he came to Tengku Tengah's house and saw her younger sister Tengku Kamariah, however, he was so smitten by her that he took the ring from his betrothed's hand, gave it to Tengku Kamariah and took her as his wife. Tengku Tengah was deeply offended. In order to avenge this insult, she enlisted the help of Opu Daéng Rilaga's sons Daéng Parani and Daéng Cellak to help her brother Sulaiman overthrow Raja Kecik.[44] Although it is uncertain if Raja Kecik already had Daéng Matekko's assistance when the Malays and Riau Bugis attacked in 1722, he was easily defeated and driven back to Siak where he reassumed his position as Sultan Abdul Jalil Rahmat Syah. Thereafter the Riau Bugis assumed an extremely important position within Johor.[45]

Given the dominance of the Riau Bugis, it behooved both Raja Kecik and Daéng Matekko to seek a reconciliation with them. Raja Kecik concluded peace with the Riau Bugis in 1727,[46] but apparently had no intention of maintaining it. On the contrary, he tried to collaborate with the Dutch to expel them from the Straits.[47] Daéng Matekko also tried to restore relations with the Riau Bugis. In 1729 or 1730, he even married a certain Engku Tengah, who may have been the widow of Daéng Parani.[48] This reconciliation was short-lived, however, and Daéng Matekko soon found himself in opposition to the Riau Bugis once again.

In the face of dominance of the Riau Bugis, Daéng Matekko tried to take advantage of alternative opportunities in the Straits. In 1731 he established himself as ruler in Selangor,[49] but he was unable to safeguard it from the designs of other Bugis groups. Later that same year, he was challenged in Selangor by another Bugis leader, To Passarai, also known as Raja Baru of Linggi.[50] Although To Passerai and Daéng Matekko were both opposed to the opu, they were never allies. In fact, To Passarai mounted an expedition against Daéng Matekko in Selangor and succeeded in expelling him after a couple of skirmishes. Daéng Matekko fled to Siak where he asked Raja Kecik for assistance. The latter provided him with 14 well-armed ships and they succeeded in driving To Passarai out of Selangor.[51] Yet shortly thereafter, the Riau Bugis under the Daéng Marewa launched an attack against Daéng Matekko, expelling him definitively from Selangor and forcing him once again to retreat to Siak.[52] After having been driven out of Selangor, Daéng Matekko was brought by Raja Kecik to Riau to ask for Daéng Marewa's forgiveness and for the return of Daéng Matekko's wife Engku Tengah. The first request was granted but not the second because of the enmity that still existed between Raja Kecik and the rulers of Riau. So fierce was this enmity that the *Tuhfat al-Nafis* records "The Raja Tua no longer believed Daeng Mattekuh [Daéng Matekko], because he had come in the company of Raja Kecik."[53] For a second time, Daéng Matekko's attempt to use marriage as a means of securing a permanent alliance failed.

The enmity between the Riau Bugis on the one side and Daéng Matekko and Raja Kecik on the other side escalated. Indeed, Daéng Matekko was so enraged and humiliated by Daéng Marewa's refusal to return his wife that he began planning with Raja Kecik to attack Riau. In 1735 they were finally prepared to launch their offensive, but it was foiled by advance warning of the attack. This enabled Sultan Sulaiman's forces to take the initiative and launch a pre-emptive strike that caused considerable damage to the invading fleet commanded by Raja Kecik and Daéng Matteko. During this engagement, the two were separated, but both managed to escape.[54] Thereafter Raja Kecik ordered his son Raja Alam, Daéng Matekko, and his naval commander Raja Emas to attack Riau again. In this battle the aggressors converted a boat into a mobile fortress but they were nevertheless defeated and retreated to Siak.[55] Raja Kecik never again threatened Riau.

Daéng Matekko's repeated attempts to forge alliances through marriages, and his lack of success with this strategy illustrates that it did not guarantee either success or assimilation. The political usefulness of his marriage to the daughter of the Pangeran Agung of Matan was thwarted by the overthrow of Pangeran Agung and the reinstallation of Sultan Muhammad Zain al-Din in 1721. Similarly Daéng Matekko's marriage to Engku Tengah was not sufficient to maintain good relations with the Riau Bugis. There was, however, one case in which Daéng Matekko successfully established a lasting marital alliance. This was when he married his daughter to Raja Kecik's son Tengku Mahmud. This marriage allowed Daéng Matekko to remain in the good graces of this branch of Siak's royal family. Tengku Mahmud also benefited from this relationship because he gained support of many Bugis on account of his wife's ethnicity.[56] The implications of this marriage, as well as the career of a son resulting from it, are discussed at greater length in chapter 6.

To conclude this discussion of Daéng Matekko, it is interesting to take a look at his relationship with his brother La Maddukelleng. They operated in different regions of the archipelago: Daéng Matekko primarily in the Straits of Melaka and La Maddukelleng primarily in the Straits of Makassar. Yet despite the physical distance between them, they looked out for each other. As brothers, they felt obliged to seek vengeance for any abuse that the other suffered. Thus after To Passarai attacked Daéng Matekko in Selangor, La Maddukelleng sought revenge on his behalf by attacking To Passarai in southeastern Kalimantan.[57] Presumably this retaliation was motivated by a combination of brotherly loyalty and anti-Bonéan sentiment.

Daéng Makkulle's Family as a Dynasty

Another compelling example of marriage and family politics comes from Western Sumatra. As previously mentioned the Wajorese pioneer Daéng Maruppa ostensibly was the brother of a ruler in Wajoq. Here again the relationship between brothers was significant. Locally recorded traditions point to the maintenance of ties between Daéng Maruppa and his brother in Wajoq and to the quickening of trade between Inderapura and Wajoq because of this connection.[58]

In Inderapura three different steps were taken to consolidate a family relationship between the Wajorese migrant and the host society. This clearly indicates a preference for dealing with relatives as opposed to dealing with strangers. First the ruler of Inderapura adopted Daéng Maruppa.[59] Such an adoption is indicative of how a family relationship was important not only to the emigrant but to the host society as well. The local ruler used the metaphor of father and son to incorporate the stranger into his ambit. Secondly, the ruler of Inderapura married Daéng Maruppa to his sister.[60] Such a marriage is especially significant within the context of western Sumatra where matrilineal traditions among the Minangkabau make marriage to the ruler's sister an exceptionally high honor. Thirdly, a son resulting from this marriage, Daéng Mabéla, was raised alongside the Sultan of Inderapura's own son. This suggests that they may have shared a wet nurse which would have made them milk relatives. As discussed in the chapter introduction, milk relations, or saudara susuan, were otherwise unrelated people who shared a wet nurse were considered to have a special bond. In this case, the boys were also cousins.

Forged at three different levels, the bonds between the ruling elite of Inderapura and the Wajorese migrants gave the Wajorese a distinct advantage from the very start. It was not, however, the only factor involved in their success. Service in the EIC was also very advantageous for the Wajorese. Successive generations served the English as both adjudicators and policy enforcement officials, and they accrued various advantages as discussed in chapter 6. What is interesting in terms of family relations is that the key position, that of Captain of the Bugis, was passed down from father to son over the course of half a dozen generations.

As a result of this hereditary distribution, there was a veritable Wajorese dynasty in western Sumatra. Eventually the power and influence of this dynasty allowed for the roles of marriage with an eye towards assimilation to be reversed. Two generations after Daéng Maruppa married the ruler of Inderapura's sister, his grandson Daéng Makkullé also married a prestigious local: the daughter of Pangeran Mangku from Balai Buntar (Sunggai Lemau).[61] Then, two more generations later, the Wajorese were so firmly entrenched in west Sumatran society that they themselves were desirable marriage partners for newcomers. Instead of marrying prestigious locals, they could afford to reverse the strategy and marry prestigious foreigners. Thus Daéng Maruppa's great-granddaughters married two newly arrived Madurese princes.

Family and Diaspora Consolidation

Whereas the discussion thus far has emphasized the use of marriage and other family relations as a means of forging bonds with host societies, it also appears that family ties were important to the maintenance of ties between Wajoq and overseas Wajorese communities. Bugis soldiers serving in western Sumatra are known to have come crying to Dutch officials about homesickness and missing their families.[62] Furloughs granted to these soldiers enabled them to visit South Sulawesi which presumably served as an important source of marriage partners for the overseas Wajorese.

The diary of the Wajorese statesman[63] who travelled to eastern Kalimantan also suggests that marital alliances were important to the maintenance of Wajoq's relations with overseas Wajorese communities. During the sixteen years covered in his diary, he married three times. Two of these marriages, to Wé Apa in Kutai and to Wé Isa in Berau, were in areas with significant Wajorese populations. Wé Isa and Wé Apa would be fascinating case studies, but unfortunately the information pertaining to them is limited to three lines in the statesman's diary. In his marriages to two people within the Wajorese political ambit, the diarist resembles the Makassarese noblewoman Karaenga ri Bontojeneq discussed in the introduction to this chapter. Whereas Wé Apa died a few short months after the marriage, the marriage to Wé Isa, however, may have been more enduring and politically more significant.

While precious few details regarding the diarist's marriage to Wé Isa are available, it is known to have taken place during a period of high tension between the Wajorese migrants and their Malay hosts in Berau. The diary records that Wé Isa was the daughter of a Pangeran in Berau. While his own name is not included in the diary, the fact that his daughter's name was Wé Isa suggests that he was Bugis. Alternatively, his daughter could have gotten her distinctly Bugis name from her mother. Either way it suggests that the Bugis already played an important role in the politics of Berau. That the diarist would marry one suggests that, in the politics of marriage, maintenance of Wajoq's relations with overseas communities was considered just as important as assimilation into host societies. Given the timing of the marriage, it was likely to have been an attempt to reinforce Wajorese presence in Berau during a politically unstable period. The need to have smoothed Wajorese-Berauan relations may have stemmed from a Wajorese desire to collect debts from the Berauans. If this were the case then there may have been an economic or commercial motive for the marriage as well. It is to the role of family in commerce that this chapter now turns.

Family and Economics

The tensions and ambiguities of commercial relationships amongst kin are exceptionally pronounced and readily apparent in the sources. On the one hand, there are countless examples of trading relationships between family members in different areas of diasporas. In fact, family networks were such an important part of early modern commerce that it has been argued that "established routes and kinship constituted the sine-qua-non of seventeenth century commerce."[64] The idea is that the presence at both ends of a trade route of trustworthy associates in the form of kin can be considered a risk reducing strategy. Common among dispersed peoples, this practice has been documented for many different groups.[65] A Wajorese instance of this practice is increased trade between Wajoq and western Sumatra that occurred after two influential brothers resided at each end of the route. Daéng Maruppa had other reasons for settling in Inderapura but once he was there, he and his brother and their respective associates chose to trade with each other as opposed to, or more likely in addition to, other potential trading partners.

On the other hand, it should not be presumed that trust was an automatic byproduct of a familial relationship. While the historiographical tendency has been to assume that early modern merchants inherently trusted their family members, recent research has revealed an imperfect congruence between kin networks and merchant networks. Rather, it appears that commercial interests, such as reputation and investment capabilities, were generally more important in the selection of business partners than family relationships.[66] Accordingly, the sources contain numerous admonitions against going into business with family. A Wajorese example is found in the law code of Amanna Gappa. This warns that when family members do trade with each other, they should do so with the utmost caution. Quite literally they are advised to negotiate the value of goods so calmly and carefully "that even the tightest cloth does not fray when pulled."[67] The need for such a warning suggests both that conflicts were commonplace and that the potential for undesirable consequences was great.

Given the advantages and disadvantages of commercial relationships with kin, and the concomitant risks, commerce may be the most tension fraught area of family relations. Arguably it was also a universal problem. The Wajorese had their own ways of dealing with the attendant challenges. These are outlined in the law code of Amanna Gappa which, as described in chapter 4, is largely concerned with fair business practices.

The law code of Amanna Gappa outlines a sharp distinction between the familial and commercial spheres. This emphasis extends to the protection of both merchants' interests from undue family interference and families' from bearing an undue share of merchants' financial responsibilities. For example, chapter 7 specifies that a merchant's wife and children may not use the goods that he obtained by means of a bagilaba pada. On the balance, it absolves the family from any responsibility for losses that a merchant incurs as a result of such loans. Among the other laws that protect a merchant's affairs from misappropriation by family members is a law in chapter 12 that prohibits the use of loaned goods to finance weddings.

There were also numerous laws designed to protect family members from possible detriments of commerce. Chapter 8 specifies that if a merchant incurs debts on a voyage, his family cannot be held responsible for these debts if he dies without telling his family about them. Furthermore, it was customary that, under certain circumstances, a wife had the option of leaving her husband because of debts he incurred. Specifically, if a merchant returned from a voyage and informed his wife of debts before they had spent a night together, she could leave him and thereby not assume any responsibility for the debts. Chapter 12 then states that a merchant's family cannot be held responsible for his debts while he is away unless there is reason to believe that he has died. Then, even if there is reason to believe he died, the family is only responsible for half of the goods. The exceptions to this rule are that the family is held responsible if he gambles it away or if he does not follow the prescriptions of bagilaba.

In a society where divorce and remarriage was commonplace, there were also laws limiting the involvement of subsequent families. Chapter 9 specifies that both the wealth and the debts that a merchant generated during one marriage belong to the spouse and children of that marriage and that the wealth and debts generated during a subsequent marriage belong to the spouse and children of that marriage. Whereas trading among family relations may have been a risk-reducing strategy in some circumstances, the more common risk-reducing strategy was likely diversification.

Among the few Wajorese merchants of whose affairs we have more than a passing reference, a cosmopolitan attitude and willingness to trade with others is readily apparent. In the legal records detailing the commerce of To Uti and To Anko, discussed at length in chapter 4, many business associates are named. These associates appear to be of a variety of backgrounds and there is no indication that they were family members. In fact, the case between Abraham Franzson and Tombo revolves around Tombo's claim that she was uninvolved and unaware of her Wajorese husband To Anko's business dealings. In this instance it is the very absence of a family tie in commerce that is remarkable.

While family ties lent strength to commercial operations in some instances, the diversity of business contacts exemplified in the affairs of To Uti and To Anko was of paramount importance. Failure to extend commercial relations beyond kin networks would have impeded and ultimately ruined Wajorese trade. Arguably, family commercial relationships are limited in all cases because, as Benjamin Arbel has argued, the very basis of international trade is contact among different groups.[68] They appear, however, to have been especially limited among the Wajorese: there is no evidence of the sorts of family firms found among other diasporic merchants nor of marriages arranged solely to enhance business cooperation. Furthermore, by codifying mutually agreed upon fair business practices, the law code of Amanna Gappa diminished any perceived need to solidify business relationships with kin.

Family Networks in Statecraft and Trade

Capable of transcending cultures and distance, family relations were a key element of traditional Bugis statecraft. Their importance is readily apparent in a variety of sources including Bugis and Makassarese diaries which, according to the eminent linguist A.A. Cense, depict the ruler as an "exalted family head of a great multitude of prominent people in the land who are bound together by many ties of marriage, ties which are not restricted to the regions, but also stretch far outside it."[70] Not surprisingly, therefore, family relations were also of tremendous significance to the Wajorese diaspora. They were widely used to forge alliances between the Wajorese migrants and the host societies, as well as between dispersed groups of Wajorese. In fact, Wajorese migrants even attempted to forge multiple family alliances simultaneously, such as Daéng Maruppa did when he was adopted by the ruler of Inderapura and married the ruler's sister while also trading with his own brother in Sulawesi.

The strength of the concomitant emotions made family relations socially very powerful. This power, however, could just as easily result in disintegration as integration. For example, the love and trust that may have been inherent in a family relationship could be permanently destroyed through misunderstandings about joint commercial enterprises or financial matters. While the historical record does not allow for a detailed examination of Wajorese familial commercial enterprises, the existence of laws to regulate commercial and financial affairs among family members clearly implies that these alliances existed and that they sometimes, if not often, went awry.

Similarly, marriage was a widely used strategy for political and social integration but it was not without its problems. For example, if one married into the wrong faction, it could result in one's expulsion from the host society as was the case with Daéng Matekko's marriage in Matan. Cultural differences also could result in irreconcilable disputes, thereby overriding the benefits of a marital alliance. This is exemplified by the marriage of the pua adu to the woman of ceremonial importance in Kutai which ultimately resulted in armed conflict.

Whereas cultural differences between the Wajorese and their host societies sometimes posed problems, in other instances they created opportunities. In such situations the migrants would emphasize their Wajorese identity. These situations were numerous enough that a Wajorese identity was maintained in the diaspora for generations, but this maintenance did not preclude adopting a second identity. It is to ethnicity as a strategic resource that this study now turns.

CHAPTER SIX

Identity and Ethnicization

Identity is crucial to diaspora. Theoretically, the continued maintenance of a distinctive identity vis-à-vis the host societies is essential to the concept of diaspora. Without what has been called "boundary maintenance," migrants assimilate and the diaspora ceases to exist.[1] Socially, identity is important because it influences the willingness of groups and individuals to act and interact with each other. A group's willingness to wage war, trade, negotiate, and intermarry all depend on the group's own identity which, it has been demonstrated, is often strengthened through contacts with other groups.[2] While qualifications about identity being fluid, multiple, and constantly renegotiated have called into question the utility of identity as a concept,[3] privileging identity as a perspective provides important insights into how a diaspora works.

This chapter looks at the ways in which Wajorese identity was created, maintained, and invoked. It describes key elements in the construction of Wajorese identity and the advantages of maintaining it in the diaspora. Then it looks at four eighteenth-century Wajorese or part Wajorese individuals who used and expressed their identity in very different ways. These individuals exemplify the process of ethnicization.

Historical, Anthropological, and Historiographical Considerations

It must be noted at the outset that the nature of ethnic identity in this discussion is at once fluid and complex. The fluidity stems from the nature of ethnicity in early modern Southeast Asia. Leonard Y. Andaya's research on ethnicization and identity in the early modern Malay world has revealed that individuals frequently assumed one ethnic identity in one set of circumstances and then adopted a different ethnic identity when they thought it would be more advantageous.[4] Given the uneven nature of available documentation, it would be impossible to quantify if this occurred more frequently in one place than another, but it was clearly possible across early modern Southeast Asia. The majority of the examples from this chapter date from the late seventeenth and eighteenth centuries when it was possible for individuals to change their identity repeatedly as acts of will. As Heather Sutherland has pointed out, "In a context where selling yourself into slavery was a recognized means of survival, acquiring a perhaps temporary ethnic label was a much less dramatic change of status."[5]

The multiplicity of Wajorese identities partially accounts for the discussion's complexity. Every Wajorese is a member of both larger groups, such as Bugis and Indonesian, and of smaller communities within Wajoq, such as Talotenréng or a village. When a Wajorese individual is asked about his or her origins, which occurs frequently and is not considered indiscreet in South Sulawesi, he or she will answer with a degree of precision relative to the circumstances.[6] Outside Indonesia, the Indonesian identity is generally the only one mentioned. Outside of South Sulawesi, but still within Indonesia, the overarching Bugis identity is likely to be emphasized. In other parts of South Sulawesi, the Wajorese identity is likely to be emphasized. Among compatriots, an individual's village and family relations are also important markers.[7] Thus individuals have a repertoire of identities from which to choose.

Wajorese identity is also difficult to pinpoint. Anthropologists have noted the difficulty of identifying specific characteristics that can be applied across the board to all Bugis.[8] Constituting the largest ethnic group of the peninsula, the Bugis form a very diverse group including aristocrats and peasants, farmers and urban merchants, devout Muslims and traditional priests. Among the Bugis themselves, Islam is considered to be a very important identity marker, but this is shared with millions of adherents across the world; furthermore there is a Christian minority in Soppéng which is also Bugis. Christian Pelras' examination of Bugis words that might be translated as "cultured" or "civilized" suggests that Bugis civilization depends on knowledge of customs and language, even more so than among Malay/Indonesian speakers[9] for whom language is an important identity marker. But even language is problematic. While the Bugis have their own language, there are numerous dialects. Those spoken in the heartlands of Wajoq, Soppéng, Boné, and Sidénréng are mutually intelligible, but the

Wajorese often have difficulty understanding certain dialects, such as that of Tellu Lupu in Boné or Sinjai.[10] Furthermore, there are populations who self-identify as Bugis but who do not speak the language. One historical example comes from southeast Sulawesi. During the 1830s, the Dutch trader J. N. Vosmaer encountered groups of Bugis in Kendari Bay who could neither speak Bugis nor be readily distinguished from the coastal Tolaki. What differentiated these Bugis from the rest of the population was their nominal acceptance of Islam, their less frequent tendency to headhunt, and their more frequent tendency to wear cotton cloth.[11]

While they might not be considered to be traditional identity markers, nor are they exclusive to the Bugis, there are a number of characteristics that form crucial elements of Bugis society. One is its permeability. According to the anthropologist Gilbert Hamonic, the Bugis never considered themselves as an isolated society. Despite the strength of their roots and their chants of autochthony, their society remains permeable.[12] A second is the importance of relative status. This is especially important among the Wajorese. It is also relevant to the discussion because emigration is commonly seen as a means of enhancing one's status. A third is a profound interest in the defense of honor. Among the Bugis this is known as siriq and it is a powerful motivator. A fourth is bilateral kinship. This is also relevant to the discussion because the larger web of kin relations that results from bilateral, as opposed to unilateral, kinship translates into a larger network of persons who can be called on in times of need or who can contribute to various enterprises. Furthermore, if an individual's kin is of a different ethnicity, this can facilitate the use of this ethnic identity.

Given these complexities, it has been argued that Bugis identity is a personal choice,[13] and that this choice invariably depends on the circumstances. These circumstances are not only geographic but also social. Different identities can be invoked in the public and private spheres, or in order to achieve any number of goals. For example, after the Makassar War there would have been Wajorese traders who used a different identity in their dealings with the Dutch so as to avoid discrimination. This identity may have been a different or more general Bugis identity or it may have been Malay. Given cultural similarities between Boné and Wajoq, it would have been more difficult for Wajorese to employ this strategy with their de facto Bonéan overlords. Nevertheless it is possible that (individual) residents of southwestern Wajoq claimed to be from Soppéng in order to avoid confiscation of their metal farm implements or other forms of persecution.

Historiographically speaking, Wajorese identity is further complicated by the tendency of outsiders to refer to all Bugis simply as Bugis regardless of their kingdom of origin. Adding another layer of complication is the fact that outside of South Sulawesi, sometimes even Makassarese, Mandarese, and Torajans refer to themselves as Bugis. Even more obscuring are references to soldiers from insular Southeast Asia, regardless of their origins, as Bugis. This generalization is so common that it even appears in a prominent reference work as the definition for Bugis:

> Name given by the Malays to the dominant race of the island of Celébes, originating in the S.-Western limb of the island; the people calling themselves *Wugi*. But the name used to be applied in the Archipelago to native soldiers in European service, raised in any of the islands. Compare the analogous use of Telinga (q.v.) formerly in India[14]

This citation documents that the ethnonym Bugis was widely used to describe soldiers regardless of their background. Thus many people described as Bugis in European sources may have had no link with Sulawesi at all. Indeed, in one instance British records even specify that there are more non-Bugis than Bugis among the Bugis soldiers.[15] The wide-spread reputation of Bugis fighters may have also encouraged people to assume a Bugis identity in order to obtain work as a soldier. Across the archipelago, local kingdoms eagerly recruited Bugis refugees because of their well-earned reputation for bravery.[16] They were known to imbibe a drink that made them fearless and were renowned for their intimidating dance known as *aruq*.

The flexibility of identity also poses historiographical complications. Since people shift identities in order to obtain a perceived advantage, the identities which they value in the private sphere and the identity that they use, and value, in a public situation can differ. If a Wajorese trader called himself or herself Malay whenever dealing with the VOC in order to avoid Dutch harassment after the Makassar War, then his or her history as a Wajorese is permanently obscured.

Despite these many complications, some sources are specific. Although the references are not common, when sources from outside Sulawesi mention a specific Bugis identity, such as Wajorese or Bonéan, one can be certain that it was a critical factor at the time.[17] That said, there is a tendency among these specific sources to mention the Wajorese component early on, and then to continue with the more salient ethnonym of Bugis. This may be a stylistic convention, or it may exemplify the tendency of South Sulawesians in general to refer to themselves as Bugis when overseas.[18] It may also indicate that a more specific identity than Bugis was not important in relationship to the other groups discussed. Presumably this is the case of the

Wajorese diarist whose connections with Wajoq were very strong but refers to his compatriots as "Bugis" in his discussions with the Sultan of Berau. This is a perfect example of the Wajorese themselves using a less specific identity when outside of South Sulawesi.

Expressions of Origins

In the development identity, one of the important choices that a group makes is to create their own canon of literature in their own language. With particular reference to Southeast Asia, Sheldon Pollack has argued that the shift from a translocal literary language to a local literary language is "the most important cultural change in the late medieval world."[19] In South Sulawesi, the sequence of events was somewhat different from the Indianized areas on which Pollack concentrates. A rich oral tradition appears to pre-date the advent of writing in South Sulawesi. After writing was introduced, presumably around 1400 CE,[20] several indigenous writing systems developed on the basis of an Indic syllabary. These were used to both preserve oral traditions and develop written ones. Despite the use of an Indic syllabary, there was never any significant degree of Indianization.[21] For example, Puranic mythology was never widespread in the original Sanskrit version in South Sulawesi. Therefore the peoples of South Sulawesi were not so much choosing a local tradition over a regional one as enhancing the pre-existing local traditions. Nevertheless, creating a literary canon in the local languages was still an important expression of group identity.

Among the many genres of Bugis literature, perhaps the most remarkable is *I La Galigo*. *I La Galigo* consists not of one single work but rather a scattered collection of tales that relate a cycle of stories with a remarkable degree of coherence and consistency. It was probably not envisaged as a collective work and it is therefore misleading to talk about its 'length.'[22] That being said, if all of the episodes were compiled it would form one of the world's longest literary works.[23] Very briefly summarized, it is the story of Batara Guru's descent from the Upperworld to the Middleworld where he becomes the first human being and the prince of Luwuq, and of the subsequent adventures of five generations of his descendants, including Batara Guru's grandson Sawérigading who is the hero of the epic. The epic is written in elaborate, archaic Bugis using five syllable units with a fair degree of regularity. It is also considered to be sacred. Many people refuse to read it without first burning incense and some people consider certain episodes to be so powerful that they must remain covered lest viewers die.[24] Moreover, the Bugis anthropologist Mattulada accords *I La Galigo* a separate status from other lontaraq (Bugis manuscripts) because it is not considered to have been created by humans.[25] Through the stories of the divine protagonists, *I La Galigo* portrays Bugis views of their past as well as the origins of the ancestors and the ancestral customs.[26]

Mattulada also considers *I La Galigo* to be "a reference book dealing with the social and cultural background of South Sulawesi people."[27] Aside from a wide variety of cultural information, it also provides guidelines for behavior such as avoiding incest, and cultivating environmental awareness. For example, in one episode Batara Guru's father, Patotoqé or 'He who directs fate,' instructs him not to eat rice while residing in the Middleworld because it had sprung forth from the gravesite of his daughter. In another episode the ruler of Tompoq Tikkaq throws rice away in a fit of anger and Patotoqé punishes him by smiting both him and his wife with a deadly disease. Both of these episodes serve as enjoinments to treat rice with respect. Whether a result of these admonishments against wasting rice or economic necessity or, more likely, both, respect of rice is an important feature of Bugis culture. Ceremonies and rituals are performed at various points during the agricultural cycle, sometime involving priests known as bissu. Once rice is harvested and ready for consumption, it is still treated with respect. Some people do not eat rice without wearing a *songkok* or skull cap and still more people are careful to always wear a shirt when carrying rice from the attic to the kitchen. Everyone avoids throwing rice out.[28] Especially when reinforced by the sacred literature, such customs form an integral part of what it means to be Bugis.

Held in high esteem, ceremonially read upon auspicious occasions, and containing guidelines for behavior and explanations as to the origins of Bugis society, *I La Galigo* forms an important part of the Bugis mythomoteur. It reasserts the group's links to sacred figures and assists in the formation of a group identity. As a text, it is also highly portable and therefore can be effective in the diaspora. *I La Galigo* is known to have been cherished outside of South Sulawesi. Several examples of *I La Galigo* texts are still held in the Mulawarman Museum in Tenggarong, East Kalimantan. In the diaspora the reading or even the mere possession of such a text reaffirms one's ties with the homeland.[29]

While *I La Galigo* provides a description of the world of which the Bugis lands are only a part, other forms of literature are more localized. Among these forms are the origin stories which help to form a sense of unity among a community. While the Wajorese origin stories do not contain explicit statements about identity like some of the texts to be examined later in this chapter, they are explicitly foundational. They usually link a particular group to shared, sacred ancestors. Bugis origin stories define the group as the descendants of mythical beings descendant from the Upperworld or ascendant from the Lowerworld. These noble ancestors are a source of communal pride. Not intended to be scientific, the mythological elements of these stories serve to establish a higher status for elite groups with in society. This in turn facilitates the patron-client relationships upon which the society is based.[30]

One example is the tale of La Matatikkaq which is contained in a Wajorese chronicle. It offers explanations for both the origins of Wajoq and Wajorese social structures. It relates the story of La Matatikkaq, a *totompo* or ascendant from the Lowerworld, who founds Cinnotabiq. He marries Lingeqmanasa, the daughter of a tomanurung and their divine origins translate into higher status to their descendants who form the ruling elite. Their great-grandsons, the brothers La Tenriba and La Tenritippeq, eventually rule Cinnotabiq together as equals. After a year of this dual kingship, the population becomes dissatisfied which makes La Tenriba angry. His three nephews leave Cinnotabiq and establish three settlements in Boliq: Tua, Talotenréng and Béttémpola. Two years later, La Tenriba and La Tenritippeq leave Cinnotabiq as well, and establish Penrang. The people of Boliq then go to Penrang and asked La Tenriba to be their ruler. La Matareng, La Tenripekka and La Tenritauq follow and their uncle appoints them as Paddanreng, the highest officials below the ruler, in the new settlement that was then named Wajoq.[31] The tale also offers a historical explanation for the social organization because the polities ruled by La Matareng, La Tenripekka, and La Tenritauq account for the confederative nature of Wajoq. Furthermore, the population's dissatisfaction with the dual rule of La Tenriba and La Tenritippeq reinforces the traditional Wajorese right to depose a ruler.

A well-known Wajorese origin myth, commonly known as *Pau Pau Rikadong* meaning "the story to which agreement is nodded," tells the story of a Luwurese princess with an incurable skin disease.[32] Her parents are desolate about her condition, but they are eventually forced to choose between their only daughter and their people. The princess is then exiled along with an entourage of servants and they wander aimlessly for forty days and nights. Finally they establish themselves under a big *bajoq* tree. Then one day, the princess encounters a buffalo who chases her around until she falls down, and he licks her entire body. After the buffalo leaves, the princess goes to bathe in the river, then she goes back into her house and falls asleep. When she awakens, she is overjoyed to discover that her skin condition has improved. She meets the buffalo every day until she is completely recovered. Subsequently the son of the ruler of Boné, who has been out hunting deer for seven days and whose provisions are exhausted, comes across the princess' settlement. When he lays eyes on the princess, immediately falls in love with her. After his hunting expedition, he returns to visit her, and is so struck by her beauty that he faints. He returns once again to Boné and cries himself to sleep because he is so lovesick. The Bonéan court is puzzled by his distress and his loss of appetite. When they finally realize that he is in love, and not physically ill, the ruler of Boné sends an armed delegation to ask the princess to marry his son. Eventually, they are married and beget children who become their subjects and who govern the different parts of Wajoq. Here again the origin story offers an explanation for the federative nature of Wajoq. In this case it also noteworthy that the princess was exiled from Luwuq for the safety of the population. This suggests that a ruling family has a responsibility to the people and that the state exists beyond their own family. Another notable feature of *Pau Pau Rikadong* is that it does not accord divine origins to the community founders. However, it states that the ruling family hailed from Luwuq which is held in high esteem. Well into the 19th century, Wajorese people spoke with pride of the Wajorese origins in Luwuq.[33]

Chronicles of more recent historical events also serve to create a feeling of pride in shared history and thereby unite the group. Tales of bravery during the Makassar War, such as the populace's continued support of the war effort, are likely to have been a tremendous source of honor. Accounts of Wajorese tenacity in the face of the Dutch attacks on Tosora in 1670 and 1741 may have served a similar purpose as well.

A good example is the manner in which Arung Matoa La Tenrilai To Sengngeng opposed signing the Bungaya Treaty as recorded in the LSW. Although Dutch records do not specify if the Wajorese leader was present at the signing,[34] according to LSW, To Sengngeng attended the ceremony. At one point he told the ruler of Gowa known as the karaéng

> The word is that you want to make an agreement with Malampéqé Gemmeqna, but what I think is better, O Karaéng, is to tell him that there will be an agreement made after he completely finishes the war with Wajoq . . . It would be good if Malampéqé Gemmeqna and I could fight alone because the war is not truly over until I am dead.[35]

The karaéng then proposed a duel with the arung matoa to Malampéqé Gemmeqna, another name for Arung Palakka, but the latter declined. This seems out of character for Arung Palakka but is certainly possible. There was a day of negotiations during which the Makassar delegation was "un-commonly friendly" with Arung Palakka,[36] thus there might very well have been an opportunity for the karaéng to bring up the arung matoa's proposal, and Arung Palakka might have declined not out of cowardice, as the Wajo-rese lontaraq implies, but rather simply because he thought it unnecessary. However, whether or not Arung Matoa To Sengngeng actually challenged Arung Palakka is of secondary importance here to the existence of the story. The episode glorifies the community's past and thereby serves to create a feeling of pride in their leader's bravery.

Almost nothing is known about how such lontaraq were used during the early modern era. However, if more recent practices can serve as any guide for the understanding the past, it is easy to imagine that they were read in a public performance with a *passureq,* a performer specialized in reading texts. Performances are likely to have been held upon special occasions such as weddings, births, the construction of a new house or the start of a new agricultural season. Given that such events are not generally linked to the courts and that texts are owned by members of all social strata, such per-formances were likely have been widespread among the populace and not just limited to elite circles.[37] Even so, the texts often present the histories of elite members of society. In this way Bugis literature exemplifies the myths, history and shared culture of Smith's *ethnie.*[38]

Nurtured with texts from the homeland, the Wajorese sense of identity and ethnic solidarity was reinforced in very practical terms overseas. The following section examines certain situations in which a Wajorese identity may have been advantageous in the diaspora.

The Advantages of Wajorese Identity

While ethnicity is not always of decisive significance in social interac-tions, historically speaking there are numerous scenarios where asserting a Wajorese identity could have been advantageous. A Wajorese identity might influence residential, professional, commercial and/or legal options. This exemplifies the process of ethnicization which has been defined as "a con-scious political decision by the group to adopt a particular ethnic identity for some perceived advantage."[39]

The Wajorese in Kutai were so numerous and powerful that the Dutch referred to Kutai as "Little Wajoq."[40] Here, then, the advantages of a Wa-jorese identity are easy to imagine. Foremost among them is the advantage of geography. After the Malay capital of Kutai moved to Tenggarong, the

Wajorese settlement at Samarinda at the mouth of the Mahakam River was located 22 kilometers downstream from the Malay capital. This afforded the Wajorese an enhanced degree of control over trade which was the life-blood of the sultanate. It also gave them considerable leverage in their dis-putes with Kutai, most of which were about trade.[41] Their geographic posi-tion enabled them to blockade the river and obstruct the transport of salt or other essential commodities to the Malays and the people farther inland with whom the Malays traded.

There may also have been political advantages to being Wajorese in Kutai. As previously mentioned, the Wajorese community in Kutai was headed by an elected official known as pua adu. While his power was considerable, it was held in check by two assistants known as the tau abeyo and tau atau discussed in chapter 3. The fact that these assistants were appointed by the kapala maneng, or people's leaders,[42] indicates that the Wajorese tradition of representative politics was continued abroad. Thus by identifying as Wa-jorese, people came to live under their own leaders and within their own political tradition rather than under a hereditary sultan.

In Makassar, asserting a Wajorese identity entitled one to live in the so-called Kampong Wajoq.[43] In Kampong Wajoq, the Wajorese had their own mosque, palace, and meeting hall.[44] Living in a close-knit community of-fered obvious advantages, such as mutual assistance and increased contacts with Wajorese merchants who could be potential trading partners. The ex-istence of Kampong Wajoq also gave the Wajorese in Makassar a sense of autonomy. There even appears to have been a limited degree of territo-rial sanctity in Kampong Wajoq. In the event of a royal visit to Makassar or Gowa, the Bonéans would send a messenger to summon the Wajorese rather than enter Kampong Wajoq themselves.[45] It may have offered the Wajorese other reprieves from Bonéan demands as well.

There also appears to have been external pressure for the Wajorese in Makassar to reside in Kampong Wajoq. The Wajorese leaders in Tosora, the Bonéans and the Dutch all encouraged them to do so. During the reign of Arung Matoa La Tenrisessuq To Denra (1699–1702), the Wajorese leaders decided that the Wajorese in Makassar should all live in Kampong Wajoq.[46] In the second half of the eighteenth century, the Bonéans also demanded that the Wajorese live there. This was during the administration of the Wa-jorese matoa La Madeq (r. 1757–1772) who had particular problems with the tyrannical character of Bonéan rulers. The datu of Baringeng, whose position uniquely straddled Wajorese and Bonéan spheres of power, made it clear to the Wajorese that it would be desirable if they lived more in one place. There were objections about the cost of relocating, as well as about the excessive corvée labor demanded of the Wajorese. Out of fear for Boné, La Madeq often brought cases which he should have resolved himself to the ranreng Tua.[47] Presumably Dutch encouragement was of a more general nature and not specifically directed towards the Wajorese because the Dutch wanted all the residents of Makassar to inhabit ethnically organized villages. Raffles had a similar plan for the ethnic groups in Singapore, but it was never realized.[48] Thus, aside from the practical advantages of co-residence, there was pressure from outside the Wajorese community for Wajorese to self-identify and reside together.

Asserting a Wajorese identity might have opened up professional and commercial options as well. Presumably a Wajorese identity facilitated using the law code of Amanna Gappa, discussed in detail in chapter 4, to regulate commercial transactions and participate in the expansive Wajorese networks. Given the law code's emphasis on mutually advantageous or at least fair business practices, participation could have provided important commercial advantages. Furthermore, work as a sawi (trading sailor) may also have been easier to acquire for those who asserted their Wajorese identity. This would have been an important advantage for people with limited financial means and commercial opportunities because it allowed them to go into trade with little or no capital of their own.

In western Sumatra, a distinctly Bugis identity entailed certain political and economic advantages that actually increased over time. The political and economic climate in western Sumatra afforded opportunities to middlemen that the Wajorese fulfilled. Eventually they rose to such tremendous power that the pengeran of Krui believed that the "Tooan-tooan de Buncouloo" (the gentlemen at Bengkulu) were the EIC Magistrate H. R. Lewis and Daéng Mabéla.[49] To understand the opportunities that a Bugis identity afforded in Bengkulu, it is necessary to elaborate on the political and economic climate of Western Sumatra.

After the arrival of the British in 1685, two rival European companies were present in Western Sumatra. The EIC adamantly desired to implement a policy of forced pepper cultivation but they did not properly understand the local political climate. Much of the population of western Sumatra was organized into fairly independent tribal communities, the members of which submitted voluntarily to their leaders. If the leaders were oppressive, they would lose their followers. Not understanding that the heads of these communities did not have sufficient authority to enforce control of the land and manpower needed for enforced pepper cultivation, Europeans in western Sumatra attributed the local leaders' lack of coercive power to personal weakness.[50] Consequently, the English sought to establish alternative local authority. Believing that the Bugis were more trustworthy and capable than the local leaders, the English asked them to assume increasingly important mediating, surveying and adjudicating duties.

In exchange for their services, Wajorese and other Bugis in the service of the Europeans received remuneration, presents and other privileges. For example, in 1695 the EIC gave a present to the "Serjant of the buggesses" in order to reward his diligence and fidelity and to encourage similar loyalty among others.[51] The EIC and the VOC also paid handsome salaries to the Bugis in their service. When the English recruited Bugis soldiers in the 1680s, the Dutch raised the pay of those in their service at Air Haji in order to retain their services.[52] Such a pay increase is remarkable in the context of the VOC, which did not raise the basic pay of its common sailors from 1602 until 1799.[53] The English also valued the presence of the Wajorese. So valuable were the services of the Bugis in the EIC that they demanded to be paid in silver and threatened to leave the EIC's service if they were not.[54] Indeed, Sultan Selan's wife was even able to obtain an advance on her husband's salary for her own maintenance in 1699.[55] Thus in western Sumatra a Bugis identity could help procure money and gifts, and perhaps even help escape the drudgery of forced pepper cultivation. Given such incentives, it is reasonable expect that people would have asserted their Wajorese identity enthusiastically.

Wajorese leaders also accrued more significant privileges as a result of their service to the EIC. One of these was formal judicial authority within the English settlements. Since early on, the EIC had tried to involve local leaders in the administration of justice. The British granted Daéng Mabéla authority over other Bugis in the service of the EIC and within the British settlements, Captain of the Bugis became a hereditary position. For Daéng Mabéla's son and grandson, the EIC expanded this jurisdiction to include all of the Bugis within the EIC settlements. Although the Bugis captain and the EIC would not have been involved in all of the disputes, the hierarchy of appeals[56] nevertheless established an important precedent of both the Bugis captain's and the EIC's mutual involvement in the local judicial system. The Bugis captain would have garnered considerable respect within the community as a result. Another privilege accorded by the EIC was the license to trade in opium issued to Daéng Maruppa II.[57] As opium was an important commodity within the Bugis community, this license doubtlessly enhanced his opportunities for personal financial gain and can be considered as a mark of the EIC's favor.

Aside from, or perhaps because of, the privileges that the Europeans accorded the Wajorese and other Bugis, the autochthonous inhabitants of

Sumatra also exhibited tremendous respect for them. The late eighteenth century observer William Marsden describes how they looked up to the Bugis migrants:

> The Makassar and Bugis people, who come annually in their praws from Celebes to trade at Sumatra, are looked up to by the inhabitants, as their superiors in manners. The Malays are affect to copy their style of dress, and frequent allusions to the feats and achievements of these people are made in their songs. Their reputation for courage, which certainly surpasses that of all other people in the eastern seas, acquires them this flattering distinction. They also derive part of the respect paid them, from the richness of the cargoes they import, and the spirit with which they spend the produce in gaming, cock-fighting, and opium-smoking.[58]

To further inspire the Sumatrans' admiration and respect, the Bugis used the title *Daéng,* not just for the captain of the Bugis Corps but also for his male descendants. Female descendants used the Arabic title *Siti* as a female equivalent in order to distinguish themselves from the Sumatrans.[59]

Clearly in western Sumatra asserting a Wajorese identity linked individuals to a powerful group. Thus people with only one Wajorese grandparent, or great grandparent, might be inclined to claim a Bugis identity. Elsewhere in the archipelago, however, a Wajorese identity was not always the most advantageous.

Emphasizing Malayness: Raja Ismail

As previously mentioned, using one ethnic identity in one situation and another ethnic identity in another situation was a common practice in the early modern Malay world.[60] The career of Daéng Matekko's grandson Raja Ismail illustrates this phenomenon perfectly. Having both a Wajorese and a Malay grandfather, he could employ whichever identity he felt most advantageous in any given circumstance. While the Malay identity served him more frequently, his Wajorese heritage was not forgotten.

As described in chapter 5, Daéng Matekko was steadfastly opposed to the Riau Bugis and tried to carve out his own niche in the Malay world. While the Riau Bugis controlled the valuable tin-producing areas on the peninsula from 1743 until 1784, there were other opportunities for accruing wealth and power in the Straits. Daéng Matekko's family was among those who pursued these alternate opportunities. While information regarding Daéng

Matekko's wife and daughter is lacking, it is known that the latter married Raja Kecik's son Tengku Mahmud. It will be remembered from chapter 3 that ancestry is an important part of traditional politics in the Malay world. Because Raja Kecik claimed to be the son of Sultan Mahmud who was the last ruler capable of tracing his ancestry to the mythically powerful rulers of Melaka, association with Raja Kecik afforded political advantages; hence Daéng Matekko's desire to marry his daughter to Raja Kecik's son Tengku Mahmud. The son of Tengku Mahmud and Daéng Matekko's daughter, Raja Ismail, parlayed his prestigious Malay ancestry into political power in the Straits, a tactic that the Riau Bugis could not similarly employ.

Raja Ismail implemented his strategy against the backdrop of the rivalry that had existed between the various Bugis factions in the Malay world. After Raja Kecik's attacks on Riau having failed, his mental state deteriorated and he gradually lost control of Siak. Civil war ensued between his two sons Raja Alam and Tengku Mahmud. Again in this instance, there was rivalry between the Wajorese and the Riau Bugis. Through his marriage to Daéng Khatijah, the daughter of Opu Daéng Parani and the sister of Daéng Kamboja,[61] Raja Alam was affiliated with the Riau Bugis. Tengku Mahmud, on the other side, was married to Daéng Matekko's daughter and received support from him and his allies during the conflict. Tengku Mahmud eventually forced Raja Alam to retreat and, upon his father's death, assumed the title Sultan Mahmud. His rule was short-lived, however, because it was not long before Raja Alam returned and ousted Sultan Mahmud, forcing him and Daéng Matekko to retreat to Lawan. From there, Tengku Mahmud and Daéng Matekko traveled from place to place trying to seek support for their cause, an attempt that the unsettled character of the region during the first half of the eighteenth century encouraged.

When Raja Ismail's father Tengku Mahmud was expelled from Siak, it did not mark the end of his involvement in Siak's affairs. He regained Siak only to lose it again to Raja Alam in 1753.[62] In an attempt to end the strife between him and his half-brother Tengku Mahmud, Raja Alam then married his son Raja Muhammad Ali to Tengku Mahmud's eldest daughter, Tengku Embung Besar who previously had been married to Daéng Matekko.[63] Although the marriage initially infuriated Tengku Mahmud, he sought the support of Sultan Sulaiman and the VOC, and eventually regained control of Siak yet again, at which point he accepted Raja Muhammad Ali as his son-in-law and accorded him the position of Yang Dipertuan Muda.[64] When Sultan Mahmud died in 1760,[65] his son Raja Ismail, who was the grandson of both Raja Kecik and Daéng Matekko, assumed leadership in Siak. His rule was short-lived, however, because the following year, Raja Alam formed an alliance with the VOC and attacked and subdued Siak. Raja Alam reassumed paramount leadership in Siak and his son Muhammad Ali retained his position as Yang Dipertuan Muda.

After fleeing from Siak, Raja Ismail sought his fortune in the greater Malay world. In doing so he exploited the advantages afforded by both his Malay and his Wajorese ancestry. His grandfather Raja Kecik claiming descent from the prestigious Melaka-Johor line, and his father Tengku Mahmud having made numerous alliances in the Malay world, Raja Ismail related to and drew considerable support from the Malay community in the Straits. He also established connections with Wajorese communities, such as the one in Mempawa. He tried to exploit various niches and alliances in the Malay world in order to exert his own conception of power and authority that transcended traditional land-based politics.

Claiming not to want to rule Siak, Raja Ismail sought to become "Prince of the Seas." The sea-based polity that he tried to establish was constructed on a combination of alliances and coercion, loyalty and raiding. He and his brothers raided various settlements along the coasts of eastern Sumatra, western Borneo and the Malay Peninsula.[66] Eventually they settled in Trengganu where they were very well received. The ruler of Trengganu, Sultan Mansur Syah, was a long-standing enemy of the Riau Bugis,[67] and as such he was prepared to ally with another enemy of the Riau Bugis. Raja Ismail even was married to Tengku Tipah, Sultan Mansur Syah's daughter, in 1763. Again the importance of marriage politics is clearly evident. After the marriage Raja Ismail and his followers demonstrated their loyalty to their host community by assisting in an attack on Kelantan.[68] Raja Ismail then used Sultan Mansur Syah as an intermediary to reestablish contact with his cousin Muhammad Ali and to propose an alliance.[69] Raja Ismail also obtained the loyalty of certain groups of orang laut (mobile sea populations) because of his prestigious ancestor Raja Kecik, and secured this loyalty through riches obtained by raiding and through an alliance with the orang laut leader Raja Negara.[70] With Raja Negara by his side, Raja Ismail gradually built up a network of supporters in the region. He secured the support of the ruler of Palembang by assisting him in subduing a rebellious cleric in Mempawa.[71] He then conducted a raid in southern Thailand where he captured more than a hundred people whom he presented to the Sultan of Palembang. In exchange for these services, he was granted numerous gifts and permanent residency in Palembang, complete with a monthly allowance.[72] Eventually Raja Ismail felt strong enough to reassert his authority in central east Sumatra and he established a base in Rokan.[73] He and his cousin Raja Muhammad Ali then developed a strategy for sharing authority in the region, where environmental diversity allowed for multiple rulers.[74] Raja Ismail then returned briefly to Trengganu where he married his daughter Tengku Kamariah to Said Umar, a prominent Arab trader,[75] thereby bolstering both his prestige and his commercial power. Although Raja Ismail had claimed not to want to rule Siak, with the support of his new son-in-law he felt confident to challenge his cousin's authority. In 1779 he launched an attack, and took control of Siak. Muhammad Ali initially fled, but the two cousins later shared authority in Siak, and Raja Muhammad Ali was reinstalled as Yamtuan Muda. Despite the tensions caused by the presence of a deposed ruler in the court, Siak prospered during their joint rule. Eventually, however, tensions led to the replacement of Muhammad Ali with Raja Ismail's son Yahya in 1781. Raja Ismail died shortly thereafter.[76]

The grandson of both Raja Kecik and Daéng Matekko, Raja Ismail related to both his Malay and Wajorese heritage. Because of Raja Kecik's alleged ties to the prestigious Melaka-Johor line, it was often in Raja Ismail's political interest to emphasize this ancestry. The *Tuhfat al-Nafis* records that after a defeat at the hands of the Riau Bugis, Raja Ismail went to the grave of his paternal grandfather Raja Kecik and danced, presumably as an expression of loyalty.[77] Emphasizing this prestigious ancestry apparently was an effective political tactic because the *Tuhfat al-Nafis* also records how orang laut in Siantan were influenced by the fact that "the royal blood of Johor flows in his veins."[78] Yet Raja Ismail did not deny his Wajorese heritage.

That Raja Ismail maintained a conceptual connection with the home of his maternal grandfather Daéng Matekko is suggested in the proposed exile of Raja Ismail's brother Raja Daud. Raja Daud and his half-sister Tengku Saliah were accused of incest. For this crime, Tengku Saliah was ritually executed.[79] When Tengku Abdullah, another brother of Raja Ismail, sought permission to execute Raja Daud, Raja Ismail suggested that he be exiled "to the Bugis lands" instead.[80] In light of the fact that Raja Daud could have been exiled to any number of lands in the western archipelago, Raja Ismail's proposal of "the Bugis lands" suggests that he and his brothers maintained a sense of their Bugis heritage. While their loyalty to their Malay heritage may have been greater, clearly they had not forgotten from where their maternal grandfather originated. On the contrary, they maintained a sense of being Wajorese and exploited it whenever they deemed it appropriate.

Another example of the importance of Raja Ismail's Wajorese connections is found in the *Hikayat Siak*. This text relates how Siak and Palembang launched a joint attack on Mempawa and successfully defeated the Penembahan of Mempawa who then ran away. Thereafter the Wajorese in Mempawa approached Raja Ismail.[81] While no further details are given, presumably this involved not only mutual recognition of their shared heritage but also a feeling of pessé. The *Hikayat Siak* also recognizes Raja Ismail's Wajorese origins in this passage, referring specifically to his Wajorese ethnicity.[82] While these references are made only in passing, their inclusion suggests that not only Raja Ismail but also other Wajorese in Mempawa must have emphasized their Wajorese heritage. There would be no mention of Wajoq in the *Hikayat Siak,* which is essentially a Minang text, were Raja Ismail and his followers not making an issue of their connections to Wajoq.

Conflicting Loyalties: Haji Hafiz and Daéng Mabéla

While Raja Ismail demonstrated considerable flexibility in the use of his Malay and Wajorese ancestry, for other overseas Wajorese individuals identity and loyalty posed a greater dilemma. One of these individuals was Haji Hafiz, as associate of Raja Ismail's grandfather Daéng Matekko in Mempawa on the southwest corner of Kalimantan. A conflict between two rival factions, both of which he felt loyal to, made it difficult for him to choose sides.

Described in chapter 5, the conflict was essentially a succession dispute between the sons of Sultan Muhammad Safi al-Din of Mempawa. The Riau Bugis supported the older son known as Sultan Muhammad Zain al-Din and the Wajorese sided with the younger son Pangeran Agung. The Riau Bugis and Sultan Muhammad Zain al-Din prevailed and, when his benefactor Pangeran Agung was imprisoned, Daéng Matekko fled to Siak.

The encounter between the sons of Opu Daéng Rilaga who, it will be remembered, appears to have been in service of Boné, and Daéng Matekko illustrates the manner in which tension between the Boné and Wajoq was felt overseas. That the different Malay factions within Mempawa tried to manipulate this animosity for their own purposes attests to the fact that the animosity was no secret. Perhaps because the opu also had relations with the royal family of Pammana, Haji Hafiz felt conflicting loyalties to both the opu and to Daéng Matekko. In an impassioned speech, however, he blamed the opu's family for ruining his own family, thereby making an indirect reference to Boné's ruin of Wajoq.

> I am a Bugis and Daéng Matekko is like my lord and the five brothers Opu Daéng are like my lord as well. I fear committing treason, and if I commit treason I will return to Bugis lands. And my family in the Bugis lands that I miss and love has probably been destroyed by the family of the five Opu Daéng.[83]

While Haji Hafiz is known to have been Wajorese, in this statement he self-identifies less specifically as a Bugis. By doing so, he relates to the opu as well as to Daéng Matekko. His dilemma is not so much one of ethnic identity as political loyalty; and by identifying with the overarching group, he can express his sentiments of loyalty to both factions. Yet circumstances forced Haji Hafiz to choose. Whether he was more influenced by feelings of loyalty to the Wajorese as a group, or to Daéng Matekko as a friend and compatriot, or whether he simply felt that his own interests were best served through an affiliation with Daéng Matekko, is unknown. Ultimately however Haji Hafiz took Daéng Matekko's side and urged him to escape. Daéng Matekko heeded Haji Hafiz's advice and fled to Siak. The five opu then proceeded to depose the Pangeran Agung and reinstall Sultan Muhammad Zain al-Din in 1721.[84]

Just as Haji Hafiz considered himself to have two lords, so did Daéng Mabéla. Despite Daéng Mabéla's family's prominence within the EIC, it did not hinder the family from serving its adversaries, both European and Asian. When the English temporarily evacuated Bengkulu in 1719, Daéng Mabéla immediately offered his services to the Dutch company. He apparently entered the VOC's service and departed for Java while his son Daéng Makkullé, grandson Daéng Maruppa and great-grandson Daéng Mabéla II a.k.a. Oenoes a.k.a. Raja Bangsawan continued to serve the EIC.

The EIC's evacuation of western Sumatra in 1719 was preceded by deterioration in the condition of its military force and in the quality of relations with local rulers.[85] Its immediate catalyst was an insurrection resulting from a dispute between the *dipati* (village head) of Bentiring, a hamlet located six miles from Bengkulu on the Bengkulu River, and a Chinese community leader who raised sugar and distilled alcohol nearby. When the Kapitan China killed some of the dipati's buffaloes that had wandered into his sugar plantation, the dipati's brother avenged the loss by killing one of the Kapitan China's slaves. When this was reported to the commander he sent five soldiers to apprehend the murderer who then was made to sit in shackles. Although he was set free after two or three days, the dipati viewed this imprisonment as an insult and set fire to the sugar mills of both the EIC and the Kapitan China. The English then sent a contingent of 70 soldiers to attack Bentiring, but they retreated to Bengkulu after only three hours. A number of local leaders who had previously sided with the EIC then joined the dipati of Bentiring and launched a counterattack on Fort Marlborough. The English, unable to defend themselves, withdrew from Bengkulu.[86]

In this conflict, the Bugis sided with the dipati of Bentiring. Daéng Mabéla and his followers tried to provide the Sumatrans with guns, powder, bullets and money, and lost the trust of the English in the process.[87] Daéng Mabéla then wrote to the Dutch in Batavia, and informed them of these events. He offered his services to the VOC and referred to himself throughout the letter as "your High Honors' servant." He also demonstrated the flexibility of overseas Wajorese allegiance by writing:

> Next to God, the highest is the Company and the Governor together with the Council at Batavia with whom I take refuge and to whom I have given my life because whom else could I serve? According to me and the opinion of all the Bugis in Bengkulu, we do not have any other ruler besides the company in Batavia. In the land of the Bugis, our king is our ruler, but overseas the Company is our ruler.[88]

Although it is possible that Daéng Mabéla was unaware of the extent of the rivalry between the EIC and the VOC, his sincerity is questionable. Especially given his previous service in the EIC, it is much more likely that he considered serving the VOC to be the most strategic of numerous options than that he could not conceive of serving any other party outside of Sulawesi. Thus his and his followers' willingness to switch allegiance and serve the EIC's arch rival exemplifies their adaptability and resourcefulness. They were not loyal to the EIC as an institution. Rather, not unlike communities in South Sulawesi, they sided with the power with whom they believed their best interests lay. Nevertheless, his loyalty to his homeland remained an in issue. Even when applying for a job with the VOC he felt compelled to mention his ruler in "the land of the Bugis."

Identities are widely known to be multiple. From Daéng Mabéla's letter and Haji Hafiz's statement it would appear that loyalties can be multiple as well. Daéng Mabéla's letter suggests that, like Haji Hafiz, he considered himself to have two rulers. In Haji Hafiz' case, both rulers were overseas. In Daéng Mabéla's case, one ruler was in Sulawesi and one overseas. While he may have emphasized this dual loyalty in order to convince the VOC to employ him, it is clear from his letter that he had not forgotten his origins. The dual nature of Daéng Mabéla's and Haji Hafiz's identity is indicative of the flexibility and permeability of Wajorese identity: An individual is generally not required to give up a Wajorese identity when acquiring another identity.

The Wajorese in Berau also appear to have had overlapping identities and loyalties. In this case, however, the available source discusses the identities of the group instead of the identities of individuals. It appears that the Wajorese were willing to consider themselves to be one with the Berauans, to be Berauans themselves, so long as the Wajorese and the

Berauans co-existed peacefully. In the face of conflict, however, this joint identity proved unstable.

The diary of the Wajorese statesman[89] introduced in chapter 3 records a dialogue between the Wajorese statesman and the Sultan of Berau, the leader of the hosting community. The two leaders are trying to resolve a conflict over the wrongdoings of the Bugis La Kamsa. In their discussion, both leaders refer to the earlier agreement in which it was specified that Berauans were like Bugis, and that Bugis were like Berauans. Both leaders also specifically refer to each other as family, which may be metaphorical, literal or both. It appears that the two groups were both happy to merge their identities as long as they were enjoying a mutually beneficial commercial arrangement. Being Wajorese or being Berauan was not an important issue until there was something to be gained by hardening the boundary between the two groups.

When tensions arose, the community leaders started delineating their ethnic boundaries. In their dialogue they both specifically refer to deaths within their own communities. The statesman mentions crimes between the communities such as Bugis stealing from Berauans and Berauans needing to repay their debts Bugis. Such references clearly indicate that both leaders conceive of their communities as separate from each other. If they truly considered their communities to be one, then their references to crimes and deaths would not be made in terms of ethnicity. Thus no matter how they addressed each other or who married whose daughter, on an essential level, both communities considered themselves distinct from the other. The separateness of the communities is further underlined by the fact that both leaders contemplated and discussed waging war against each other.

There does appear to be some level of recognition of the mutual benefits of maintaining their relationship. The negotiations recorded in the diary are protracted, and are likely to have been even longer in actuality. Furthermore, the Wajorese leader also explicitly distinguishes between the actions of an individual and of the community, the presumption being that the wrongdoings will be pardoned and the community not held responsible if the guilty individual is punished. He states that he is willing to exile a guilty Wajorese because he has very high hopes for his family in Berau, and he suggests cooperative efforts to capture and exile wrong-doers. Nevertheless, despite the leaders' previous formal agreement that Bugis and Berauans should be as one people, they both maintained distinct ethnic identities. So distinct were these identities that both parties were ready to dissolve the hosting relationship in the event of unsuccessful conflict resolution. In this case the conflict was resolved. However, one cannot

help wonder what would have happened to the Wajorese statesman's Berauan wife in the event of a Wajorese attack on, or retreat from, Berau. No
indication is given in the sources.

This episode suggests that, while identities may be multiple, one particular identity can be stronger or more enduring than another. In this case it is
the Wajorese or Bugis identity which the Wajorese held before they came
to Berau that prevailed over the Berauan identity that they claimed to have
adapted. This episode also demonstrates how an ethnic identity can be invoked as a protective mechanism to safe-guard a group's well-being.

Maintaining Wajorese Identity

Aside from this dialogue about the importance of conflict resolution to
group identity, the diary of the Wajorese statesman contains information as
to how Wajorese identity and group cohesion were maintained. The diarist
recorded his participation in a number of rituals that would have promoted
group cohesion such as ear piercings, circumcision, and placenta burials.
While some, such as cockfights, may have been held primarily for the sake
of entertainment, they still would have had important social functions. In
other parts of the archipelago, cockfights are known to serve as forums
for displaying not only wealth but also honor, dignity, and respect.[90] Other
ceremonies, such as a flag ceremony, probably served more directly to reinforce the community's identity.

Flags or banners are widely used as symbols of a polity in Bugis society.
While the Bugis word for banner is "baté," they are commonly referred
to in Bugis texts as "tanra-tanra limpoé," meaning "signs or evidence of
the territorial entities." More than emblems, banners were considered to
embody the spirits of powerful ancestors. As such they were incorporated
into the regalia of some Bugis polities.[91] Elsewhere in eastern Indonesia,
banners are known to have signified community identity. For example, in
1695 when a group of nomadic fishermen arriving in Mondono in Central
Sulawesi were asked to show their VOC passes, they produced flags that
showed their relation to two princes.[92] Among the Wajorese, three different
colored flags represented the three different limpo within Wajoq: Béttémpola, Tua, and Talotenréng. The Wajorese chronicles state that they were
made at the suggestion of Luwuq,[93] and this affiliation with Luwuq would
have lent them extra prestige.

What is striking about the diarist's participation in these ceremonies is
that it occured both in Kalimantan and in South Sulawesi. Furthermore, the

flag ceremony, which presumably had the greatest potential for promoting groups cohesion, was held in Pasir in eastern Kalimantan and not in Wajoq. Given the significance of flags in Wajorese politics, it is unfortunate that the diary does not specify which flag was involved. The diarist also recorded that when he arrived in Kutai from Sulawesi, there was a sort of formal reception that regrettably is not described.[94] Similar ceremonies to welcome the Bugis are also mentioned in modern histories of east Kalimantan. In one text from Pasir, a display of local arts is explicitly mentioned.[95]

While the diarist did not record the presence of traditional Bugis priests known as bissu at these ceremonies, this priesthood is known to have existed overseas. In Pegatan, a polity founded by the Wajorese in southeastern Kalimantan, the bissu endured until well into the twentieth century.[96] It appears that the people of Pegatan maintained Bugis, specifically Wajorese, customs and language with tremendous tenacity.[97] The bissu would have played an important role in the maintenance of identity and group cohesion because they promoted both traditional Bugis beliefs and respect for rulers.

Another manner in which identity is maintained is through writing. While origin myths trace the origins of communities in prehistoric times, there are other stories that detail the foundation of communities in the more recent past. Community sentiment is drawn from these stories. This is especially so because the community fathers are sometimes accorded a status tantamount to ancestors and worshipped accordingly.[98]

One example of valorizing a community through writing is the history that Daéng Mabéla wrote of the Wajorese in western Sumatra. Named after his great grandfather, Daéng Mabéla was the great-great-grandson of the original pioneer in western Sumatra and thus the fifth generation of a Wajorese dynasty. As previously discussed, a Bugis identity was extremely advantageous in parts of western Sumatra. It is also the one place known where the family's lineage was emphasized through the repeated use of names: Daéng Mabéla, Daéng Maruppa and Daéng Makkullé. It is no coincidence that this happened in the area that the Wajorese were most privileged. This genealogical legacy serves to connect the past to the present and to establish order and continuity and thereby reinforce the family's privileged position.

Both known versions of the text are primarily occupied with the position of the author's family.[99] They discuss the noble origins of the family Wajoq, and the manner in which both the local society and the English empowered this family. From one text it appears that Daéng Mabéla had adopted a particular view of local politics in which Bugis authority was necessary. The desirability of stricter authority than is the tradition in western Sumatra is reflected in his description of local politics around the time of the arrival

Figure 3: Mid-nineteenth-century drawing by Heinrich von Gaffron of Bugis cockfighters in Pegatan, Southeast Kalimantan. Source: KITLV Image Library

of his own family and prior to the advent of the British. He writes that the inhabitants of Bengkulu were unhappy, that there was no respect for authority, and that the population suffered from the continually wanton behavior of a large group of nasty people.[100] Daéng Mabéla also discusses his family's links to local society. One version of the text emphasizes how Daéng Mabéla I grew up alongside the son of the ruler of Inderapura.[101] The other version of the text emphasizes the manner in which Pangeran Mangku Raja in Sungai Lemau gave his daughter in marriage to Daéng Makkullé and then publicly recognized him as his own son. It also emphasizes the hereditary nature of the position by repeating the names of the people who held it, listing their ages at death and describing their relationship to each other.[102]

Daéng Mabéla's emphasis on his family's long history of service to the English company is not surprising given the loss of prestige that he endured at the hands of the British. After he replaced his father Daéng Maruppa as Captain of the Bugis[103] and head of all non-European foreigners, Daéng

Mabéla was extremely influential. He controlled the Malay bazaars in Fort Marlborough[104] and participated in the judicial system. As previously mentioned, he also received an eighth of the revenues collected by the court and was responsible for distributing another eighth among various datuks.[105] Although Daéng Mabéla was officially third in rank after the pengeran of Sungai Lemau and Sungai Itam, in practice he was the most important member of the court.[106]

Despite Daéng Mabéla's power and prestige, his position was not guaranteed. In 1807 the British resident Thomas Parr found Daéng Mabéla guilty of embezzlement from money that he had been commissioned to transport to an outlying district. Daéng Mabéla was discharged from both his position as Captain of the Bugis Corps and adjudicator in the Fort Marlborough pengeran court. Presumably feeling tremendous siriq or humiliation, he seemingly withdrew from the public sphere.[107] While the English recalled him later the same year out of need and he continued to serve them until the

Figure 4: Four *bissu*, presumably photographed by A.A. Cense ca, 1930. Source: KITLV Image Library

left western Sumatra, he never regained his prestige and wealth. None of these circumstances are mentioned in his family history. Instead, the text attributes his impoverishment to loss of his license to trade opium and French theft.[108] In his family history, his family is essential, his genealogy is prestigious and his reputation is untarnished.

A second example of valorizing a community through writing is from Makassar. This is the history of the Wajorese matoa in that city that forms part of the manuscript NBG 106 held in the Leiden University library. The entire manuscript is a sort of notebook in which the owner recorded anything and everything that was of interest to him, including random texts such as the history of a Syrian king. The sections dealing with the Wajorese matoa in Makassar could be compared to the chronicles of Wajoq because it organizes all of its historical content around the administrations of the matoa. Spanning more than a century and a half, it records names, origins, and accomplishments of fourteen officials who held this post. In some instances it includes the author's or the community's perception of these leaders, a record of their interactions with other community leaders, their challenges, and the manner in which they left office. The text also provides details about the Wajorese community as a whole. It also records various community events, such as the construction of a house of worship, and regulations, such as freighting charges.

The goals of this text are multifold. It provides a record of the community, and thereby lends a sense of antiquity and legitimacy to Wajorese presence in Makassar. It also emphasizes the role of the matoa as the community leader. One stylistic element suggests that the text attributes more authority to the Wajorese matoa than he actually had. That is the use of introductory expression such as "During the reign of this monarch, it also happened that [. . .]"[109] Without actually specifying who is responsible for a given accomplishment such as the construction of a palace or meeting house, the text suggests that it was the initiative of the matoa. This valorizes the community's leaders and by extension the Wajorese community in Makassar. Given the fact that Makassar functioned as the heart of the Wajorese community during the very early eighteenth century, legitimizing the community there was very important.

A third example of writing to legitimize a community comes from twentieth-century eastern Kalimantan. Several recent histories offer explanations for the Bugis presence there. Their point of reference is La Maddukelleng who is portrayed not as a ruthless conqueror but as a founding father. This portrayal may be indicative of local efforts to have La Maddukelleng canonized as a national hero of Indonesia which occurred in 1998.

Published in 1981, D. Adham's *Salasilah Kutai* relates the manner in which La Maddukelleng's son Petta Sebengareng settled in Kutai from where he ordered the kidnapping of Andin Ajang, the daughter of the ruler of Pasir. They married and had a daughter named Andin Duyah, later known as Aji Putri Agung, who then married the ruler of Kutai's son Aji Muhammad Idris, later known as Sultan Aji Muhammad Idris. After a long sojourn in Kutai, Petta Sebengareng grew remorseful for having kidnapped the princess and for not having visited his own parents, so he, his wife Andin Ajang, their daughter Aji Putri Agung and her husband Sultan Aji Muhammad Idris all traveled first to Pasir and then to Pénéki. They were feted in both places and stayed for more than a year in Pénéki where Aji Putri Agung gave birth to Aji Imbut. Born in Bugis lands, he would later have the support of the Bugis community in Kutai. When he reached the age of one, he and his parents returned to Kutai where Sultan Muhammad Idris resumed his rule. Meanwhile Petta Sebengareng and Andin Ajang remained in Pénéki.

Family relations firmly established, the royal families of Kutai and Pénéki remained close. After a few years, a messenger from Pénéki came to Kutai with a request from Petta Sebengareng that Sultan Muhammad Idris return to assist Pénéki in a war. Aji Putri Agung could not accompany him because she was pregnant, so Sultan Muhammad Idris went alone to Sulawesi where he was victorious in battle but died while hunting. His followers did not want to return to Kutai so Raja Pénéki granted them land in Akkotengeng. Sultan Muhammad Idris' kris and headband were returned to his wife Aji Putri Agung, who fainted when she learned of his death, and all of Kutai mourned for forty days. Aji Kado, who had been ruling in Sultan Muhammad Idris' absence then assumed the title Sultan Aji Muhammad Aliyeddin, and married Aji Putri Agung. Fearing for the safety of her late husband's three children, she sent them all to Pénéki. Believing that Aji Imbut was the rightful ruler of Kutai, the Bugis in Samarinda Seberang did not accept Sultan Aji Muhammad Aliyeddin and they refused to assist him defend the country from an attack from Sulu until after his reputation had been irreparably damaged by his inability to defend the land. The Bugis then sent for Aji Imbut. Aji Kado a.k.a. Sultan Aji Muhammad Aliyeddin was executed and Aji Imbut was installed as Sultan Aji Muhammad Muslihuddin. Owing his reign to the Bugis, Sultan Aji Muhammad Muslihuddin concluded an agreement with them that safeguarded both his rule and the position of the Bugis in Kutai's society. D. Adham dates Sultan Aji Muhammad Muslihuddin's reign with a letter he purportedly wrote to the VOC in 1739 requesting the establishment of trading relations.[110]

While D. Adham's account is difficult to corroborate with Wajorese lontaraq, it can be corroborated with Dutch sources regarding aid from Pasir during the Pénéki War.[111] What is more important for the present discussion, however, are the clues that D. Adham's account provides clues regarding the legacy of the Wajorese. It points to the power of the Bugis community in Samarinda and implicates their lack of support in Sultan Aji Muhammad Aliyeddin's demise. By presenting the Bugis as the restorers of Sultan Aji Muhammad Muslihuddin to his rightful throne, it serves as a justifying myth for Bugis presence in Kutai. In this sense, it resembles the works of Raja Ali Haji such as the *Tuhfat al-Nafis,* which was written in the nineteenth century. *Salasilah Kutai*'s relatively recent publication date, 1981, suggests that the need to justify Bugis presence in Kutai is still strongly felt.

Identity as an Essential Diaspora Mechanism

In that a group's identity often arises or is strengthened by contacts with outsiders, a diaspora is an exceptionally fruitful field for the study of identity. The Wajorese diaspora is no exception. Wajorese migrants found themselves in a wide variety of circumstances and made various choices regarding their identity, presumably according to what they perceived as being most advantageous at any given time and place. So prevalent was this practice that ethnicization or identity manipulation, regardless as to whether it was done consciously, can be considered as a strategy for success overseas.

Implementing identity required different things in different areas. In Wajoq itself, the origin stories and specific histories were used to distinguish the Wajorese from their neighbors. The claim of descent from a princess of Luwuq and fidelity to Gowa were sources of pride and strengthened the Wajorese identity. Other stories, such as certain episodes of *I La Galigo,* provided guidelines for behavior and reinforced the social structure.

Outside of Wajoq there was room for more flexibility. Individuals and even communities could change their ethnic identity in order to obtain a perceived advantage; and they could even do so repeatedly. Daéng Matekko used his Wajorese identity to forge alliances with anti-Bonéan elements in the Straits of Melaka. His grandson Raja Ismail then employed the prestigious Malay lineage acquired through his maternal grandfather in an attempt to acquire political caché in the Malay world. When he was confronted with the crime of his brother Raja Daud, however, he relied upon their Wajorese heritage to find a solution: exile to Bugis lands. In eastern Kalimantan, the Wajorese used their distinct identity as a community in order to reside under their own elected leaders and to gain commercial advantages over their Malay hosts.

The sources show that ethnicization was conceived of in terms of "being" Wajorese or Bugis or of having a particular lord. Doubtlessly it was not conceived of as "implementing identity" for personal or communal gain. Nevertheless there were various ceremonies, processes and texts that the Wajorese used on a regular basis so as to maintain and fortify their own identity. These are documented in the diary of the Wajorese statesman who participated in such ceremonies as circumcisions and placenta burials. Logistically this culture is also reinforced by the importation of marriage partners, priests and other new migrants, as well as regular travel and commerce. The development of a distinctive literary canon, including Daéng Mabéla's history of his family and the records of the Wajorese matoa in Makassar, also appears to have been key. Despite the contact with a wide variety of other ethnic groups, these behaviors in which the Wajorese engaged kept their identity alive and they were able to employ it when desired.

It is no coincidence that these markers were most pronounced on the western coast of Sumatra. Here the advantages of a Bugis identity over a local identity were the greatest and could even include exclusion from forced cultivation, special trading licenses and judicial privileges. Consequently it was also in western Sumatra that the most mechanisms for maintaining a Bugis identity were maintained. These included the use of the titles Daéng and Siti and particular styles of dress. In this area there was also a veritable dynasty of Wajorese leaders who bore the names Maruppa, Mabéla, and Makkullé across the generations so as to ensure their family's, and their community's, special status.

Identity was also significant to the manner in which the diaspora functioned. Far from being mere sentiments, community ties could be used to mobilize political and military power. A case in point is the help offered by the Wajorese on Sumbawa in the campaign of La Maddukelleng. The queen of Boné reported that the Wajorese allies in Sumbawa supplied them with large quantities of gunpowder, shot and provision and that ten ships stood ready to go to Sumbawa in 1736.[112] Wajorese lontaraq also state that the Wajorese from Sumbawa provided Wajoq with guns and blunderbusses.[113] Nor was this a one-time event. The Wajorese community on Sumbawa also lent their support during the Pénéki War during the mid-eighteenth centu-ry.[114] That a Wajorese merchant residing, or maybe even born, on Sumbawa would support a military effort in the homeland attests to the survival of a Wajorese identity across both time and space.

With the return of La Maddukelleng from Kalimantan and his assumption of leadership in Wajoq, the role of overseas communities in Wajorese af-fairs became increasingly important. It is to this episode in Wajorese history that this study now turns.

CHAPTER SEVEN

The Repatriate Arung Matoa

Interaction between the overseas communities of Wajorese and Wa-joq itself intensified during the early eighteenth century when successive arung matoa deliberately encouraged expatriates to contribute assistance to the homeland. It culminated in the 1730s with the return to Wajoq of the exiled La Maddukelleng. After being tried and acquitted by the Tel-lumpocco, he attracted a huge following and freed Wajoq from Bonéan interference. Thus after a long period of subordination to Luwuq, then Gowa and then Boné, Wajoq assumed a position of paramountcy in South Sulawesi. It did not last. After his unsuccessful attempt to unite the peoples of South Sulawesi and expel the Dutch from Makassar, La Maddukel-leng's actions caused a period of turmoil not only in Wajoq but also across the lands of the Tellumpocco.

The extremely complex political situation reveals long-distance political participation on many levels. By the eighteenth century, many Wajorese had been overseas for a generation. Nevertheless, they still participated in the affairs of the homeland. Their contributions and repatriation exemplify the bonds that they still felt with Wajoq. While such participation was a widespread phenomenon, involving communities from Sumbawa, Makassar, eastern Kalimantan, and elsewhere, La Maddukelleng's return and campaign against the Dutch are the clearest example of the argument that diasporic Wajorese communities continued to feel close ties with the homeland and participate in its political life. La Maddukelleng's interference directly at Wajoq's center was not "external" intrusion but part of the politics of Wajorese society.

The Flight of La Maddukelleng

La Maddukelleng, the older brother of Daéng Matekko, fled from Wajoq as a young man. The vast majority of lontaraq provide no details about his early life.[1] Typically, the LSW fills in some of the gaps. As previously discussed, this lontaraq has a high level of accuracy with regards to such matters as the dating of important events, but the story of La Maddukelleng's early life is somewhat muddled. This episode begins by recounting a ceremonial event critical to La Maddukelleng's early life and describes it as having been held during the reigns of both Arung Matoa La Saléwangeng (r. 1715–1736) and Arumponé La Patauq (r. 1696–1714), which do not coincide. Since this story of the youthful La Maddukelleng and why he fled Wajoq is not included in the vast majority of Wajorese chronicles, it is therefore likely that the author of the LSW simply included the legendary background of this historic figure.

According to legend, La Patauq held an ear-piercing ceremony in Cenrana for his daughter I Waleq, at which there was also a cockfight and a deer hunt. La Maddukelleng, who just recently had been circumcised and therefore presumably was in his early teens, was charged with carrying Arung Matoa La Saléwangeng's betelnut box. During the cockfight, a Bonéan threw the head of a dead cock that hit the arung matoa. La Maddukelleng was so offended by this act that he stabbed the offending Bonéan. A brawl ensued in which 19 Bonéans and 15 Wajorese were killed, forcing the Wajorese to swim across the river to safety. After they returned to Tosora, a messenger of the arumponé arrived asking for the person who started the stabbing to be brought to Boné for judgment. Wanting to protect La Maddukelleng, the arung matoa replied that the person had not returned to Wajoq. At first the arumponé was not satisfied with this reply. When the arung matoa reminded the arumponé that, according to the Treaty of Timurung, they were not supposed to doubt each other, the arumponé acquiesced.

Fearing that the Bonéans might attack Wajoq in order to find him, La Maddukelleng decided to flee. After La Maddukelleng paid his parting respects to the arung matoa, the ruler of Bénténg told La Maddukelleng not to forget Wajoq. La Maddukelleng then paid his respects at the grave of Petta Cinnotabiq, said a silent prayer, and departed.[2] Aside from the typescript *A Short History of the Arrival of the Bugis in Samarinda Seberang,* there is no further mention of La Maddukelleng until 1726.

La Maddukelleng Abroad

After leaving South Sulawesi, La Maddukelleng may have traveled to Sumbawa and elsewhere, but the Dutch first became aware of La Maddukelleng's presence in Kalimantan in the 1720s. According to Dutch records, he settled in Pasir where the Wajorese were already on good terms with the local rulers, and quickly became involved in regional trade and politics through both strategic marriages and commercial maneuvers. He married a daughter of the ruler of Pasir, Aji Patti, and his growing influence attracted increasing numbers of Wajorese[3] who placed themselves under his protection in Pasir. La Maddukelleng used the immigrants to strengthen his own power base by creating what amounted to his own private army and navy. Eventually La Maddukelleng's ambitions led to a war in which his force drove Aji Patti and his Malay followers out of Pasir to Baja Baja and Kutai. La Maddukelleng then assumed the title of Sultan Pasir himself and demanded the Malays who had fled from Pasir be returned to face his justice. The ruler of Kutai refused to comply, and so La Maddukelleng sent his collaborator Panglima To Assa under the title of Kapitan Laut, together with his younger brother Gusti, in six well-manned ships to Kutai to seize the Malays by force. Upon hearing of this impending attack, the ruler of Kutai and almost all of the inhabitants fled into the mountains. La Maddukelleng's force then captured the remaining inhabitants, sold the men and kept the women and girls as wives, and burned Kutai down.[4] Some escaped, however, and came to Makassar as refugees.[5] The dethroned ruler of Pasir himself came to Makassar and appealed to the VOC for help. In the 1720s, however, the VOC could not see sufficient reason for getting involved and denied his request.[6] There was no way that the company, or anyone else, could foresee how influential La Maddukelleng would later become in the affairs of South Sulawesi.

In 1728 after the attacks on Kutai and Pasir, To Assa was reported sailing back and forth at the mouth of the Banjarmasin River. This alarmed the Banjarese who feared an attack on Banjarmasin. They appealed to the VOC for help in defending themselves, but the company would agree only to build a lodge in Banjarmasin, and this only if it received an exclusive pepper contract.[7] The company did its best to convince the ruler of Banjarmasin that such an arrangement would prevent To Assa from attacking Banjarmasin.[8] Rumors of To Assa's impending attack scared the uplanders thereby enabling the king to buy all of their pepper at very low prices,[9] a deal from which the VOC presumably also profited. Thus it was that the VOC, at minimal expense, was able to turn the rapine of La Maddukelleng, To Assa, and their followers to its own interests. Then again in 1730, To Assa spent a month and ten days cruising the Banjar River with 60 ships manned with 500 or 600 people. When this force approached Banjarmasin, the Banjarese attacked and, after a small skirmish, To Assa fled.[10]

Meanwhile in Wajoq, La Saléwangeng anticipated a war with Boné and wrote a letter to La Maddukelleng in Pasir asking him to return and help.[11] Arung Taq La Dallé took the letter to La Maddukelleng in Pasir. Although it would have been impossible for the author to know the contents of a letter kept confidential, according to the LSW, which presumably was recording a legend, La Saléwangeng's letter to La Maddukelleng read as follows:

> It would be good if you returned to Bugis lands. Later if you return to Wajoq, your pardon will be requested from Boné. If Boné does not want to pardon you, then let Boné attack you because there is already much ammunition in Wajoq, as well as lead, guns and funds. The guns in Wajoq number more than 1500, excluding those in Wajoq's *liliq* or vassals. When you get this letter, after you have read it, do not show it to anyone else. Do not tell this to anyone else, either, just appear suddenly in Bugis lands.[12]

When La Maddukelleng read the letter, he immediately started gathering weapons and tools of war and he reportedly assembled a force of forty ships loaded with arms and troops. He returned to Sulawesi with Arung Taq La Dallé, Kapitan Laut To Assa, and Puanna Pabbola, as well as people from Pasir who wanted to accompany him.[13]

The Return of La Maddukelleng

At the time of La Maddukelleng's return, the Tellumpocco alliance was already considerably weakened. As Boné's power had declined, the balance of power in South Sulawesi had not adequately adjusted. No one had been able to replace the charismatic Arung Palakka La Tenritatta as lord of South Sulawesi, and the Dutch were still not firmly enough entrenched to rule the peninsula independently. La Maddukelleng took advantage of this power vacuum, further undermining the Tellumpocco alliance.

La Maddukelleng's violent career, particularly his acts of piracy during the reign of La Saléwangeng, was widely known.[14] There was a song about La Maddukelleng that went as follows: "The buffalo eats at sea. Its tail is so heavy that it does not move. Its horns don't butt. If it moves its tail just once, Wajoq will be troubled, Soppéng will be made to sit lost in thought and Boné will lose its perspective."[15] This song, which may have been composed at a later date by the writer of the lontaraq, emphasizes the impact that La Maddukelleng had on the politics of South Sulawesi in its prediction that his return would be a troublesome burden to Wajoq, paralyze Soppéng and disenfranchise Boné.

As La Maddukelleng began making his presence felt in South Sulawesi, the Dutch also grew concerned. In 1735, he set fire to houses on an island across from Fort Rotterdam. The Dutch Governor Sautijn reported that La Maddukelleng and To Assa, with a fleet of about 19 double masted-gorabs and a few other smaller ships, were seen in broad daylight going from one island to another setting all the houses on these islands on fire.[16] In early March 1735, the Dutch tried to blockade La Maddukelleng and his followers but the latter managed to escape. Rumor then had it they were headed for Sumbawa, but instead they invaded Sabutung, burning part of it.[17] The Dutch then grew alarmed by the prospect that La Maddukelleng and his followers might do the same in Vlaardingen, a residential section near the fort. On March 12 at 8 a.m., La Maddukelleng and To Assa appeared within sight of Castle Rotterdam, about four or five miles from the wall with a considerable fleet of about 27 to 28 boats, 14 of which were double-masted. Dutch allies in Bontualaq, an area in Makassar, and Gowa swore that they had advised their people to be on guard, and to make sure that La Maddukelleng and To Assa were not permitted in any rivers or on land, and that they should not be given even the slightest assistance.[18]

Rallying Support in South Sulawesi

The Dutch did not suspect that Wajoq would support La Maddukelleng or even allow him to take shelter.[19] Indeed, when La Maddukelleng returned to Bugis lands, he was not immediately well received. Not only was he barred from disembarking off the coast of Doping but also he was also put on trial. Within a short period of time, however, he overcame these obstacles and gained tremendous support.

In late 1735 La Maddukelleng appeared on the coast of Mandar with Arung Taq La Dallé,[20] Puanna Pabbola, To Assa, and 40 ships. According to one lontaraq, the ships were exceptionally large and mounted with heavy cannons that the Mandarese could not withstand.[21] Coincidentally, La Pasonriq Arung Lipukasi (Tanété) was also there with a force from Magindanao in the southern Philippines.[22] Armed conflict ensued. Some lontaraq relate that To Assa seized a ship from Mangngarancang and then was surprised in Binuang. Other lontaraq say that La Maddukelleng went southwards along the coast, moored at Sabutung, then attacked two islands near Makassar. Perhaps both are true but the latter attack is confirmed in Dutch records[23] and the Diary of Gowa.[24] Certain accounts also relate that the Tellumpocco considered attacking him, but were scared of entering a naval engagement with this famous pirate.[25] La Maddukelleng then went to the coast of Boné where he was refused entrance to Wajoq, and from there proceeded to Doping on the coast of Wajoq. He was not permitted to land there, but instead was forced to wait on board his ship for forty days. Finally a messenger arrived bringing him permission to land on the condition that he submit himself to trial by the Tellumpocco.[26]

Once on land, La Maddukelleng went to Séngkang. According to most lontaraq, his progress thereafter was marked by the acquisition of a larger and larger following at every turn. He disembarked at Doping with 40 men; by the time he reached Lawesso they had increased to at least a hundred, and more and more continued to join him as he proceeded to Pénrang and Séngkang. When he reached Séngkang, his command had swollen to more than 500,[27] or, according to one account, almost a thousand.[28] Such popularity might be attributable to a widely felt social desire to undermine Bonéan paramountcy or to the manner in which the Wajorese population was able to relate to a repatriate. This instant popularity is not, however, depicted universally in the lontaraq. One source, Leid Cod Or 1923 VI, deemphasizes La Maddukelleng's initial popularity, making his eventual acquisition of entire Wajoq's support all the more striking.

In Tosora, there was a conference of the Tellumpocco in which Boné accused La Maddukelleng of seven different crimes. Different lontaraq name different crimes, but their number and general nature are in all cases the same. In an article specifically about La Maddukelleng and this trial, Noorduyn analyzes the various Bugis texts and translates one in its entirety.[29] According to this text,[30] these crimes were: murdering a Bonéan noble named To Passarai in the village of Tobonio on the southeastern coast of Borneo; killing a Bonéan messenger; frightening the ruler of Mandar, a Bonéan ally, by cockfighting and threatening Mandar with his artillery; setting Baranglompo on fire; firing on Fort Rotterdam in Makassar; frightening the ruler of Boné by entering the River Cenrana aboard strange ships; and ordering six assassinations in Kera, a village in northern Wajoq. He was then called to trial to account for his actions.

La Maddukelleng made a seven-point argument in his defense. He claimed that he was justified in killing To Passarai because he had murdered a Wajorese man in Pasir. He then argued that it was not he but his subjects who killed the Bonéan messenger, and that because this occurred at sea, they could not be held accountable. He explained that by positioning his guns in Mandar, he was only trying to protect himself from the possibility that the ruler of Mandar would unjustly claim victory in a cockfight, and that when his subjects burned houses in Baranglompo and Balangcaddi, they did so for religious reasons because the houses were empty. He justified firing on Fort Rotterdam by saying that he was only returning fire. He also claimed that he did not change ships before entering the River Cenrana and that he killed people in Kéra for the sake of revenge.[31] Either La Maddukelleng's replies were sufficient to satisfy the court, or his armed followers swayed the court's opinion. Either way he was acquitted of the charges brought against him and permitted to leave Tosora.

Following La Maddukelleng's acquittal, the power shift within the Tellumpocco accelerated. For a long time, Boné had been the most powerful of the three united lands. The Treaty of Timurung, which created this alliance, specified that Boné was the oldest of the three brothers. Following the Makassar War, Boné under La Tenritatta and La Patauq was certainly the most powerful. This state of affairs began to change after the rule of La Patauq and this new power balance was reflected in the acquittal of La Maddukelleng. His arguments in defense of himself were far from indisputable. Indeed, according to Zainal Abidin, they actually angered the Tellumpocco,[32] but it acquitted him nevertheless. Thus his acquittal may have been dictated more by the power that La Maddukelleng now wielded rather than by the persuasiveness of his defense.

La Maddukelleng did not remain long in Séngkang because the city was surrounded by the forces of the Tellumpocco. He then went to Pénéki where he was inaugurated as arung Pénéki. Thereafter he asked the Bonéans to leave Pénéki,[33] thereby precipitating a war with Boné. The Bonéans first retaliatory act was to invade Pénéki, following which they made the strategic mistake of burning other places in Wajoq. The population was enraged by these acts which are described in the lontaraq as Bonéan aggression, with the result that many of its members rebelled and joined forces with La Maddukelleng. Boné was no longer fighting a pirate but the Wajorese population.

The Tellumpocco's unity suffered tremendously as a result.[34] Eventually, La Maddukelleng would assume leadership of the Tellumpocco, but first he waged war on Boné. The Wajorese were able to seize the Bonéan fort south of Pénéki, but there was dissent within the ranks. Several of Wajoq's constituent polities opted to side with Boné because at this early stage in the conflict they perceived their best interests as lying with Boné.[35] Their switch exemplifies the manner in which polities within Wajoq could choose their allegiance according to the manner in which they perceived their best interests.

Word of the conflict between Boné and Wajoq reached Makassar on July 5, 1736.[36] Although the Dutch sided with their traditional ally Boné, their attention was focused on Maros where the Makassarese Karaéng Bontolangkasa and Arung Kaju were leading a rebellion against them. They nevertheless supported the Bonéan queen Arung Timurung with weapons, powder, and supplies, and even sent a small contingent to Cenrana under the command of Captain Steinmetz. Steinmetz' efforts to assist the Bonéans against the Wajorese met with resistance from Wajorese-inclined ministers within the Bonéan court. He reported that the queen, Arung Timurung, had at first been determined to fight the enemy, but had lost some of her resolve because her ministers advised against it.[37] Eventually he realized that three of the principal Bonéan ministers, the Makkedangng Tana, the Maddanrang, and the To Marilaleng, were all conspiring with the Wajorese. One example of their treachery was postponing the bombardment of Tosora on the pretext that they were not yet fully prepared, though they were actually giving the Wajorese time to prepare their defenses.[38] When the attack was finally launched, the To Marilaleng falsely reported that they had run out of powder. Steinmetz tried to keep this information from the Bonéan queen, but at this point Sautijn recalled him to Makassar in order to avoid further calamity. Seeing that the war was going badly, the queen herself also took refuge in Bontualaq with the pretext that things could be better resolved from there.[39]

In his outgoing report for his successor, Sautijn expressed his amazement that the Wajorese could resist without help and weapons from the VOC. Part of their ability stemmed from their overseas connections. Besides the support that La Maddukelleng had brought with him from Kalimantan, the Wajorese also received help from allies in Sumbawa. La Maddukelleng's staunch ally Karaéng Bontolangkasa had lived in Sumbawa following his exile from Gowa and had married the daughter of the Sumbawa ruler Amas Madina (1688–1725).[40] The queen of Boné reported that there were Wajorese allies in Sumbawa who supplied them with large quantities of gunpowder, shot and provision. To this end ten ships stood ready to go to Sumbawa in 1736.[41] The importance of this connection is also documented in certain lontaraq which state that the Wajorese from Sumbawa provided Wajoq with guns and blunderbusses.[42]

While waiting for reinforcements from Sumbawa, La Maddukelleng assumed Wajoq's leadership. Shortly after the confrontation with Boné, he replaced La Saléwangeng as arung matoa. The lontaraq describe how La Saléwangeng resigned. At a meeting in Tosora, he suggested that he was old and tired and that Wajoq should find a new ruler. The people replied that as long as he was alive, they did not want him to go because Wajoq had prospered under his rule. But La Saléwangeng persisted, and so the people suggested that he select one of his grandchildren to lead Wajoq. La Saléwangeng replied, "I do not see anyone who could lead the Wajorese in fighting as well as La Maddukelleng."[43] Arung Bénténg then went to speak to La Maddukelleng at Paria, which he was helping to defend. La Maddukelleng agreed to accept the appointment, and on November 6, 1736,[44] became the thirty-first arung matoa of Wajoq.[45] La Saléwangeng, whose rule had already lasted for twenty years, remained an advisor until his death eight years later.[46] In contrast to the Wajorese lontaraq, letters from Bugis rulers found in VOC archives suggest that the transition might not have been so peaceful. Letters from Datu Baringeng and Arung Timurung report that La Saléwangeng was in fact dethroned.[47] Given the record of La Maddukelleng's previous and subsequent activities, this version is more likely accurate.

As arung matoa, La Maddukelleng took a vow to free Wajoq from all of its oppressors.[48] He encouraged all the Wajorese to take up arms against all those attacking Wajoq.[49] He also sought reimbursement of the money, people, and goods seized by Boné in 1670, and repeatedly launched attacks on northern Boné. He was not, however, immediately successful. In March 1737 the Makkedangng Tana reported to the Dutch that the Bonéans attacked the Wajorese and won over ten constituent polities. Nine hundred Wajorese perished in that battle, which led them to seek a ceasefire from the Bonéan queen Arung Timurung which she granted.[50] Wajorese lontaraq describe other conflicts in which the Wajorese were more successful against Boné and its allies, such as their numerous attacks on northern Boné and Sidénréng, and when Soppéng requested a ceasefire.[51] They also describe how, during these engagements, La Gau Datu Pammana, only recently installed as Pillaq Wajoq, proved himself to be particularly valiant and loyal to La Maddukelleng during this war.[52] In mid-1737, an agreement was finally reached in which Boné and Soppéng reimbursed Wajoq for the goods, people, and money seized by Arung Palakka and Arung Bélo in 1670.[53] The fact that such payments were demanded more than 50 years after the offense testifies to the strength of Wajorese resentment and pride. Boné and Soppéng began recompensating Wajoq in installments[54] and Wajoq grew in strength.[55]

Yet La Maddukelleng's ambitions extended beyond the restoration of Wajoq's lost people, territory, and goods. He sought to mobilize Wajoq and its neighbors, especially Boné, which he viewed as having brought the Dutch to Sulawesi, to expel the Dutch from Makassar. At a meeting of the Tellumpocco in Timurung in October 1737, he stated this explicitly. "Wajoq wants Boné to force the Dutch to leave, for as long as they're here, the Tellumpocco will be in decline."[56] It was two years, however, before La Maddukelleng was able to launch an attack.[57]

Conflict and Negotiations with the Dutch

Having heard rumors of a possible attack,[58] and aware of the increasingly large role that Wajoq was playing in the affairs of South Sulawesi, the Dutch grew concerned about what these events might portend for them.[59] Their response therefore was an attempt to establish a lasting, albeit unequal, peace with the Wajorese. On October 7, 1738, Dutch Governor Smout received a communication from Wajoq brought him by the Wajorese messenger La Using, to which he replied that he would like Arung Matoa La Maddukelleng to come to Makassar. Smout further stated that he wanted to promote peace in Sulawesi and to improve the situation so that the Wajorese merchants could once again prosper commercially. Finally he expressed the hope for a reliable report from Wajoq since the governor was trying his best to rectify the problems in Sulawesi.[60]

The Wajorese messenger returned to Makassar on October 25 bearing the message that the arung matoa had never considered the VOC as an enemy but rather as a friend, and that he had always had love for the company and had adhered faithfully to their treaty. The governor's response was that the VOC first and foremost wanted to restore peace to Celebes, which was the reason he had sent the letter in the first place. He added that the Dutch wanted to understand the reasons for the troubles between the rulers of Boné and Wajoq. The messenger quickly answered that the differences between Wajoq and Boné were settled and that they were now friends. He also informed the governor that it was necessary for a European envoy to be sent to Wajoq to meet the arung matoa, and that if this were done, there could be little doubt that the arung matoa himself would then come to Makassar.[61]

The Dutch thought that it would be very beneficial if the arung matoa were to come to Makassar, and so they decided to send Lieutenant Philip Lodewijk Figera, and senior interpreter Jan Hendrik Vol to Wajoq.[62] They were instructed not to complete negotiations with the rulers of Wajoq but instead simply to announce their presence. In order to show the company's willingness to receive the arung matoa in Makassar they were to inform him that they had come on the advice of the Wajorese messenger. They were expected to remain for one to six days in order to see how their message was received, but they were instructed to avoid staying for eight to ten days. In the event that they were not admitted or that the arung matoa could not decide if he would come to Makassar or not, then the expedition was instructed to return to Makassar forthwith. Under all circumstances, however, they were to try and ascertain exactly how large Wajoq was and how the conflict with Boné had developed.[63]

Dutch records relate that Figera and Vol departed for Wajoq on November 3. On November 10, they reached Cempaga where they were hospitably greeted by To Assa, La Maddukelleng's collaborator. The next day, they arrived in the capital of Tosora. There they had an audience with the arung matoa, together with representatives from the Tellumpocco and the lesser nobles of Wajoq. They delivered the VOC's letter, and the arung matoa promised to consider it and inform them of his decision. Two days later they were told that the arung matoa and four of the forty Wajorese rulers would indeed go to Fort Rotterdam, the VOC headquarters in Makassar. The arung matoa made it clear, however, that he was not aware of any binding contract between the Wajorese and the VOC later than the one signed when the Wajorese went to Fort Rotterdam after the attack on Tosora in 1670. He added that he was prepared to come to Makassar in person to meet with the Dutch as long as the Tellumpocco was permitted to maintain its sovereignty.

The Dutch emissaries also gathered information outside official channels and learned from the messenger La Using that the arung matoa wanted to nullify the old contract between the Wajorese and the Dutch. Indeed, had the Dutch not brought a copy of it with them, he would not have known that it even existed. The emissaries found it difficult to give credence to this account, and so they asked their confidant Daéng Mangili to learn more about La Maddukelleng's intentions. He spoke confidentially with La Using, who informed him that the arung matoa intended to restore the ruler of Gowa to his former authority and glory. Furthermore, in order to satisfy the Tellumpocco, the arung matoa wanted the VOC to restore all of the territories that it had acquired from the Gowan ruler. Figera's commission also learned from the Bonéan Tomarilaleng that troubles with the Bonéans could be expected to continue. In his opinion, however, the arung matoa's courage would vanish if Boné and Tanété were united. On November 16, they had another audience with the arung matoa and were given a letter.[64] The latter explained that this letter was just a formality and that it contained no other information than what they had already been told. That same afternoon, they left Tosora.[65]

When Figera's expedition returned to Makassar, they brought with them a Dutch sailor named Jan Lambregts who had been residing in Tosora. The story of his kidnapping attests to the power and bravery of the Wajorese in the 1730s. According to his own account, he and one of his mates were abducted in July 1737, while trying to procure provisions for their ship (*De Goswiena*). They were immediately stripped of their clothing and taken to Batu Putih where they were held captive for three months with no hope of escape. One night Lambregts was forced onto a ship, where he was blindfolded until the ship was on the open sea. When the ship landed, he could not say where he was, but from there he was brought over land to Tosora. There he was given by his captors as a present to the paramount ruler of Wajoq. He was kept there for four or five days before he was forcefully brought to a temple where he was shaved and circumcised, indicating his conversion to Islam. He was then forced to remain in Wajoq for eight months, during which time he observed that the Wajorese twice received shipments of gunpowder, but from whom or where he could not say.[66]

Certain Bugis accounts of the relations between Wajoq and the Dutch differ substantially from Dutch sources. According to *Lontarak Wajoq III,* the Dutch sent a messenger with greetings from Makassar, together with the promise that the Dutch were willing to supply the Wajorese with anything they needed. Arung Matoa La Maddukelleng replied that Wajoq did not want to ask the VOC for presents, but only sought security and peace for the Tellumpocco.[67] The Leid Or Cod 1923 VI, on the other hand, describes an exchange of letters, after which the Dutch sent an interpreter asking if Wajoq remembered its friendship with the Company. It goes on to record that La Maddukelleng replied, "Wajoq denies being friends with the Company. To Unruq only acquainted Wajoq with the Company, but To Unruq is now dead. We do not know each other anymore. If the Company wishes, then we will renew our mutual acquaintance; let them come here or we will go to Makassar." According to this lontaraq, the interpreter returned to Makassar on November 16, 1738,[68] which is confirmed in Dutch records.

Regardless of what transpired between the Dutch and the Wajorese, any attempt at reconciling their differences was too late. The Wajorese had already begun sending weapons to their allies in Gowa.[69] No matter what he said or did not say, clearly La Maddukelleng was more determined than ever to force the Dutch out of Makassar. In February 1739 he and his allied army departed for Makassar to attack the Dutch. Almost immediately there was dissent among the ranks. When someone dared to suggest to La Maddukelleng that he reconsider attacking the Dutch, La Maddukelleng replied, "Fine, Tellumpoccoé, go back to your village if you do not want to go to war. The Dutch in Ujung Pandang only have 500 soldiers and I also have 500. So I'll go alone to fight them. Hopefully I can get them to leave Ujung

Pandang (Makassar)." Although some people retreated, La Maddukelleng remained steadfast.[70]

La Maddukelleng arrived in Makassar on April 5, 1739. There he found more unrest and considerably less support than he had expected. When he and Karaéng Bontolangkasa approached the rulers of Gowa for their support, they were told that the rulers must consult their ministers before granting the request. La Maddukelleng apparently rejected this temporizing, saying that they did not know exactly who their friends were.[71] This led the minister, the karaéng matoa named I Mappasanreq, to defect to the Dutch, absconding at night with the Sudannga (a sword, the regalia of Gowa) and storing it with the Dutch. Another minister, Karaéng Garassiq also went over to the Dutch. Karaéng Bontolangkasa was then made ruler of Gowa, but only four ministers gave him their support.[72]

Leid Cod Or 1923 VI provides a detailed Wajorese account of La Maddukelleng's attack on Makassar. It relates that during the first half of May, La Maddukelleng tried to negotiate the return of the Sudannga. The Dutch response was to claim that they had to consult with Batavia before taking any such action and that they continued to uphold the provisions of the Treaty of Bungaya. Frustrated, the Wajorese and Karaéng Bontolangkasa marched on Makassar on May 16, 1739, but were repulsed. Thereafter the Makkedangng Tana fled to Kampong Berru with the Bonéan flags, the Samparaja, and the Pajumpulaweng. This convinced the Wajorese that the Bonéans were on the side of the Dutch.[73] During the next three weeks, they launched three more attacks on the Dutch at Makassar, all of which were repulsed.[74] During the campaign, Karaéng Bontolangkasa was injured by a bullet from within his own ranks. He called for La Maddukelleng, and blamed their failure on the lack of unity between the Makassarese and Bugis. He therefore advised his friend to withdraw because he believed that Gowa was lost.[75] Yet La Maddukelleng refused to accept defeat. On the night of July 20, 1739, there was a total eclipse of the moon that darkened the sky for two hours and allowed the Wajorese forces to move about without detection. They invaded Gowa,[76] but were unable to achieve the total victory for which they were hoping. When they also failed to expel the Dutch, they retreated to Wajoq to await a Dutch counterattack. Meanwhile, Karaéng Bontolangkasa died in Bontoparang on September 8, 1739. The Bugis lontaraq explain that he refused to let his wounds be treated because of shame (siriq) at the demise of Gowa.[77]

La Maddukelleng's mission failed in large part because he was unable to secure the loyalty of the Gowan and Bonéan people. The Gowan rulers in Kampong Berru and the Bonéans under Batari Toja all sided with the

Dutch. The dissent among the various factions stemmed in part from personal disagreements, and in part from different interpretations about who
was responsible for bringing the Dutch to Sulawesi in the first place. One
lontaraq blames Gowa for treating its vassals too harshly and thereby forcing Arung Palakka to seek assistance.[78] Other lontaraq blame Arung Palakka entirely[79] and thus justify La Maddukelleng's deeds.

After retreating from Makassar, La Maddukelleng joined Arung Bénténg
and attacked Tanété. The Wajorese lost the ensuing battle in part because
the Soppéng contingent deserted on the battlefield. The Wajorese were desperate and had to retreat.[80] After seventeen days in Tosora, the Wajorese
launched an attack on Soppéng. According to one source, this was to punish Soppéng for having deserted in the middle of the battle in Tanété.[81]
Datu Lumpulle led this expedition, and succeeded in subduing Soppéng in
a single day.[82] La Pacau was then reinstated as ruler of Soppéng.[83] Twenty
months later, La Maddukelleng married Datu Lompulleq We Tompi, the
sister of a prominent noble in Soppéng,[84] thereby reaffirming Wajoq's alliance with Soppéng.

Counterattack

One year after La Maddukelleng married Datu Lompulleq, the Dutch
under Smout, aided by people from Boné, Buton, Luwuq, and Soppéng,
launched a counterattack against Wajoq. They departed on December 3,
1740, and arrived at Cenrana on December 24. 1740. Many of Wajoq's liliq
immediately switched loyalties and sided with the Dutch and the Bonéans.[85]
The Wajorese tried to buy them off, but the Dutch would not accept either
redemption money or a *pappasoroq,* a gift consisting of buffalos, rice, and
fruits, a gift which the Wajorese hoped would make the Dutch turn around
and go home.[86] Prior to the Makassar War, Speelman had said that Dutch
lives could be repaid only in blood and not in money.[87] Smout may have felt
the same way, because he rejected the Wajorese offer of a peaceful settlement.[88]

Fighting began in January of the following year. Wajorese lontaraq record that the Wajorese took numerous Bonéan heads and drove away both
the Bonéans and the Dutch.[89] Smout's report states that the Dutch did not
press this first attack against the Wajorese. They had just received news of
the Chinese rebellion in Batavia, which caused a commotion and distracted
them from the affair at hand. The Dutch were also disheartened by lack of
provisions. They went hungry for almost five days because the surround-

ing land had been laid waste, and because a supply ship was detained.[90] Furthermore, they suffered from illnesses. Smout's report further mentions a second battle in which the Bonéans torched southern Wajoq.[91] Indeed, there appear to have been numerous other skirmishes that did not involve the Dutch directly. Described in the Wajorese lontaraq, these encounters include a battle in which the Wajorese were defeated because their allies ran away before there was even any bloodshed; an attack at Patila and Patampeng where the Wajorese chased the Soppéngers back home;[92] and Wajorese attacks on northern Boné.[93] Smout's report also mentions how the Bonéans attacked Tosora against his orders.[94] Thus the conflict turned out to be as much a war between Boné and Wajoq as it was a Dutch reprisal against the Wajorese.

With the exception of Leid Cod Or 1923 VI,[95] most of the lontaraq do not mention the rather lengthy negotiations that took place between the Wajorese and the Dutch. For twenty-five days, messengers went back and forth between the two camps. According to Leid Cod Or 1923 VI, the Dutch demanded that Wajoq return Boné's cannons, provide compensation for the people from Maccongkiq who had been killed or kidnapped, and reimburse the Company for its expenses. Wajoq, however, would not agree to these terms.[96] Both Wajorese lontaraq and Dutch records describe numerous other Dutch attempts to resolve the conflict by negotiation, but record no success in these efforts.[97]

Dutch records describe how, while the negotiations were at a standstill, Arung Tanété La Oddang had requested Dutch assistance in mounting an attack against Lagusi. The Dutch were very happy to oblige because this would enable them to leave the swamps of Cenrana which were making them sick. After this village had been captured, Smout expressed his desire for a Dutch withdrawal. The Bonéans strongly objected, saying that if the Dutch left them today, the Wajorese would attack them tomorrow. Furthermore, the Bonéans emphasized how they had attacked Tosora at their own peril and that the Dutch therefore should not desert them now. Smout agreed to provide them with six soldiers and three cannons. Then the Dutch moved their camp to Lagusi in Pammana where they built a number of fortifications from which to fire upon Tosora. Lagusi was just across from Tosora and it was possible to fire upon the capital with cannons and mortars. Smout records the consternation of the Wajorese when they saw the Dutch so close to their capital. Yet the fortifications which the Dutch built in Lagusi did not serve their purpose as well as they had hoped. They were struck by fierce storms and tempests and then flooded by torrential rains and floods that destroyed the encampment. The Dutch therefore were forced to withdraw.[98]

With no secure base of operations, and provisions running low, the Dutch were now in danger, and Smout therefore wanted more than ever to end the conflict peacefully. Presumably, however, the Wajorese understood this and were in no hurry to conclude a peace treaty that would limit their freedom.[99] When negotiations were resumed, the Dutch proved to be much less demanding than previously. According to lontaraq, the Wajorese objected to the idea of an alliance or *assobakeng*.[100] According to Smout's report, the Wajorese stated that they were not anyone's slaves.[101] They said that they would never be slaves of the Company but that if they were free, rather than subservient allies, like Boné and Gowa, then they would have no objections to signing the treaty. The Bonéans, on the other hand, said that if the treaty made the Wajorese their equals, then they would not sign either. Smout assured the Wajorese that subservient ally could never mean slave in the Dutch language, but he was still unable to get their agreement regarding this point.[102]

The Leid Or Cod 1923 VI records that the Wajorese and the Dutch both became bored and dissatisfied with the unsuccessful negotiations and that the Dutch simply walked away from them.[103] Dutch records, on the other hand, state that an oral agreement was finally reached on March 25, 1741. The agreement was recorded by the Dutch as follows: 1) The contract, made in Ujung Pandang at Castle Rotterdam on the 23rd December 1670 between Maximiliaan de Jong of the VOC and Arung Matoa Puanna La Gelleng together with the other rulers and nobles of that country who are included, is completely renewed, as if it were inserted here word for word. 2) The Wajorese agree to restrict their travels, and in particular not to travel in the Bay of Tomini. 3) Wajoq promises Boné to leave Timurung to the Bonéans, as was agreed in 1737. 4) Wajoq will restore any Bonéan goods that are now being held in Tosora. 5) Henceforth Boné and Wajoq shall be equals and shall not interfere with each other's internal affairs. Although they may comment on each other's administrations, they will let each other's rulers reign peacefully and undisturbed, without exceptions. 6) In reverence for this treaty, both Wajoq and Boné shall ask the Company to mediate in any dispute between them rather than independently take revenge upon each other. 7) All acts of war and enmity will cease, and be forgiven and forgotten on both sides. Peace will be fully restored as if there had never been any problem.[104]

The Dutch punitive expedition did not achieve the results for which they had hoped. In practical terms the verbal agreement, which the Wajorese refused to sign, was nothing more than an honorable retreat for the Dutch.[105] Thus in December 1742 the Wajorese merchants, who had fled from Makassar with La Maddukelleng, were allowed to resettle there.[106] Never did the

Wajorese limit their travels as agreed upon in the second article. On the contrary, as described in chapter 4, Wajorese enterprises blossomed to the detriment of Dutch trade. Thus, in sharp contrast to the defeat of 1670, the Wajorese emerged from the conflict of 1739–1741 relatively unscathed.

Civil War

The departure of the Dutch did not mark the end of violence in Wajoq. On the contrary, La Maddukelleng launched a period of civil conflict that endured for decades. Just three days after the departure of the Dutch from Tosora on March 29, 1741, La Maddukelleng sent out his personal guard of pirates (*paggoraq*) to punish the vassals who had been disloyal and gone over to the Dutch side as soon as Smout had approached.[107] A number of them were fined while others were shown pity and regarded as a "child" of Wajoq. Yet there remained internal dissent in Wajoq as well as among its vassals.

One of the main conflicts during this period pertained to the relationship between Wajoq and its vassals Pammana and Sidénréng. This became personified in a conflict between La Maddukelleng and Datu Pammana La Gau, who was also the Pillaq of Wajoq. Whereas La Gau had displayed particular bravery in La Maddukelleng's attack against the Dutch in 1739, in the 1740s he incited Sidénréng against Wajoq because his brother-in-law La Wawo was the ruler or Addatuang of Sidénréng. Flexing his muscles for display, La Gau insisted that nobody outside his family would rule Sidénréng as long as he lived.[108] Arung Bénténg (Bénténg being the former palace center of Rappang, another part of Ajattappareng north of Sidénréng) advised La Gau not to create problems in Wajoq but the damage was done. When Sidénréng tried to make amends, La Maddukelleng refused to accept Sidénréng's surrender. Instead he insisted that Sidénréng appoint someone else as the ruler of Sidénréng that very day, otherwise La Maddukelleng would attack tomorrow. Sidénréng preferred armed conflict to abandonment of its adat.[109] Eventually armed conflict ensued between Sidénréng and Wajoq and it lasted for more than eight months. When Sidénréng and Pammana under La Gau sought reconciliation, the gravity of La Gau's and La Maddukelleng's crimes was debated. La Gau was accused of undermining the paramount ruler and La Maddukelleng was accused of acting arbitrarily. At this point, however, La Maddukelleng was still arung matoa and held the upper hand. La Maddukelleng insisted that La Gau's crimes could not be exonerated through remuneration and that he must be exiled or executed. Opinion in Wajoq was split, with some people agreeing with La Maddukelleng and others saying that La Gau should just be fined. Before consensus could be reached, La Maddukelleng shot La Gau who then escaped to Sekkanasu, probably to the south of Wajoq. Thereafter Sekkanasu and Sidénréng become the main targets of La Maddukelleng's aggression. When Sekkanasu tried to ally with Pammana, and when La Gau went to Pammana and stabbed the representative of the Cakkuridi who was also La Maddukelleng's wife, Wajoq attacked Pammana. For six months, the people of Pammana were unable to procure provisions but La Gau did not want to surrender. Instead La Gau and his wife Datu Watu tried to make peace by marrying their relative to Arung Bénténg's sister, because Arung Bénténg was an ally of La Maddukelleng. Arung Bénténg accepted the request and the marriage took place a month later, but even this was not enough to mend the rift between La Gau and La Maddukelleng. Arung Bénténg advised La Gau to ask La Maddukelleng's pardon one more time, promising that if it is not accepted, then they would attack La Maddukelleng together. La Gau then went to Tosora and once again asked La Maddukelleng for forgiveness. This time his apology was accepted.[110]

Another conflict from this period involved Mojong, a community north northeast of Lake Sidénréng which had traditionally been part of both Belawa and Sidénréng. People from both Belawa and Sidénréng sought gardening privileges in Mojong, and they would often fight over the garden until someone was wounded or killed at which point the victor would garden and his or her opponent would retreat. This happened year after year until they eventually thought that maybe they should not fight each other so much and agreed to seek arbitration. The issue was deliberated at length in Wajoq. After both sides of the story were heard repeatedly, it was decided to consult the lontaraq. While they were checking, however, La Maddukelleng decided unilaterally that Mojong was part of Belawa and awarded compensation to Belawa. Sidénréng was jealous, but the most infuriating aspect of La Maddukelleng's behavior was his blatant disregard for the deliberation process and thus for Wajorese adat.[111]

Through his arbitrary and contentious behavior in these and other situations, La Maddukelleng gradually lost the support of the Wajorese population. In 1754 when he tried to attack Sidénréng again and failed for lack of support, he relinquished his title in the middle of the campaign. One lontaraq records him as saying, "You appointed me on the battlefield to be arung matoa but if you don't want me to lead wars, then take Wajoq back on the field."[112] He was replaced by La Maddanaca (r. 1754–1755) who, like La Maddukelleng, was ostensibly selected for his ability to lead military campaigns. La Maddanaca is remembered for undertaking discussions with the Dutch in Makassar where he was later killed. In turn he was replaced by La Pacauq (r. 1755–1757.)[113]

La Maddukelleng as Arung Pénéki

Even after he left the office of arung matoa, La Maddukelleng still held the office of arung in Pénéki and he still tried to influence Wajoq. He wrote a letter from Pénéki arguing that if the Wajorese council punished him for breaking Wajorese customs, then they themselves would be ruining Wajoq. He also warned them against listening to Pilla La Gau, and promised that he would never hurt Wajoq as long as he lived. Because opinion was split, the Wajorese council replied with apparent difficulty, declaring that they treasured and followed Wajorese adat. They also emphasized that decisions regarding Wajoq were not made privately. During this period of tremendous anxiety, Wajoq lost numerous vassals; consequently La Pasawung stepped down as arung matoa.[114]

Around this time the Dutch also grew anxious about the manner in which La Maddukelleng and his band of robbers, as well as other Wajorese constituents, were causing poverty and troubles for the Bonéans. Having assumed a position of authority in Makassar with the help of Boné during the late 1660s, and believing they had no other trustworthy ally in the peninsula, the Dutch wanted Boné to be more powerful than Wajoq. Adding to their concern were Wajorese demands for Timurung and Wajorese attempts to renew their alliance with the Makassarese.[115]

Also around this time, La Maddukelleng's son La Pakka stole the horse of the arumponé,[116] and pillaged parts of Boné. When La Maddukelleng refused to surrender his son, Boné retaliated by attacking Pénéki. This escalated into what the Dutch called the Pénéki War. Boné attacked Pénéki for more than a year, there was a failed attempt at negotiation, and the war continued for two more years. Unable to reach an agreement within the Tellumpocco, Boné sought help from the Dutch. The arumponé visited Governor Sinkelaar and said that he was obliged to help the Bonéans bring the Wajorese to reason. When Sinkelaar tried to argue that this was not his responsibility and the arumponé chastised him for his unfriendliness.[117] Apparently this worked because the Dutch did lent Boné assistance in the form of supplies and loans. The Dutch wanted the war to end quickly and to reinstate the Bungaya Treaty. The Dutch were even willing to exclude several clauses, especially those that restrict freedom of navigation and Wajorese alliances with Gowa.[118] Wajoq, however, was more interested the renewal of the Tellumpocco.

During the course of the war, the Dutch grew frustrated with the Bonéans for prolonging the conflict and for not fighting wholeheartedly. While there was some Bonéan reluctance to attack Pénéki,[119] Pénéki was a difficult opponent because they received reinforcements from Wajoq, Pasir, Sumbawa, and Timor.[120] La Maddukelleng also exhibited his typical tenacity. Wajorese chronicles describe how, when a messenger tried to convince La Maddukelleng to surrender, he replied that he did not mind being attacked into desperation by the Tellumpocco and that he did not want to give up.[121] This corresponds with Dutch sources reporting that the Pénékians would rather die than leave.[122]

After numerous attacks and limited success, the Bonéans finally launched a devastating attack on Pénéki in which La Maddukelleng's son La Tobo died. Desperate for help, Pénéki appealed to Wajoq and Wajoq complied. Wajoq also asked for the surrender of La Pakka and La Maddukelleng agreed in word but never actually delivered his son. This unfulfilled promise caused people to rebel against La Maddukelleng, but before it became a major issue La Pakka died during another successful attack on Pénéki.[123]

There are then two different stories about how the war ended. Wajorese sources relate that the death of La Pakka inspired La Maddukelleng to surrender. Not convinced that his surrender was genuine, Boné suggested asking him to return everything he has stolen to test his sincerity. Considering this a breach of sovereignty, Wajoq objected, saying that Pénéki was a vassal of Wajoq; and the Tellumpocco agreed.[124] A letter from the arumponé to the Dutch tells a different story, however. It says that Wajoq came to Pénéki's aid with a large force including some of the 40 Lords. Despite this aid, Boné captured La Maddukelleng. Wajoq then sent a messenger to Boné asking for the release of La Maddukelleng and the Bonéans granted this request. From this letter it also appears that the Bonéans were not as clement with the rest of the Pénékians as with La Maddukelleng; they sold part of the population into slavery to repay their debt to the Dutch.[125] Whether La Maddukelleng surrendered or was captured by the Bonéans, he was eventually left in Wajorese custody.

Around 1763, the Tellumpocco met to discuss La Maddukelleng's manifold crimes and his possible punishment. A lontaraq in the Leiden University library, NBG-Boeg 125, describes this meeting day by day. Wrongdoings dating back more than 20 years were discussed. Wajoq said that it agreed with some of La Maddukelleng's doings and Boné pointed out that La Maddukelleng was not entirely responsible because previous rulers had also played a role. Wajoq further conceded that La Maddukelleng did let the Tellumpocco fall and that Wajoq did not remind him of previous agreements as they should have according to existent treaties because they were scared of him; he was threatening decapitation. The Tellumpocco adjourned and then reconvened and read texts about his crimes which were too numerous to count. Eventually Wajoq declared La Maddukelleng to be a destructive force for pillaging on land and sea and for being wholly uncompromising. When Wajoq offered to compensate for his damage, Boné replied that, if La Maddukelleng had only stolen, then Wajoq could pay back half of the value in jewels but La Maddukelleng had also broken the Tellumpocco. In turn, Soppéng argued that traitors should be crushed with stones. Boné then asked whether the pertinent adat of Boné, Soppéng, and Wajoq were all the same. Boné said that according to its adat, once a ruler is appointed, he or she cannot be contradicted. Even if the arumponé says that white is black, then it is black. Soppéng responded that they have the same custom in Soppéng. Wajoq then stated that it is also the same way among the Wajorese. This statement is unexpected because the nature of Bonéan rule during the late seventeenth and early eighteenth century was generally more autocratic that of the Wajorese; thus it may indicate that the Wajorese earnestly sought to restore the Tellumpocco. Thereafter they adjourned for the day. At their concluding meeting, a message arrived from the arung matoa saying that it is better to try to come to agreement another day. Boné countered that if they adjourn, then Wajoq would have to take all of the anger upon itself, but Wajoq did not object. All three parties agreed that, when and if they could agree upon an appropriate punishment for La Maddukelleng, they would send word to him. Here ends the lontaraq describing this series of meetings. From other sources, it would appear that such an agreement was probably never reached. These simply state that La Maddukelleng died without specifying the circumstances.[126]

It was unusual for Wajorese lontaraq to record the death of a former arung matoa without any mention of the manner in which he died, especially the LSW which was an attempt to write an all-inclusive history. The manner in which it portays the controversy surrounding La Maddukelleng suggests either that already at the time of writing there was confusion about the events surrounding La Maddukelleng's demise or that his story was intended to serve a didactic purpose. Pages and pages are devoted to debates about La Maddukelleng's crimes and these provide an occasion to present laws and customs about returning stolen property, deliberation, and other important social concerns.

La Maddukelleng is generally remembered as having restored some of the greatness and power that Wajoq lost during the Makassar War. He is also commemorated for never having surrendered to the Dutch, and for this reason in 1998 he was made a National Hero. Yet La Maddukelleng has not escaped criticism. Indeed, La Maddukelleng is accused of ruining the very foundations upon which Wajoq was established. The statement of the first Arung Matoa Petta La Paléwo To Palippu that Wajoq was brave, rich, clever, strong, and capable has legendary status among the Wajorese. One lontaraq accuses La Maddukelleng of thinking that he alone had these five characteristics, thereby leading him to act to Wajoq's detriment. It goes on to level other charges against him: he stripped Wajoq of its bravery by always declaring war without following the custom of first consulting with the three Baté. He put an end to Wajoq's cleverness because he indepen-dently corresponded with the Dutch, and he weakened Wajoq's capabilities by judging liliq very harshly and attacking those he thought were misbehav-ing, without even consulting Wajoq. By acting independently without con-sultation, he undermined Wajoq's strength. When questioned or criticized by part of Wajoq, he simply replied that if they did not want to participate, then they were not needed.[127] This arrogance was condemned by his critics.

A Diasporic Leader

The interaction between Wajoq, its overseas communities, and its vassals in South Sulawesi during the first half of the eighteenth century shows that Wajoq's various constituents functioned in a similar manner, regardless as to whether they were located in South Sulawesi or not. At times they will-ingly provided assistance to the center, but at other times, they changed their focus according to their perception of their own needs. Within Wajoq itself in South Sulawesi, this is exemplified by various constituents that switched allegiance according to their own interests. On the diasporic level it is exemplified by the overseas Wajorese communities, which participated in Wajorese affairs whenever it served their interests or when their sense of loyalty inspired them to do so. In some instances, perhaps in the case of La Maddukelleng,[128] expatriates were even recalled to help their homeland in times of need. In fact Dutch records attest that it was common practice among the Wajorese for rulers to ask their "overseas subjects" to return when necessary.[129]

La Maddukelleng's return and assumption of the arung matoaship can best be seen as the culmination of overseas participation in the Wajorese government. From around the time of La Maddukelleng's birth, expatriates began playing an increasingly large role in Wajorese society. Successive arung matoa actively encouraged entrepreneurship and overseas commerce in particular as a means of strengthening Wajoq. State-supported entrepreneurs were expected to give back to Wajoq and in this manner Wajoq not only recovered from the traumatic aftermath of the Makassar War, but also attained a paramount position within the hierarchy of states in South Sulawesi.

This paramountcy, however brief, would not have been possible without the cooperation and contributions of Wajorese overseas communities. La Saléwangeng's refortification policies depended upon the purchase of arms overseas, a process which the overseas communities could facilitate. Similarly, La Maddukelleng's campaigns depended upon the involvement of the Wajorese diaspora communities. He returned from eastern Kalimantan with both ships and people. Having arrived in Sulawesi, he then depended upon the cooperation of the Wajorese communities in both Makassar and Sumbawa for weapons and other support. Whereas such cooperation pre-dated La Maddukelleng's return, his attempt to oust the Dutch from Makassar is still a prime example of how the Wajorese diaspora functioned. By the mid-eighteenth century, many Wajorese overseas communities had begun to identify with their host communities, but they remained involved in the activities of their homeland. It is this factor that made the diaspora communities an indispensable part of Wajorese statecraft.

CHAPTER EIGHT

The Wajorese in Comparative Perspective

Among the numerous nineteenth-century observers who noted the tendency of the Wajorese to migrate was the missionary cum philologist B. F. Matthes. He described the people of Wajoq as "born traders [who] wander around everywhere in the archipelago and settle in those places where they can find the most advantage and at least be safe from the rapacity of a host of petty rulers, [a situation] which in their own country all too often leaves much to be desired."[1] While Matthes explains Wajorese emigration in terms of a flight from government, this study takes a contrary view. It argues instead that the Wajorese diaspora resulted from particular features in the nature of Wajorese government and society that encouraged migration. Moreover, Wajorese rulers' passive encouragement of migration and active encouragement of overseas commerce enabled the polity as a whole to benefit by tapping the economic and military power of its emigrants. Shared cultural attributes and family ties further strengthened the cooperative relationship between the people in Wajoq and the overseas Wajorese.

As this book has shown, at the base of traditional Wajorese statecraft were several mechanisms including personal and familial relationships, representative councils, and a shared culture. These could be extended to geographically disparate locations and were in fact transposed to such an extent that physically dispersed Wajorese communities were sometimes able to function in concert. Together they worked towards common military, political, commercial, and social goals. While individuals and separate settlements had their own concerns, they were willing to participate in and contribute to the greater Wajorese community.

Both family relationships and identity were significant to the bonds uniting the Wajorese and to the manner in which they operated as a group. Family ties were used as a means of forging and consolidating politically significant relationships. While marriages between the Wajorese and their hosts were not always untroubled, marrying into the host community was still a widespread strategy. Other sorts of family relationships, such as adoptions and brother-hoods, were politically significant as well, both between the Wajorese and their hosts and between different groups of Wajorese. In addition to family relation-ships, a shared sense of identity was important to the functioning of the dias-pora. Being Wajorese distinguished individuals from other groups and could afford significant advantages, especially in western Sumatra. This identity also made it possible for Wajoq to harness the power of emigrants who would have been unlikely to contribute to the homeland if they did not still consider them-selves Wajorese. As attested in various Malay texts from the western archipel-ago, the Wajorese sense of identity was strong. Significantly, however, it was not rigid. Shedding their Wajorese identity or assuming an alternative identity when circumstances dictated were widespread practices among emigrants.

The strength of the Wajorese community facilitated the establishment of a far-flung commercial network. Their enterprises spread from Aceh to the Bird's Head and to countless points in between. They shared intelligence concerning market conditions and trade routes, and they developed a mutu-ally agreed upon legal system to ensure fair business practices. So success-ful were their commercial operations that the Dutch in Makassar found it difficult to compete. In turn, the strength of their trade enabled the Wajorese to refortify their homeland in the early eighteenth century. A series of arung matoa appealed to the larger Wajorese community for manpower, weapons, and money to refortify the homeland. As a result of their success, Wajoq eclipsed Boné as the paramount power in the peninsula for a brief period during the mid-eighteenth century.

Despite the many ways in which Wajoq and the Wajorese diaspora coop-erated, there was one area in which they were completely distinct from each other: political representation. The council of overseas Wajorese leaders appears to have consisted of representatives of different places at differ-ent times. These locations include Pontianak, Pasir, Makassar, Sumbawa and Kutai, but Wajoq itself is absent from all available lists of participants. Meanwhile, the Arung Patampulu only accorded direct representation to the Wajorese limpo or districts of Talotenréng, Tua, and Béttémpola. Thus there was no overlap between the council of overseas community leaders that agreed upon commercial laws and the political council that governed Wajoq. The two councils could, however, be considered as two distinct lay-ers of political bureaucracy.

Regardless of this distinction, there was a great deal of interaction between Wajoq and the Wajorese diaspora. Indeed, the intensity of this interaction was a defining characteristic of the early modern Wajorese diaspora.
In that the eighteenth-century Wajorese simultaneously participated in two
societies at once, they constitute an early example of a now widespread
phenomenon. Their participation was facilitated by geographic, political
and cultural circumstances.

Geographically, the interaction among Wajorese communities was facilitated by their proximity. While there may have been Wajorese individuals in
Sri Lanka or South Africa, the early modern Wajorese diaspora was largely
confined to insular Southeast Asia. Thus the areas of overseas settlement were
relatively close to the homeland, especially in comparison to other groups
such as the Hadramis who crossed the Indian Ocean or the Africans who
crossed the Atlantic. Consequently emigrating overseas was not necessarily
seen as a once in a lifetime relocation. Instead, it could be seen as a temporary measure undertaken for the purpose of acquiring wealth or prestige.
Many individuals, such as the diarist and soldiers in the service of the VOC,
would have travelled to and from various points in the diaspora repeatedly.

There was also a key political factor that greatly influenced relations between Wajoq and the Wajorese diaspora: the homeland was relative acces-
sibility. Briefly during the late seventeenth century, intolerable conditions
gave reason for an exodus but these abated within a matter of decades.
Moreover the homeland continued to exist. This gave the diaspora and
the homeland the opportunity to cooperate synergistically, an opportunity
which was not afforded to other early modern diaspora such as the Armenians or the Jews.

Culturally, the exceptional permeability of early modern Southeast Asian
societies facilitated biculturalism. Across the archipelago, boundaries to
the assimilation of the Wajorese were low. Cultural and physiological similarities with Malays and other groups in the archipelago allowed the Wajorese to adopt another identity or adapt their own as they saw fit. Nowhere
did the Wajorese experience the sort of insurmountable obstacles to assimilation or persecution that other racially or religiously more distinct diaspora sometimes faced. Consequently, they were not forced to stop being
Wajorese in order to assimilate, and could even change identities repeatedly as acts of will. This made simultaneous participation in two societies
culturally feasible.

The permeable, fluid nature of early modern Southeast Asia enabled other
diaspora to maintain close relations to their homeland as well. One example
is the Minangkabau diaspora. Like the Wajorese, the Minangkabau diaspora

developed relatively close to the homeland in the highlands of western Sumatra. Its members typically had multiple allegiances including their own community leader, the ruler of their host society and the Minangkabau ruler in Pagaruyung.[2] In both the Wajorese and the Minangkabau cases, the proximity of the homeland, the nature of traditional politics and the ability to adopt more than one identity allowed the diaspora to function as an extension of the homeland.

The Wajorese case exhibits features common to other diaspora as well. One such commonality is the presence of multiple layers of diaspora. In his voluminous book *Diasporas within a Diaspora: Jews, Crypto-Jews and the World Maritime Empires (1540–1740)*,[3] Jonathan Israel has thoroughly documented the co-existence of numerous smaller groups within the Jewish diaspora. There were also subgroupings within the Wajorese diaspora based on the sub-polity of origin. For example, Wajorese people from Talotenréng residing in Makassar tended to reside with other people from Talotenréng. Furthermore, the Wajorese diaspora itself was part of a larger Bugis diaspora consisting of both Wajorese and other sorts of Bugis, like the Bonéans.

A second similarity between the Wajorese and other diaspora lies in the extensive but not exclusive use of kin as partners in commercial endeavors. Use of kin networks was a prevalent strategy, as is indicated by the need to codify laws to govern it and as is exemplified by the increase in trade between Wajoq and western Sumatra that occurred after two influential brothers resided at each end of the route. Yet family networks alone were insufficient for the establishment and maintenance of successful commercial networks because merchants who confined themselves to their own groups missed valuable trading opportunities. The notion of a self-contained trading diaspora is thus untenable. Recent studies, therefore, have moved beyond notions of insular and cohesive communities and emphasized the cosmopolitan nature of early modern trade and the global outlook of the merchants themselves. For example, Francesca Trivellato's research on Sephardic networks reveals that commercial alliances were formed according to business interests regardless as to whether the most effective or best-connected traders were co-religionists or strangers.[4] Wajorese merchants exhibited a similar cosmopolitan attitude and willingness to trade with others.

A final yet particularly important similarity between the Wajorese case and other diaspora is the unbounded nature of its spheres of social activity. Commercial pursuits, social considerations and local circumstances were more important to diaspora communities like the Wajorese than political boundaries. Like all enduring diaspora, when circumstances changed, the Wajorese adapted accordingly.

Using a variety of intertwined mechanisms to link geographically dispersed communities, the Wajorese optimized their dispersion. Indeed, Wajorese commerce was actually more remarkable after their establishment of overseas settlements than beforehand. The manner in which Wajoq deliberately encouraged this commerce and then harnessed its power for political and military purposes exemplifies how Wajoq and the overseas Wajorese sometimes acted in concert. Although Wajoq lacked the ability to coerce the overseas communities, the support that they provided voluntarily was enough to alter the course of Wajorese history.

Glossary

adat: Customs and traditional practices

arumponé: Paramount ruler in Boné

arung: Lord, ruler

arung matoa: Paramount ruler in Wajoq

Arung Patampulu: (Wajorese council of) Forty Lords

aruq: Bugis war dance

bagilaba pada: Equal sharing of profits

bagilaba samatula: Sharing of profits with an agreement

baruga: Meeting house

bendahara: Principal official in a Malay polity, second to the sultan

bicara: Public discussion

bissu: Traditional Bugis priests

burghers: Former VOC servants entitled to trade in Asia

darat: Minangkabau heartland

datuk: Non-royal leader in the Malay world

datu: Paramount ruler in Soppéng

daulat: Sovereignty

EIC: (English) East India Company **hikayat:** Historical chronicle

inreng pettu: Loan without interest or loss

inreng réweq: Loan of goods

inreng ripasa: Small loans without a formal contract

kabupaten: Regency (division of modern Indonesian provinces)

kalula: Apprentices to the captain who traded on behalf of the *matoa*

kampong: Village

kapala maneng: Community leaders

kenduri: Ritual meal

kerajaan: Kingdom

kris: Dagger or short sword

laloang: Commissioned goods

limpo: People or village (lit. surround)

liliq: Vassals

lontaraq: Manuscripts

matoa: Head, ruler

orang asli: Non-Malay peoples residing on the Malay peninsula

orang laut: Peoples residing along the rivers and coasts

payung riLuwuq: Paramount ruler in Luwuq

pengeran: Prince, governor, chief

Petta Wajoq: Wajoq's highest ruling council

pessé: Solidarity or commiseration

rantau: Areas outside the Minangkabau heartland

real: Spanish silver coin

rijksdaalder: Dutch silver coin

salasilah: Genealogy

sawi: Traders who worked as sailors without receiving a salary

siriq: Single concept encompassing shame and self-worth

taroanang: Deliberation among prominent community members

tau abeyo: Wajorese official in Kutai

tau atau: Wajorese official in Kutai

tau matoa: Term for Bugis community leaders

tomanurung: Descendant from the Upperworld

tomaéga: The populace

totompo: Ascendant from the Lowerworld

VOC: Vereenigde Oost-Indische Compagnie (United Dutch East India Company)yang dipertuan: Title of Malay rulers literally meaning 'The One who is Lord'

Notes

1: Amongst Diasporas and States

1. Vijay Mishra, "The Diasporic Imaginary: Theorizing the Indian Diaspora," *Textual Practice* 10, 3 (1996): 426.

2. Joseph Conrad, *The Rescue* (London: Dent, 1920).

3. Nur Asiah, *Ensiklopedia Pahlawan Nasional Indonesia* (Jakarta: Mediantara, 2009), 65.

4. These texts were rewritten after the wars of the 1730s. Therefore, the resounding declarations attributed to fifteenth-century Wajorese rulers may be a better reflection of eighteenth-century concerns more than fifteenth-century values. See Anthony Reid, "Merdeka: The Concept of Freedom in Indonesia," in *Asian Freedoms: The Idea of Freedom in East and Southeast Asia*, David Kelly and Anthony Reid, eds. (Cambridge: Cambridge University Press, 1998), 148.

5. Zainal Abidin, *Persepsi Orang Bugis Makasar tentang Hukum, Negara dan Dunia Luar* (Bandung: Penerbit Alumni, 1983), 243–44.

6. Stephen Druce's research suggests that the five constituent polities of Ajattappareng might have concluded an agreement stating that people of Ajattappareng "could enter and leave whichever part they wished, but must remain loyal to their own ruler." See Stephen C. Druce, *The Lands West of the Lakes: A History of the Ajattappareng Kingdoms of South Sulawesi 1200 to 1600 CE* (Leiden: KITLV Press, 2009), 167.

7. Benedict Anderson, *Imagined Communities: Reflections on the Origins and Spread of Nationalism* (London: Verso, 1991).

8. David A. Bell, *The Cult of the Nation in France: Inventing Nationalism, 1680–1800* (Cambridge: Harvard University Press, 2001), 3, 200–01.

9. China, where the relationship between sovereignty and territory has long been recognized, is the most notable exception.

10. On print capitalism see Anderson, *Imagined Communities*, and on industrialization see Ernest Gellner, *Nations and Nationalism* (Ithaca: Cornell University Press, 1983).

11. Victor Lieberman, "Transcending East-West Dichotomies: State and Culture Formation in Six Ostensibly Disparate Areas," in *Beyond Binary Histories: Re-imagining Eurasia to c. 1830*, ed. Victor Lieberman (Ann Arbor: University of Michigan Press, 2001), 24.

12. Ibid., 52.

13. James B. Collins, "State Building in Early-Modern Europe: The Case of France," in *Beyond Binary Histories*, ed. Lieberman, 160.

14. Thongchai Winichakul, *Siam Mapped: A History of the Geo-Body of a Nation* (Honolulu: University of Hawai'i Press, 1994), 77–79.

15. Clifford Geertz, *Negara: The Theater State in Nineteenth-Century Bali* (Princeton: Princeton University Press, 1980), 25.

16. O. W. Wolters, *History, Culture, and Region in Southeast Asian Perspectives* (Singapore: Institute of Southeast Asian Studies, 1982); Benedict Anderson, "The Idea of

Power in Javanese Culture," in *Culture and Politics in Indonesia*, ed. Claire Holt (Ithaca: Cornell University Press, 1972); S. J. Tambiah, *Culture, Thought, and Social Action An Anthropological Perspective* (Cambridge: Harvard University Press, 1985); S. J. Tambiah, *World Conqueror and World Renouncer: A Study of Buddhism and Polity in Thailand against a Historical Background* (Cambridge: Cambridge University Press, 1976.)

17. Wolters, *History, Culture, and Region*, 17.

18. O. W. Wolters, *The Fall of Srivijaya in Malay History* (Ithaca: Cornell University Press, 1971), 8–13.

19. Soemarsaid Moertono, *State and Statecraft in Old Java: A Study of the Later Mataram Period, 16ᵗʰ to 19ᵗʰ Centuries* (Ithaca: Modern Indonesia Project, 1963), 71.

20. Anderson, "The Idea of Power in Javanese Culture," 31.

21. Ibid., 7–8.

22. Tambiah, *Culture, Thought, and Social Action*, 252; Tambiah, *World Conqueror and World Renouncer*, 115.

23. Tambiah, *World Conqueror and World Renouncer*, 123.

24. Ibid.

25. Ibid., 117–18; Tambiah, *Culture, Thought and Social Action*, 272.

26. Tambiah, *World Conqueror and World Renouncer*, 114.

27. Aidan W. Southall, *Alur Society: A Study in Processes and Types of Domination* (Cambridge: W. Heffer & Sons Limited, 1956), 250–52.

28. Burton Stein, "The Segmentary State: Interim Reflections," in *De La Royauté à l'Etat: Anthropologie et Histoire du Politique dans le Monde Indien*, J. Pouchepadass and H. Stern, eds. (Paris: Ecole des Hautes Etudes en Sciences Sociales, 1991), 217.

29. Thomas M. Kiefer, *The Tausug: Violence and Law in a Philippine Moslem Society* (Prospect Heights, IL: Waveland Press, Inc., 1986), 109–11; James Francis Warren, *The Sulu Zone, 1768–1898: The Dynamics of External Trade, Slavery, and Ethnicity in the Transformation of a Southeast Asian Maritime State* (Singapore: Singapore University Press, 1981), xxii–xxvi.

30. While there are numerous Indian influences in the languages, belief systems, and technologies of South Sulawesi, the region did not undergo the profound social transformation of Indianization that, according to Coedes, is "characterized by Hinduist or Buddhist cults, the mythology of the Puranas, and the observance of the Dharmasastras" as expressed in the Sanskrit language. See G. Coedes, *The Indianized States of Southeast Asia* (Honolulu: University of Hawai'i Press, 1968), 15–16.

31. See Ian Caldwell, "The Myth of the Exemplary Centre: Shelly Errington's Meaning and Power in a Southeast Asian Realm," *JSEAS* 22, 1 (1991):109–18.

32. Thongchai Winichakul, *Siam Mapped*, 75–76.

33. Leonard Y. Andaya, *The World of Maluku: Eastern Indonesia in the Early Modern Period* (Honolulu: University of Hawai'i Press, 1993), 83–98.

34. Shankar Aswani and Michael W. Graves, "The Tongan Maritime Expansion: A Case in the Evolutionary Ecology of Social Complexity," *Asian Perspectives* 32, 2 (1998): 141, 153.

35. This increase has been documented in numerous ways. For example, Stéphane Dufoix counted the number of times per decade that the word "diaspora" has appeared in the titles of French doctoral dissertations. See his article "Généalogies d'un lieu commun: "diaspora" et sciences sociales," (*Actes de l'histoire de l'immigration*, vol. 2, http://barthes.ens.fr/clio/revues/AHI/articles/preprints/duf.html).

36. For a comprehensive history of the word "diaspora." see Stéphane Dufoix, *La Disporaion. Une Histurie des Usages du Mot* Diaspora (Paris: Editions Amsterdam, 2011).

37. Stéphane Dufoix, *Diasporas* (Berkeley and Los Angeles: University of California Press, 2008), 11, 16–17.

38. Gregory Bienstock, *The Struggle for the Pacific* (New York: Macmillan, 1937), 51.

39. Abner Cohen, "Cultural Strategies in the Organization of Trading Diaspora," in *The Development of Indigenous Trade and Markets in West Africa*, ed. Claude Meillassoux (Oxford: Oxford University Press, 1971).

40. Philip Curtin, *Cross-cultural Trade in World History* (Cambridge: Cambridge University Press, 1984), 230.

41. Ibid., 2.

42. "The traders were specialists in a single kind of economic enterprise, whereas the host society was a *whole* society, with many occupations, class stratification, and political divisions between rulers and ruled." Curtin, *Cross-cultural Trade in World History*, 5. Emphasis in the original.

43. Oxford: Clarendon Press, 1989.

44. Sanjay Subrahmayam, "Iranians Abroad: Intra-Asian Elite Migration and Early Modern State Formation," *Journal of Asian Studies* 51, 2 (1992): 340–63.

45. Ina Baghdiantz-McCabe, *The Shah's Silk for Europe's Silver: The Eurasian Silk Trade of the Julfan Armenians in Safavid Iran and India* (Atlanta: Scholar's Press, 1999).

46. Barbara Watson Andaya and Leonard Y. Andaya, *A History of Malaysia* (London: Macmillan Press Ltd., 1982), 80. Other works that deal directly with the role of overseas Bugis without referring to a "Bugis diaspora" include Khoo Kay Kim, "Raja Lulu/Sultan Salehuddin: The Founding of the Selangor Dynasty," *JMBRAS* 58 (1985): 1–13.

47. Robin Cohen, "Diaspora: Changing Meanings and Limits of the Concept," in W. Berthomière and C. Chivallon, eds., *Les diasporas dans le monde contemporain* (Paris: Karthala and Maison des Sciences de l'Homme, 2006), 47.

48. Stathis Gourgouris, "Concept of 'Diaspora' in Contemporary World," in *Diaspora Entrepreneurial Networks: Four Centuries of History*, Ina Baghdiantz McCabe, Gelina Harlaftis and Ioanna Pepelasis Minoglou, eds. (New York: Berg, 2005), 389.

49. Ibid., 386.

50. Epeli Hau'ofa, "Our Sea of Islands," *The Contemporary Pacific* 6, 1 (1994): 147–61. While Hau'ofa has been criticized for romanticizing cultural and economic realities, this critically acclaimed essay has been hailed as "the most visionary piece ever to emerge in Pacific Studies." See Teresia Teaiwa, "L(o)osing the Edge," *The Contemporary Pacific* 13, 2 (2001): 346; and David A. Chappell, "Transnationalism in Central Oceanian Politics: A Dialectic of Diasporas and Nationhood?" *Journal of the Polynesian Society* 108 (1999): 280.

51. Subramani, "The Diasporic Imagination," in *Navigating Islands and Continents: Conversations and Contestations in and around the Pacific*, Cynthia Franklin et al., eds. (Honolulu: College of Languages, Linguistics and Literature, University of Hawai'i and the East West Center, 2000), 177.

52. Hau'ofa, "Our Sea of Islands," 160.

53. Ilana Gershon, "Viewing Diasporas from the Pacific: What Pacific Ethnographies Offer Pacific Diaspora Studies," *The Contemporary Pacific* 19, 2 (2007): 474.

54. Subramani, "The Diasporic Imagination," 174.

55. Joel Bonnemaison, "The Tree and the Canoe: Roots and Mobility in Vanuatu Societies," *Pacific Viewpoint* 26, 1 (1985): 30.

56. Bruce Robbins, "Actually Existing Cosmopolitanism," in *Cosmopolitics: Thinking and Feeling Beyond the Nation*, Pheng Cheah and Bruce Robbins, eds. (Minneapolis: University of Minnesota Press, 1998), 2–3.

57. David Hollinger, *Postethnic American: Beyond Multiculturalism* (New York: Basic Books, 1995), 106, 116.

58. David Hollinger, "Nationalism, cosmopolitanism, and the United States," in *Immigration and Citizenship in the Twenty-first Century*, ed. Noah M. J. Pickus, (Lanham, MD: Rowman and Littlefield, 1998), 87.

59. The Bugis script is derived from an Indian prototype, the Pallava script of southern India that spread to Southeast Asia in the fourth or fifth century. The script was modified and used to write indigenous languages; in Java this resulted in the development of the Kawi script which is named for its association with texts in Old Javanese or Kawi. The so-called "ka-ga-nga" syllabaries, of which the Bugis syllabary is one, seem to have originated with the Kawi script. In South Sulawesi, two different "ka-ga-nga" syllabaries developed from a common source which was related to Kawi but which now is extinct. One of its derivatives, the Makasarese script, also known as Old Makasarese, is now obsolete. The second syllabary, the Bugis script, also called Bugis/Makasarese, is now used to write Makasarese and Mandarese as well as Bugis. The precise origins of the forerunner script are impossible to trace. It is likely to have originated from trading contacts with the north coast of Java, or from Javanese trading contacts in the Lesser Sunda Islands. See Ann Kumar and John H. McGlynn, eds., *Illuminations: The Writing Traditions of Indonesia* (New York and Tokyo: Weatherhill, Inc., 1996) especially Thomas M. Hunter, Jr., "Ancient Beginnings: The Spread of Indic Scripts," 3–7; Ann Kumar, "Introduction," xvi; Roger Tol, "A Separate Empire: Writings of South Sulawesi," 213–14; as well as Ian Caldwell, "South Sulawesi A.D. 1300–1600: Ten Bugis Texts" (PhD diss., Australian National University, 1988), 183–84.

60. It is impossible to determine with absolute certainty when writing was introduced to South Sulawesi, but qualitative and quantitative shifts in historical data suggest that writing arrived on the scene around 1400. Written historical records for South Sulawesi apparently date back to about 1300 but those for the fourteenth century are much sketchier than those for the fifteenth and sixteenth centuries. Records for the fourteenth century do not allow for the cross-referencing of individuals, nor do they contain the same type of biographical and anecdotal information that is found in records for the fifteenth and sixteenth centuries. Based on this marked increase in the details of historical records, and on counting generations and reigns and assigning these with an average lifespan, Ian Caldwell and Campbell Macknight approximate that writing arrived in South Sulawesi around 1400. See Caldwell, "South Sulawesi A.D. 1300–1600," 169–171; and C. C. Macknight, "The Emergence of Civilisation in South Celebes and Elsewhere," in *Pre-Colonial State Systems in Southeast Asia*, A. Reid and L. Castles, eds. (Kuala Lumpur: Malaysian Branch of the Royal Asiatic Society, 1975), 132.

61. There are two main collections of Bugis texts. The Nederlandsch Bijbelgenootschap's (Dutch Bible Society) collection consists in large part of manuscripts that were collected by B. F. Matthes or copied by hand under his commission. It is housed at the Leiden University Library and is described in B. F. Matthes' *Kort Verslag aangaande alle mij in Europa bekende Makassaarsche en Boeginesche Handschriften* (Amsterdam: C. A.

Spin & Zoon, 1875). Numerous excerpts are also published in his *Boegineesche Chres tomaihle, Oorspronkelijke Boeginesche geschriften in proza en poëzij*, Vol. 1–3 (Makassar: Het Nederlandsch Gouvernement, 1864–1873). The other main collection consists of microfilmed copies of more than three thousand privately owned manuscripts. It was assembled by a team from Hasanuddin University in Makassar with funding from the Ford Foundation and is now available on microfilm at a number of research libraries around the world, including the Center for Research Libraries in Chicago, the Leiden University Library, and the Makassar branch of the Indonesian National Archives. Smaller collections of Bugis documents are held in London, Washington and Berlin, and the Australian National University library has a substantial holding of microfilmed materials from various sources.

62. Bugis historical sources consist of rich and varied manuscripts written in indigenous scripts on European paper. The vast body of diverse Bugis and Makasarese historical records falls into several main categories including diaries, treaties, and *adat* (customary law) registers. Numerous scholars have highlighted the preoccupation with objectivity and almost scientific precision of the Bugis and Makasarese historical texts. Hindu influence is minimal and the mythological elements are contained in the beginning in an origin myth, presumably because the mythical elements are designed merely to justify the nobility's status, rather than to explain creation. Generally speaking, if anything sounds incredible, the writer denies responsibility for its veracity. Thus documents are punctuated with phrases like "According to legend . . ." When no sources are available on a particular subject, the writer will state just that. That being said, historical lontaraq are almost always written in a period later than the one they describe. While often accurate, they are historical perceptions, rather than contemporary records, and should be used with the same caution as any historical source. See A. A. Cense, "Eenige aantekeningen over Makassaars-Boeginese geschiedschrijving," *BKI*, 107 (1951): 42–60; Christian Pelras, "Les Fouilles et l'Histoire à Célèbes Sud," *Archipel*, 3 (1972): 205; C. C. Macknight, "The Rise of Agriculture in South Sulawesi before 1600," *RIMA*, 17 (1983): 98; J. Noorduyn, "Origins of South Celebes Historical Writing," in Soedjatmoko *et al*, *An Introduction to Indonesian Historiography* (Ithaca: Cornell University Press, 1965), 140.

63. A particularly noteworthy category of Bugis and Makasarese historical records are the *attoriolong* (Bugis) or *patturioloang* (Makassarese), which are generally longer works comparable to chronicles. Existing for a limited number of states, a number of characteristics are common among them. First, such chronicles are based on a variety of sources, such as diaries, legends and genealogies. They are organized around lists of rulers to which are appended important events such as wars or the conclusion or renewal of treaties. Second, chronicles generally employ a relative notion of time. For example, event B is said to occur however many months or years after event A. Third, chronicles also have particular stylistic conventions. They often use dialogues to relate how a decision was made or what public opinion was. A ruler, for example, may converse with his or her subjects. Fourth, Bugis chronicles sometimes also personify political entities, saying what a state says and what a state does; a fact which lends credence to the idea that the state existed as a concrete entity, distinct from the ruler.

64. J. Noorduyn, *Een Achttiende-Eeuwse Kroniek van Wadjo': Buginese Historiografie* ('s-Gravenage: H. L. Smits, 1955).

65. Bugis texts are commonly known as lontaraq, which originally appears to have referred to the leaves of the lontar tree (*Borassus flabellifera*) upon which early manu-

scripts were written, but eventually came to mean any written work. Lontaraq exist in a wide variety of forms, including genealogies, legal texts and medical treatises. The manner in which texts were written on such leaves is exceptional. The leaves were cut into strips and sewn together to make a long band which was inscribed and then wound onto a holder with two reels. The text was read by turning the reels to make the band advance, not unlike a cassette tape. See Zainal Abidin, "Notes on the Lontara' as Historical Sources," *Indonesia* 12 (1971): 162–63.

66. At least two copies of the LSW exist. One is owned by the Wajorese noble Datu Sangaji. Even though he reportedly will not allow his own family to see it, he permitted the Manuscript Project (*Proyek Naskah*) team from Hasanuddin University to microfilm it. See *Lontaraq Sukkuna Wajoq*, Proyek Naskah Unhas No. 01/MKH/1/Unhas UP Rol 73, No. 1–21. Another copy was owned by Zainal Abidin who translated and published parts of it as Zainal Abidin, *Wajo' Abad XV-XVI: Suatu Penggalian Sejarah Terpendam Sulawesi Selatan dari Lontara'* (Bandung: Penerbit Alumni, 1985).

67. The LSW includes a great many details that are not found in any other Wajorese lontaraq, including dates, songs, legends, events taking place in other parts of Sulawesi, and the articles of contracts made with the VOC. While some of these details appear nowhere else, many others are verifiable using Dutch sources. For example, the exact date of the famous Bonéan ruler Arung Palakka's death is given. Certain episodes also appear to have been inserted to make a point rather than to relate factual information. For example, in the LSW there is an account of a Wajorese victory in the early stage of the siege of 1670. It describes a conflict that occurred in the enemy's camp. Since it seems unlikely that the Wajorese would have clearly heard the words of songs and conversations behind enemy lines, this episode may have been inserted as an interpretive element later on, perhaps to illustrate the incredible odds which the Wajorese were facing. Another example consists of a conversation between Puanna La Gelleng and Petta Wajoq about the war, which might very well reflect the attitudes of the writer, not the people whose conversation he describes. Alternatively, these episodes may stem from oral traditions or another now lost source.

Much of the information contained in the LSW can never be verified. For example, while James Brooke did comment on Wajorese rifle practice in 1840, there was no Dutch expedition to Wajoq that coincidentally recorded the presence or absence of shooting ranges during the reign of Arung Matoa La Saléwangeng To Tenrirua Arung Kampiri (1715–1736.) Yet Dutch records and evidence from other parts of the archipelago suggest that there was indeed a conscious effort to refortify Wajoq and to seek riches overseas as described in the LSW. Furthermore, the text is reliable in a number of other cases, such as the conditions of the treaty made in between Wajoq and the Dutch in 1670. (See Rodney Mundy, ed., *Narrative of Events in Borneo and Celebes*, I: 101.)

68. A length of fifty pages is already considered long. See Noorduyn, "Origins of South Celebes Historical Writing," 140.

69. Zainal Abidin, *Wajo Abad XV-XVI*, 18. The version owned by Datu Sangaji, which contains more words per page, is 497 pages long.

70. Zainal Abidin, *Wajo Abad XV-XVI*, 32.

71. These reasons are two-fold. First of all, its inclusion of so many historical events that are not found in other lontaraq suggests a desire to elevate Wajorese historiography to a new level. While such a desire could have stemmed from Portuguese sources that influenced South Sulawesi's historiography from the sixteenth century, it could also have stemmed from a familiarity with Dutch historiography achieved much later. Given the

LSW's inclusiveness, the latter is more likely. Secondly, it is rumored in Sulawesi that there is a copy of the LSW in the Leiden University library, but no such copy exists. The claim, however, represents a desire to accord antiquity and authority to the manuscript which may have also been produced much later than other Wajorese chronicles.

72. Christian Pelras, "Les premières données occidentales concernant Célèbes-Sud," *BKI*, 133 (1977): 227–60.

73. All of the company's outposts filed regular reports on local circumstances. With the exception of documents from Gamron, the Cape of Good Hope, and after 1665 Ceylon, these reports were first sent to Batavia. Scriveners worked from six in the morning until six at night (and often later by candlelight) copying the voluminous records. See F. de Haan, *Oud Batavia* (Batavia: G. Kolff, 1922), 1: 207. A substantial part of the VOC archives were repatriated by the Dutch and are now housed in the National Archives of the Netherlands in The Hague. Other documents, such as the court transcripts used in chapter 4, remain in the countries where they were produced. While the Dutch did not consider them sufficiently important to send to the Netherlands for preservation, they are exceptionally important to local historical studies. For the purposes of this study, the archives of the English East India Company are also worthy of mention. The EIC had an outpost on the western coast of Sumatra from 1685 until 1824 where it employed numerous generations of a Wajorese family.

74. Sanjay Subrahmanyam has argued "that the idea of the 'diaspora' has severe limitations in the context of early modern Asia since it is mortgaged to a view in which commerce and state functioning are distinct spheres." (Subrahmayam, "Iranians Abroad," 341, 358). While his assertion that "trade and politics often went together in this period" is undeniably correct, his rejection of the concept's applicability implies acceptance of Curtin's model of trading diasporas, and this is not a given. Francesca Trivellato, for example, has criticized Curtin's tendency to assume group cohesion. See Francesca Trivellato, *The Familiarity of Strangers: The Sephardic Diaspora, Livorno, and Cross-Cultural Trade in the Early Modern Period* (New Haven: Yale University Press, 2009), 11–12.

2: Wajorese History and Migration

1. David Bulbeck and Ian Caldwell, *Land of Iron: The Historical Archaeology of Luwu and the Cenrana Valley* (Hull and Canberra: Center for South-East Asian Studies and School of Archaeology and Anthropology, 2000), 5.

2. The technical abilities that enabled the Bugis to participate in these trading networks is beyond the scope of this study. See instead C. C. F. M. Le Roux, "Boegineesche Zeekaarten van den Indischen Archipel," *Tijdschrift van het Aardrijkskundige Genootschap* 52 (1935): 687–714 and Gene Ammarell, *Bugis Navigation* (New Haven: Yale Southeast Asian Studies, 1999).

3. Smout to Loten, 1.6.1744, NA, VOC 2628: 242.

4. Jacqueline Lineton, "'Pasompe' Ugi': Bugis Migrants and Wanderers," *Archipel* 10 (1975): 177.

5. Christian Pelras, *The Bugis* (Cambridge: Blackwell, 1996), 9.

6. Anthony J. Whitten, Muslimin Mustafa and Gregory S. Henderson, *The Ecology of Sulawesi*, (Yogyakarta: Gadja Mada University Press, 1987), 85; Pelras, *The Bugis*, 7.

7. At odds with both linguistics studies and local perceptions, this rudimentary classification has a powerful hold on the identities of individuals. Stephen Druce relates how a Pattinjo speaker from an ethnically very diverse region of South Sulawesi distinguished himself from the Bugis because of the difference in language, but then concluded that "as there are just four ethnic groups in South Sulawesi I suppose that we must be part of the Bugis ethnic group." See Druce, *The Lands West of the Lakes*, 136.

8. Bulbeck and Caldwell, *Land of Iron*, 14, 103–07.

9. Abdurrazak Daeng Patunru, *Sedjarah Wadjo* (Makassar: Jajasan Kebudajaan Sulawesi Selatan dan Tenggara, 1965), 40.

10. On the importance of leadership abilities and status to social order, and in particular their relevance to political history, see Susan Bolyard Millar, *Bugis Weddings: Rituals of Social Location in Modern Indonesia* (Berkeley: Center for South and Southeast Asia Studies, 1989), especially chapter three.

11. Issues of status have long attracted the attention of scholars of South Sulawesi. H. Th. Chabot's pioneering work *Verwantschap, stand en sexe in Zuid-Celebes* (Groningen and Jakarta: J.B. Wolters, 1950) has been translated into English and published as *Kinship, Status and Gender in South Celebes* (Leiden: KITLV Press, 1996). More recent works include Millar, *Bugis Weddings* and Lucie van Mens, *De Statusscheppers Sociale Mobiliteit in Wajo, 1905–1950*, (Amsterdam: Centre for Asian Studies, 1989).

12. This distinction became less pronounced following the establishment of the *Arung Pitu*, or "Seven Lords," during the reign of the tenth arumponé, I Tenrituppu Matinro riSidénréng (r. 1602–1611.). (See C. C. Macknight and Mukhlis, *The Chronicle of Boné*, forthcoming).

13. Campbell Macknight, pers. comm., January 1, 2013.

14. A notable exception is the paramount ruler of Wajoq known as the *arung matoa* or "senior ruler."

15. David Bulbeck has demonstrated that, in terms of multi-linear cultural evolution, the kingdoms or polities of South Sulawesi are actually complex chiefdoms. The only exception is Gowa-Talloq which was a state from the late sixteenth century until 1669. See Francis David Bulbeck, "A Tale of Two Kingdoms: The Historical Archaeology of Gowa and Tallok, South Sulawesi, Indonesia" (PhD diss., Australian National University, 1988), 469–72, and his review of *A Chain of Kings: The Makassarese Chronicles of Gowa and Talloq* by William P. Cummings, ed. and trans., *Review of Indonesian and Malaysian Affairs* 42 (1): 207–20.

16. *Limpo* literally means "surround" and it is also used to mean "people" or "village." As no plurals exist in the Indonesian or Bugis languages, I have not attempted to pluralize Indonesian or Bugis words.

17. Ian Caldwell, "Power, State and Society Among the Pre-Islamic Bugis," *BKI* 151, 3, (1995): 395; Ian Caldwell, pers. comm., November 11, 2002.

18. Boné is generally considered more autocratic than Wajoq. This was especially the case during the reigns of Arung Palakka and Sultan As-saleh. (See Leonard Andaya, "The Nature of Kingship in Bone," in Anthony Reid and Lance Castles, *Pre-colonial States Systems in Southeast Asia*, 124–125; Pelras, *The Bugis*, 180; and Rahilah Omar, "The History of Boné A.D. 1775–1795: The diary of Sultan Ahmad as-Salleh Syamsuddin" (PhD diss., University of Hull, 2003).)

19. Anthony Reid, "A Great Seventeenth Century Indonesia Family: Matoaya and Pattingalloang of Makassar," *Masyarakat Indonesia* 8, 1 (1981): 3.

20. Abdurrazak, *Sedjarah Wadjo*, 56–57

21. This is a sharp contrast to concepts of statecraft in the Malay world where the ruler and his lineage justified the existence of the state and the hierarchy of nobles. Matheson points out that there is "no evidence for the existence of the state as a concept, as abstract ideal above and beyond the ruler, which was to be sustained and protected . . ." in the Malay *Tuhfat al-Nafis*. See Virginia Matheson, "Concepts of the State in the *Tuhfat al-Nafis* [The Precious Gift]" in Reid and Castles, *Pre-colonial States Systems*, 21. The differences between statecraft in the Malay world and the Bugis can be accounted for in part by the overlay of Indic ideas that is far more prevalent in the western archipelago than in Sulawesi.

22. Christian Pelras, "Hiérarchie et Pouvoir Traditionnels en Pays Wadjo'," *Archipel* 1 and 2 (1971): 170.

23. Wajorese historical sources record that these banners were made at the suggestion of Luwuq when Wajoq and Luwuq concluded an alliance (Abdurrazak, *Sedjarah Wadjo*, 42; Noorduyn, *Een Achttiende-Eeuwse Kroniek van Wadjo'*, 168–69).

24. Noorduyn, *Een Achttiende-Eeuwse Kroniek van Wadjo'*, 164–65, and B. F. Matthes, *Over de Wadjorezen met hun Handels- en Scheepswetboek* (Makassar: P. van Hartrop, 1869), 5. This practice is defended in certain *lontaraq*, specifically in stories about To Taba's contract with the Wajorese. See Noorduyn, *Een Achttiende-Eeuwse Kroniek van Wadjo'*, 62.

25. Pelras, *The Bugis*, 178.

26. Ibid. and Pelras, "Hiérarchie et Pouvoir," 171–72. The Council of Forty Lords only convened on certain occasions, such as when the need arose to select and pay homage to the arung matoa. Although it was difficult to reach consensus in such a large council, its decisions were final, with no appeal from them except in the conclusion of peace or declaration of war. See Matthes, *Over de Wadjorezen met hun Handels- en Scheepswetboek*, 6; and Speelman to High Government, 1670, NA, VOC 1276: 874, 882.

27. Pelras, "Hiérarchie et Pouvoir," 218–23.

28. Mundy (ed.), *Narrative of Events in Borneo and Celebes*, I: 73.

29. As Leonard Andaya points out, "Even a "slave" state in South Sulawesi treaty traditions retains its identity and its self-esteem." See L. Andaya, "Treaty Conceptions and Misconceptions: A Case Study from South Sulawesi." *BKI* 134 (1978): 282–83.

30. Ian Caldwell, pers. comm., March 22, 2013.

31. Abdurrazak, *Sedjarah Wadjo*, 31–34.

32. Noorduyn, *Een Achttiende-Eeuwse Kroniek van Wadjo'*, 250–53.

33. Pelras, "Hiérarchie et Pouvoir," 181–83.

34. Speelman to High Government, 1670, NA, VOC 1276: 873.

35. While historical evidence is lacking, modern anthropologists have noted that these minute gradations themselves were a source of flexibility in Wajorese society. So complex was the system that its implementation proved difficult. Acciaioli notes "Whereas in Mandar and Goa only subdivisions of the nobility are created by these means, in Wajo' distinct status levels that are intermediate between pure nobility and commoners are generated. By such means the entire system is open to more variant interpretations, as the exact boundaries where nobility has become so diluted as no longer to warrant the title are rendered more obscure. As divisions multiply in systems like that of Wajo', the boundaries between gradations are blurred. The possibility of status mobility is thereby entrenched more firmly in the entire system." See Greg Acciaioli, "Distinguishing Hierarchy and Precedence: Comparing

Status Distinctions in South Asia and the Austronesian World, with special reference to South Sulawesi," in *Precedence: Social Differentiation in the Austronesian World*, ed. Michael P. Vischer, (Canberra: ANU ePress, 2009,) 70.

36. Matthes notes that among the Wajorese "a fortune earned through diligent industry is worth more in their eyes than prestige and birth. For example, in Boné and other Bugis lands, marrying with a man of lower descent would cause a princess great shame; but in Wajoq, a man, even though not of royal birth, can marry a queen without compunction." See Matthes, *Over de Wadjorezen met hun Handels- en Scheepswetboek*, 30.

37. *Lontaraq Sukkuna Wajoq*, Proyek Naskah Unhas No. 01/MKH/1/Unhas UP Rol 73, No. 1–21: 228.

38. "Mythomoteur" is a concept developed by Ramon d'Abadal i de Vinyals and popularized by Anthony Smith who defines it as the "constitutive myth of the ethnic polity." See Anthony D. Smith, *The Ethnic Origins of Nations* (Oxford and New York: Basil Blackwell, 1986), 15, 58.

39. Peter Bellwood, "Hierarchy, Founder Ideology and Austronesian Expansion," in *Origins, Ancestry and Alliance: Explorations in Austronesian Ethnography*, James J. Fox and Clifford Sather, eds. (Canberra: Department of Anthropology, ANU, 1996), 24.

40. Gilbert Hamonic, *Le Langage des Dieux: Cultes et Pouvoirs Pré-Islamiques en Pays Bugis, Célèbes-Sud, Indonésie*, (Paris: Centre National de la Recherche Scientifique, 1987), 157–59.

41. Pelras, "Hiérarchie et Pouvoir," 183.

42. Van Mens, *De Statusscheppers*, 27.

43. See B. F. Matthes, "Over de Bissoe's of heidensche priesters en priesteressen der Boeginezen" in H. van der Brink ed., *Dr. Benjamin Frederik Matthes: zijn leven en arbeid in dienst van het Nederlandsch Bijbelgenootschap* (Amsterdam: Nederlandsch Bijbelgenootschap, 1943); Gilbert Hamonic, *Le Langage des Dieux*; and Leonard Y. Andaya, "The Bissu: Study of a Third Gender in Indonesia," in Barbara Watson Andaya ed., *Other Pasts: Women, Gender and History in Early Modern Southeast Asia*, (Honolulu: Center for Southeast Asian Studies, 2000), 27–46.

44. While bissu use *I La Galigo* to affirm their position in society, are mentioned some of the episodes, and are asked to read and translate manuscripts of which they have their own collections, the link between the two is incidental. See Sharyn Graham Davies, *Gender Diversity in Indonesia; Sexuality, Islam and Queer Selves*, (Oxon and New York: Routledge, 2010), 67–69.

45. Andaya, "The Bissu: Study of a Third Gender in Indonesia," 36.

46. On the influence of the bissu as advisors in Wajoq, see Mundy, ed., *Narrative of Events in Borneo and Celebes*, I, 83.

47. Leonard Y. Andaya, *The Heritage of Arung Palakka: A History of South Sulawesi (Celebes) in the Seventeenth Century* (Den Haag: Martinus Nijhoff, 1981), 15–16.

48. Zainal Abidin, *Wajo' Pada Abad XV–XVI*, 65.

49. Pelras, *The Bugis*, 96. Another example comes from the Chronicle of Sidénréng in which brothers left their homeland and formed new settlements. See Caldwell, *Ten Bugis Texts*, 187.

50. The Cinnotabiq Treaty between Arung Cinnotabiq La Rajallangiq To Patiroi on the one side and the matoa pabbicara with the people on the other side was one of the formative treaties of Cinnotabiq, Wajoq's predecessor. In it, La Rajallangiq agreed to protect the people from trouble, listen carefully to their concerns, correct them when they were

wrong, support them when they are right and ensure that the customs of the country are up held for everyone's benefit. The people, in return, are promised guidance and support from the ruler who bears responsibility for Cinnotabiq's welfare. Furthermore, the ruler could not act arbitrarily towards the people, nor could the people assume or abuse the powers of the ruler. In essence, this was a social contract between the ruler and the ruled, establishing the foundations of the Cinnotabiq polity. See Abdurrazak, *Sedjarah Wadjo*, 27–28.

51. The Lappadeppaq Treaty between the Wajorese people and Arung Béttémpola La Tiringeng To Taba was concluded following a leadership crisis in Wajoq. It clarifies the position of the ruler, stating that wherever he went his people surrounded him, that when he called they would come, and that what he ordered they would obey. See Abdurrazak, *Sedjarah Wadjo*, 37–39.

52. Zainal Abidin, *Persepsi Orang Bugis Makasar tentang Hukum, Negara dan Dunia Luar*, 243–44.

53. Aliamir, "Tinjuan Historis Politik Pemerintahan Kerajaan Puang Rimaggalatung di Wajo," (master's thesis, Hasanuddin University, 1993); Pelras, *The Bugis*, 112–13; Abdurrazak, *Sedjarah Wadjo*, 44.

54. Andaya, *The Heritage of Arung Palakka*, 22.

55. For a discussion concerning the rise of the twin kingdoms of Gowa and Talloq, see Bulbeck, *A Tale of Two Kingdoms*, 113–74; Anthony Reid, "The Rise of Makassar," *RIMA* 17 (1983): 117–60; and William Cummings, "'Only One People but Two Rulers': Hiding the Past in Seventeenth-Century Makasarese Chronicles," *BKI* 155 (1999): 97–120.

56. Pelras, *The Bugis*, 116; Noorduyn, *Een Achttiende-Eeuwse Kroniek van Wadjo'*, 75.

57. Andaya, *The Heritage of Arung Palakka*, 31.

58. Using the substantial quantities of rice at their disposal, the royal families of Gowa and its twin-kingdom Talloq made international trade a conscious goal. This commerce brought considerable wealth and fame to Makassar. When the rulers of Gowa and Talloq converted to Islam in 1605, the prestige of the twin kingdoms grew. Although there is evidence to suggest that Luwuq converted to Islam a year before Gowa, Gowa played a more important role in its spread, and championing the new faith increased its prestige and influence. Gowa waged a series of wars between 1608 and 1611 to convert the other kingdoms of South Sulawesi. In 1609 Gowa forced Sidénréng to convert. Soppéng followed suit later that same year, as did Wajoq in 1610 and Boné in 1611. Gowa also continued its aggrandizement following the so-called Islamic Wars and conquered areas extending southward to Sumbawa, westward to Lombok and western Kalimantan, eastward almost as far as Ternate, and northward as far as Menado. See John Villiers, "Makassar: The Rise and Fall of an East Indonesian Maritime Trading State 1512–1669," in*The Southeast Asian Port and Polity*, eds. J. Kathirithamby-Wells and John Villiers, eds. 145; and "Materials for a History of the Company's Factory at Macassar from the Year 1613 to 1667 with Some Resulting Incidents until the Year 1674," Celebes Factory Records, India Office Library, London (microfilm, University of Malaya Library), 1826: 36; Noorduyn, "De Islamisering van Makasar," *BKI* 117 (1956): 254–56; Andaya, *The Heritage of Arung Palakka*, 33; Bulbeck, *A Tale of Two Kingdoms*, 120–21.

59. Andaya, *The Heritage of Arung Palakka*, 37–38.

60. Ibid., 39–41; Pelras, *The Bugis*, 142–43.

61. Andaya, *The Heritage of Arung Palakka*, 40.

62. Ibid., 40–42.

63. Ibid., 39–41; Pelras, *The Bugis*, 142–43.

64. So successful was this policy of free trade that Moluccan spices were sometimes sold more cheaply in Makassar than in Maluku. See F. W. Stapel, *Het Bongaais Verdrag* (Leiden: University of Leiden 1922), 9.

65. The Makassarese ruler is recorded to have said that trading restrictions were against the will of God "who created the world so that all people could enjoy its benefits, or do you mean that God has reserved these islands, so far away from your own land, for your trade only . . ." Ibid., 62.

66. Ibid., 62–66; Andaya, *The Heritage of Arung Palakka*, 50.

67. Stapel, *Het Bongaais Verdrag*, 74–77, 81–83, and Andaya, *The Heritage of Arung Palakka*, 62–63.

68. Speelman had personal reasons for wanting to achieve more than was expected of him. See Andaya, *The Heritage of Arung Palakka*, 68–70, and F. W. Stapel, *Cornelis Janszoon Speelman* (The Hague: Martinus Nijhoff, 1936), 34–35.

69. F. David Bulbeck, "The Landscape of the Makassar War," *Canberra Anthropology* 13, 1 (1990): 82–83.

70. Andaya, *The Heritage of Arung Palakka*, 100–1.

71. Andaya, "The Bugis-Makassar Diasporas," *JMBRAS* 68 (1995): 120. Dutch sources make special reference to the Wajorese who are recorded as having departed for Jambi and not returning. See Speelman in Makassar to High Government in Batavia, 1670, NA, VOC 1276: 878v.

72. Both the Dutch and the Makassarese blamed the other side for each other for the resumption of hostilities. See C. Skinner (ed.), *Sja'ir Perang Mengkasar: The Rhymed Chronicle of the Macassar War by Entji'Amin*, (Den Haag: Martinus Nijhoff, 1963), 18, 292–93.

73. Andaya, *The Heritage of Arung Palakka*, 126–35.

74. William Cummings, *Making Blood White: Historical Transformations in Early Modern Makassar*, (Honolulu: University of Hawai'i Press, 2002), 34; and William Cummings, *A Chain of Kings: The Makassarese Chronicles of Gowa and Talloq* (Leiden: KITLV Press, 2007), 8.

75. Others were Lamuru and Mandar.

76. Andaya, *The Heritage of Arung Palakka*, 124.

77. *Lontaraq Sukkuqna Wajoq*, 218.

78. *Lontarak Akkarungan (Wajoq) I*, (Makassar: Pemerintah Daerah Tingkat I Sulawesi Selatan, 1985), 83. These high numbers of casualties and the mass decapitations run contrary to ideas of warfare in the archipelago. They were probably intended to convey the desperateness of the situation in a symbolic manner.

79. Stapel, *Cornelis Janszoon Speelman*, 56.

80. Andaya, *The Heritage of Arung Palakka*, 126.

81. *Lontarak Akkarungan (Wajoq) I*, 83. See also Matthes, *Over de Wadjorezen met hun Handels- en Scheepswetboek*, 23.

82. Andaya, *The Heritage of Arung Palakka*, 138–39.

83. Noorduyn, *Een Achttiende-Eeuwse Kroniek van Wadjo'*, 120. According to *lontaraq* it was built in the reign of La Tenrilai To Sengngeng 1658–1670. See *Lontarak Akkarungan (Wajoq) I*, 83–84; and Abdurrazak, *Sedjarah Wadjo*, 60.

84. More than 280 houses and the city's gunpowder magazine were destroyed. See Speelman to High Government, 1670, NA, VOC 1276: 882.)

85. Abdurrazak, *Sedjarah Wadjo*, 60–61.
86. *Lontarak Akkarungan (Wajoq) I*, 85.
87. *Lontaraq Sukkuqna Wajoq*, 217. In this version, a more complete list of vassals which went over to Boné is provided than in most versions. The mention of vassals of the extreme edge of the land, probably referring to Timurung, suggests that some of these were inserted after the war. This version also makes a distinction between vassals which went over to Boné before and after To Sengngeng's death which is not explicitly made elsewhere.
88. *Lontaraq Sukkuqna Wajoq*, 217.
89. Ibid., 215.
90. One source claims that Tosora held out for three years! See Abdurrazak, *Sedjarah Wadjo*, 60.
91. Noorduyn, *Een Achttiende-Eeuwse Kroniek van Wadjo'*, 123.
92. de Jongh to Council, 10.4.1671. NA, VOC 1281: 736.
93. Andaya, *The Heritage of Arung Palakka*, 140.
94. Contract between the VOC and Wajoq, Makassar, 10.1.1671, ANRI, Makassar 274/14.
95. de Jongh to Council, 10.4.1671. NA, VOC 1281: 737.
96. The NBG's collection at the Leiden University library has five copies of it. See Noorduyn, *Een Achttiende-Eeuwse Kroniek van Wadjo'*, 28, 124.
97. *Lontaraq Sukkuqna Wajoq*, 219.
98. Water stirred with a kris and thereby given supernatural powers.
99. de Jongh to Council, 10.4.1671. NA, VOC 1281: 737–737v.
100. Contract between the VOC and Wajoq, Makassar, 10.1.1671, ANRI, Makassar 274/14. See also, J. E. Heeres and F. W. Stapel, eds., *Corpus Diplomaticum Neerlando-Indicum. Verzameling van Politieke contracten en verdere Verdragen door de Nederlanders in het Oosten gesloten, van Privilegebrieven, aan hen verleend, enz.* (The Hague: Martinus Nijhoff, 1907–1955), II, 426–430.
101. W. Ph. Coolhaas, ed., *Generale Missiven van Gouverneurs-Generaal en Raden van Heeren XVII der Verenigde Oostindische Compagnie*, (Den Haag: Martinus Nijhoff, 1960– . . .), III, 752.
102. Coolhaas, ed., *Generale Missiven*, III, 752.
103. Andaya, *The Heritage of Arung Palakka*, 141–42; *Lontaraq Sukkuqna Wajoq*, 222.
104. Noorduyn, *Een Achttiende-Eeuwse Kroniek van Wadjo'*, 276–77.
105. *Lontaraq Sukkuqna Wajoq*, 222.
106. Ibid., 221.
107. Andaya, *The Heritage of Arung Palakka*, 142.
108. Coolhaas, ed., *Generale Missiven*, III, 752.
109. Andaya, *The Heritage of Arung Palakka*, 141.
110. Coolhaas, ed., *Generale Missiven*, III, 752–53.
111. Coolhaas, ed., *Generale Missiven*, IV, 56.
112. Cops to Gov. Gen. van Goens, 20.7.1679, NA, VOC 1347: 392–94v.
113. Andaya, *The Heritage of Arung Palakka*, 192.
114. *Lontaraq Sukkuqna Wajoq*, 222. Such explicit statements are not universal in Wajorese *lontaraq* as is sometimes claimed. See Jacqueline Lineton, "An Indonesian Society and Its Universe: A Study of Bugis of South Sulawesi (Celebes) and Their Role within

a Wider Social and Economic System" (PhD diss., University of London, 1975), 17. The most obvious example of a Wajorese chronicle which does not refer to emigration at this time is Noorduyn, *Een Achttiende-Eeuwse Kroniek van Wadjo'.*

115. Many other Bugis, as well as Makassarese and Mandarese, opted to leave South Sulawesi at that time. So massive was this exodus that Dutch records mention encountering at sea "floating cities" of such refugees. See Andaya, *The Heritage of Arung Palakka*, 210.

116. Smith, *The Ethnic Origins of Nations*, 39–40.

3: Overseas Politics

1. See William Cummings, "The Melaka Malay Diaspora in Makassar, C.1500–1669," *JMBRAS* 71, 1 (1998): 106–21.

2. Anthony Reid, "Pluralism and progress in seventeenth-century Makassar," *BKI* 156, 3 (2000): 439–47.

3. Speelman Notitie 1669 fol 704, as cited in H. Sutherland, "Mestizos as Middlemen? Ethnicity and Access in Colonial Macassar," in *Papers of the Dutch-Indonesian Historical Conference held at Lage Vuursche*, Gerrit Schutte and Heather Sutherland, eds. (Leiden/Jakarta: Bureau of Indonesian Studies, 1982), 256. This is her translation.

4. Heather Sutherland, "Eastern Emporium and Company Town: Trade and Society in Eighteenth-Century Makassar," in *Brides of the Sea: Port Cities of Asia from the 16th-20th Centuries*, ed. Frank Broeze (Kensington: New South Wales University Press, 1989), 98.

5. Heather Sutherland, "Mestizos as Middlemen?" 251.

6. Christopher Healey, "Tribes and States in 'Pre-Colonial' Borneo: Structural Contradictions and the Generation of Piracy," *Social Analysis* 18, (1985): 11.

7. Victor King, *The Peoples of Borneo* (Oxford: Blackwell, 1993), 25.

8. Healey, "Tribes and States in 'Pre-Colonial' Borneo," 13.

9. Report of Francis Prins regarding his voyage to Pasir, 31.10.1674, NA, VOC 1312: 2000.

10. J. Hageman, "Geschiedkundige aanteekeningen omtrent zuidelijk Borneo," *TNI* 23, 1 (1861): 202; Constantinus Alting Mees, *De Kroniek van Koetai: Tekstuitgave met Toelichting*, (Santpoort: N. V. Uitgeverij, 1935), 17.

11. King of Pasir to Gov. Cornelis Beernink, received 2.10.1701, NA, VOC 1663: 39–40.

12. Mees, *De Kroniek van Koetai*, 17.

13. Isaacq van Thije to Gov. Gen. van Outhoorn, 30.9.1697, NA, VOC 1595: 215.

14. King of Pasir to Gov. Gerrit van Toll, undated, NA, VOC 1808: 393–94.

15. Crain Bontoramba and the Pongawas of Pasir to Gov. Bernink and Council, delivered 10.3.1701, NA, VOC 1663: 42.

16. So important was the ruler that Milner characterized Malay statecraft as the condition of having a *raja*. See A. C. Milner, *Kerajaan: Malay Political Culture on the Eve of Colonial Rule,* (Tuscon: University of Arizona Press, 1982).

17. Virginia Matheson and Barbara Watson Andaya, *The Precious Gift (Tuhfat al-Nafis)* [by Raja Ali Haji ibn Ahmad] (Kuala Lumpur: Oxford University Press, 1982), 318, f. 24n1.

18. Andaya, "The Bugis-Makassar Diasporas," 125–26; Matheson and Andaya, eds., *The Precious Gift*, 318, f. 24n1.

19. Jane Drakard, *A Kingdom of Words: Language and Power in Sumatra* (Shah Alam: Oxford University Press, 1999), 3, 17, 68, 71, and 261.

20. There are two different published accounts about the arrival of Daéng Maruppa in western Sumatra. The first appeared in W[inter], "De familie Daing Mabella, volgens een Maleisch handschrift," *TNI* 3, 2 (1874): 115–21. In this article Winter provides a Dutch translation of Daéng Mabéla's history of his own family, a copy of which was owned by the Pengeran of Belimbing. (The author of this manuscript bears the same name as his great grandfather, Daéng Maruppa's son.) The second account of the Wajorese at Inderapura appears in the Adatrechtbundels. (O. L. Helfrich, "De Adel van Bengkoelen en Djambi (1892–1901)," *Adatrechtbundels*, XXII: Gemengd, 's-Gravenhage: Martinus Nijhoff, 1923, 316–19.) This second article by the Dutch commissioner O. L. Helfrich cites Winter, but differs in some of the details that it provides. These two articles are the only known sources pertaining to the arrival of the Wajorese pioneer Daéng Maruppa.

21. Helfrich, "De Adel van Bengkoelen en Djambi," 317.

22. One detail that points to the 1670s is the birth and military service of Daéng Maruppa's son Daéng Mabéla. Daéng Maruppa married a sister of the Sultan of Inderapura and they had a son named Daéng Mabéla a.k.a. Sultan Selan. Daéng Mabéla's brother Sultan Endey, presumably another son of Daéng Maruppa and the sultan's sister, entered the service of the English East India Company as Chief Captain of the Bugis Corps in 1688. See John Ball, *Indonesian Legal History: British West Sumatra 1685–1825* (Sydney: Oughtershaw Press, 1984), 26–27. Presuming that he was a teenager at this time, this would date his birth between 1670 and 1675.

23. Andaya, "Treaty Conceptions and Misconceptions, 278–80.

24. Reid, "Pluralism and Progress," 443. Another example of this is from Buton where the rulers were addressed as 'grandchild' and the council as 'grandfather.' See Esther Velthoen, "Contested Coastlines: Diasporas, Trade and Colonial Expansion in Eastern Sulawesi, 1680–1905" (PhD diss., Murdoch University, 2002), 39.

25. Pelras, "Hiérachie et Pouvoir Traditionnels en Pays Wadjo'," 174.

26. Matheson and Andaya eds., *The Precious Gift*, 29–30.

27. Andaya, "The Bugis-Makassar Diasporas," 132.

28. This is depicted in the *Salasilah Melayu dan Bugis* in quasi-matrimonial terms. "The Yamtuan Besar will be like a woman only, and eat only when given food. And the Yamtuan Muda will be like a man. Whatever issue is at hand, his word will be final." In *Silsilah Melayu dan Bugis*, ed. Arena Wati (Kuala Lumpur: Penerbitan Pustaka Antara, 1973), 67.

29. Nishio Kanji, "Bangsa and Politics: Melayu-Bugis relations in Johor-Riau and Riau-Lingga," in *Proceedings on the Symposium on Bangsa and Umma: A Comparative Study of People-grouping Concepts in the Islamic Areas of Southeast Asia*, Midori Kawashima, Kazuhiro Arai, and Hiroyuki Yamamoto, eds. (Tokyo: Institute of Asian Cultures, Sophia University, 2007), 101.

30. KITLV, Or. 545 No. 182 *Stukken van Intje Moehammad*, VIII; Matthes, *Over de Wadjorezen met hun Handels- en Scheepswetboek*, 34.

31. Abdurrazak, *Sedjarah Wadjo*, 64.

32. *Lontaraq Bilang Wajoq 1711–1732*, No. 01/MKH/4/Unhas/UP, Roll 35 No. 4, 32.

33. S. W. Tromp, "Eenige Mededeelingen omtrent de Boegineezen van Koetei," *BKI* 36 (1887): 167–98.

34. Anonymous, "Verslag van het Verhandelde tot Regeling der Betrekkingen tusschen de Maleische en Boeginesche Nederzettingen aan de Koetei-Rivier onder den Vorigen Sultan van Koetei,—vertaald uit het Oorspronkelijke Maleisch," *Tijdschrift voor Indische Taal-, Land- en Volkenkunde,* 24 (1877).

35. Mees, *De Kroniek van Koetai,* 15.

36. For example *Lontaraq Sukkuqna Wajoq,* 222.

37. S. W. Tromp, "Uit de Salasilah van Koetei," *BKI* 37 (1888): 17.

38. B. F. Matthes, ed., *Iyanaé sure powada-adaengi Undang-undangna sinina toWajoé, iya nawinrué matowana to-Wajoé ri Junpandang riyasengé Amanna Gappa,* (Makassar: Van Hartrop Jr., 1869), 23, 67.

39. Coolhaas, ed., *Generale Missiven,* V, 615.

40. The *Salasilah Bugis* uses the words Wajorese and Bugis interchangeably. It is known from other sources, however, that the vast majority of Bugis in Samarinda were Wajorese.

41. "Pulang pulang" meaning "go home" thus their specific destination is not mentioned. Presumably it means Wajoq, but might also mean Kampong Wajoq in Makassar. Assuming that the arrival of the Wajorese in East Kalimantan dates from the late seventeenth century, then Wajorese repatriation suggests that, despite the difficulties for Wajoq after the Makassar War, links between the homeland and overseas groups were already intense.

42. Tromp, "Eenige Mededeelingen omtrent de Boegineezen van Koetei," 182–83.

43. Ibid., 167–81.

44. Leonard Y. Andaya, "Local Trade Networks in Maluku in the 16th, 17th and 18th Centuries," *Cakalele* 2, 2 (1991): 74.

45. Coolhaas, ed., *Generale Missiven,* VII, 173.

46. Warren, *The Sulu Zone,* 85–86.

47. M. Noor, *Sejarah Pemerintahan Kabupaten Berau dari Masa ke Masa,* (Samarinda: the author, 1996).

48. *Lontaraq Bilang Wajoq 1711–1732,* No. 01/MKH/4/Unhas/UP, Roll 35 No. 4. This is one of three diaries known to record the lives of Bugis overseas. The other two are the diary of Arung Palakka that records his stay in Java and his military campaign in Tanah Toraja and the diary of an exiled Bugis noble in Maluku, Bengal, and Jakarta. See A. A. Cense, "Old Buginese and Macassarese Diaries," *BKI* 122, 4 (1966): 425–26.

49. Rahilah Omar, *The History of Boné,* 27.

50. The other one is *Catatan Harian Kerajaan Wajoq, 1832–1835 dan 1843–1848,* No. 01/MKH/28/Unhas/UP.

51. Sultan Sulaiman was the fourth sultan of Pasir. The first sultan for whom dates are readily available is the sixth sultan, Sultan Adam (1844–1861.) See H. M. Noor, *Perlawanan Terhadap Imperialisme dan Kolonialisme di Kerajaan Berau, Kutai dan Pasir* (Samarinda: the author,1997), 68.

52. This local tradition is contained in H. A. Demang Kedaton's typescript "Sedjarah Ringkas Kedatangan Suku Bugis di Samarinda Seberang" (A Short History of the Arrival of the Bugis in Samarinda Seberang) which is discussed in chapter 6.

53. *Lontaraq Bilang Wajoq,* 35.

54. Which sultan is not specified. The first Berauan leader to bear the title sultan was the twelfth ruler Sultan Aji Kuning. The first sultans for whom dates are readily available are Raja Alam Sultan Alimuddin of Sambaliung (1810–1837) and Sultan Aji Kuning II of Gunung Tabur (1810–1850).

55. The tenth and eleventh rulers of Berau bore the title Pengeran Presumably, lesser nobility used it after the ruler began to use the title sultan. That this leader's daughter's name was Wé Isa suggests that he was Bugis.

56. *Lontaraq Bilang Wajoq*, 39. Wé Isa died six months later.

57. Bugis diaries generally accord a page to each month and a line to each day. Long entries are written either in the margins, sometimes even with the text changing directions, or in the space intended for other days. The information about Wajorese-Berauan relations occupies the space originally accorded to five months in the diary. While it is more likely that the conflict intensified after the diarist had been in Berau for a year and a half than that he arbitrarily chose pages, both are possible. It should also be remembered that the diary was copied by hand into a modern notebook and the copyist could have taken liberties with the placement of the text.

58. This desire is likely to have been influenced by verse 3:110 from the Qur'an which instructs Muslims to enjoin what is right and forbid what is wrong.

59. There does not appear to be any evidence in the Wajorese chronicles to support Daéng Maruppa's claims of royal blood. His claims are likely to be an instance of inflating genealogy so as to impress the host society, a practice which was common among Bugis migrants.

60. Neither this account nor the tradition recorded by Winter specifies a year, but it appears that Daéng Maruppa arrived in western Sumatra during the 1670s. Although the military defeat which preceded Daéng Maruppa's departure is not specified, and Wajorese historical sources do not record an attack on Tosora by Bénténg, the reference is presumably to the Makassar War or to the subsequent attack on Tosora.

61. Helfrich, "De Adel van Bengkoelen en Djambi," 317.

62. J. Kathirithamby-Wells, "The Inderapura Sultanate: The Foundations of its Rise and Decline, from the Sixteenth to Eighteenth Centuries," *Indonesia* 21 (1976): 77; Drakard, *A Kingdom of Words*, 129.

63. J. Kathirithamby-Wells, "A Survey of the Effects of British Influence on Indigenous Authority in Southwest Sumatra (1685–1824)," *BKI* 129 (1973): 247–48.

64. British records assert that Sultan Endey and Sultan Selan were serving the Dutch prior to the British. See Gibbon to Bloom and Council, 1689, India Office Library, London (microfilm University of Hawai'i Library via interlibrary loan from CRL and University Malaya Library), SFR II: 42–43. Although the Dutch in western Sumatra certainly employed Bugis at this time, confirmation of Sultan Selan and Sultan Endey's service is not conspicuous in the Dutch records. Furthermore, their service with the VOC is not mentioned in the Malay language family history translated by Winter.

65. This is according to the local tradition recorded by Winter. According to Helfrich's account, the English East India Company wrote directly to Daéng Mabéla and asked him to fill this position. The ministers of Inderapura gave Daéng Mabéla their blessings to go see the English, on the condition that he return as quickly as possible. After restoring order in Bengkulu, Daéng Mabéla returned to Inderapura, but the company persuaded him to go once again to Bengkulu and enter their service. See Helfrich, "De Adel van Bengkoelen en Djambi," 317–18.

66. Winter, "De familie Daing Mabella," 117.

67. Diary and Consultations, Fort York, 30.1.1695/6, SFR, III: 229.

68. Diary and Consultations, Tryanong Factory, 15.10.1695, SFR, III: 140.

69. The European in this case was accused of robbing a sloop. See Diary and Consultations, 31.10.1695, SFR, III: 163–71.

70. See chapter 4.

71. Diary and Consultations, 8.7.1695, SFR, III: 27.

72. Sultan Muhammad Syah to Gibbon, received 12.10.1689, SFR, II: 39.

73. Dato Rajah Quasso to Collet, received 16.9.1712, SFR, VII: 54.

74. Diary and Consultations, 10.8.1702, SFR, V: 133. The volume in which this document is contained is not clearly noted in the CRL's copy of the SFR, yet it is presumably volume V.

75. W[atts] et al [at Fort York] to the EIC in London, undated, presumably January 1703.

76. It should be noted that during this period, there was a decline in the actual number of Bugis serving in the Bugis corps. British records from the 1740s mention that there were " . . . no recruits of true Bugguesses for many Years . . ." and that a number of Bugis repatriated. See Alan Harfield, *Bencoolen A History of the Honourable Easy India Company's Garrison on the West Coast of Sumatra (1685–1825)* (Hampshire: A and J Partnership, 1995), 100, 102.

77. Letters and Consultations, 30.10.1732, SFR VIII as cited in Kathirithamby-Wells, "A Survey of the Effects of British Authority in Southwest Sumatra," 249.

78. Kathirithamby-Wells, *The British West Sumatran Presidency 1760–1785: Problems of Early Colonial Enterprise* (Kuala Lumpur: Penerbit Universiti Malaya, 1977), 56.

79. Ibid., 120.

80. Winter, "De familie Daing Mabella," 119.

81. Harfield, *Bencoolen*, 195–96.

82. Ibid., 205.

83. Kathirithamby-Wells, *The British West Sumatran Presidency*, 90, 105–06

84. Winter, "De familie Daing Mabella," 119.

85. H. R. Lewis, "A Commentative Digest of the Laws of the Natives of that part of the Coast of Sumatra, immediately dependent on the Settlement of Fort Marlborough and practised in the Court of that Presidency." *Adatrechtbundel VI* (Den Haag: Martinus Nijhoff, 1913), 283.

86. Ibid., 285.

87. Kathirithamby-Wells, "A Survey of the Effects of British Authority in Southwest Sumatra," 251.

88. The exploits of this family are even commemorated in local Malay literature. In the Syair Mukomuko, Daéng Maruppa is referred to as "the mighty chief . . . Captain of the Bugis at [Fort] Marlborough." See J. Kathirithamby-Wells and Muhammad Yusoff Hashim, *The Syair Mukomuko: Some Historical Aspects of a Nineteenth Century Sumatran Court Chronicle* (Kuala Lumpur: Art Printing Works Sdn. Bhd., 1985).

89. Kathirithamby-Wells, "A Survey of the Effects of British Authority in Southwest Sumatra," 256.

90. Ibid., 258.

91. Helfrich, "De Adel van Bengkoelen en Djambi," 319. Daéng Mabéla II was, however, the last of the Bugis leaders to use the title *daéng*. See John Bastin, *The British in West Sumatra (1695–1825): A Selection of Documents, Mainly from the East India Company Records Preserved in the India Office Library, Commonwealth Relations Office, London,* (Kuala Lumpur: University of Malaya Press, 1965), 173n420.

92. Tromp, "Eenige Mededeelingen omtrent de Boegineezen van Koetei,"

93. The number of the *kapala maneng* is not known and may have fluctuated.

94. La Side, "Serba-serbi tentang Amanna Gappa dan Penangkatan Matowa Wadjo di Makasar dalam abad ke-17," *Bingkisan* 2, 8, (1969): 22.

95. Ibid., 491–92.

96. La Side, "Serba-serbi tentang Amanna Gappa," 22.

97. Matthes, *Over de Wadjorezen met hun Handels- en Scheepswetboek*, 31.

98. These were agreed upon during the administration of the first matoa To Pabukiq (c.1671–1676/1681), and were formalized after his successor To Pakkalo (1676/1681–1697/1702) had served for three years. Only during the inauguration of the third matoa Amanna Gappa (1697–1723) were they incorporated into the actual ceremony.

99. It was later added to this that they must share their profits with the matoa even if the sale takes place quickly, without his knowledge.

100. Later this pertained specifically to ships traveling to Batavia or Tana Bareq = Pulau Pinang.

101. J. Noorduyn, "The Wajorese Merchants' Community in Makassar," *BKI* 156, 3 (2000): 478–79, 493–94.

102. The VOC's victory in the Makassar War was due to a large part to Arung Palakka's participation, and after the war the Dutch continued to rely heavily upon the rulers of Boné for advice about the politics of South Sulawesi. Thus, after the 1667 Bungaya Treaty, the Bonéan rulers took up residence in Bontualaq, close to Casteel Rotterdam. From there, they assisted the Dutch in local political affairs. From the signing of the Bungaya Treaty to the death of Arung Palakka in 1696, Boné was paramount among the polities of South Sulawesi. This was demonstrated time and time again, most notably in the Luwuq-Boné War of 1676 and in the Toraja Wars of 1683. See Andaya, *The Heritage of Arung Palakka*, 177–81, 258–62.

103. Arung Palakka's successor and nephew La Patauq (1696–1714) was also the great-grandson of To Ali, the fifteenth arung matoa of Wajoq. Beginning with La Patauq, the king of Boné also bore the title of ranreng Tua which La Patauq had inherited from his father Pakokoé who in turn had inherited it from his mother Khadijah Da Salleq. The office of ranreng Tua was unique among positions in the Wajorese government in that it was often held by two people simultaneously. This practice had begun in the early seventeenth century when two brothers, To Appamadeng and To Pasawei, had jointly held the office of ranreng Tua. Perhaps because of this legacy, the tradition of sharing the office of ranreng Tua lasted into the eighteenth century. Yet it assumed quite a different character. See Noorduyn, "The Wajorese Merchants' Community in Makassar," 476; Noorduyn, *Een Achttiende-Eeuwse Kroniek van Wadjo'*, 108.

104. Noorduyn, "The Wajorese Merchants' Community in Makassar," 477.

105. Ibid., 494, La Side, "Serba-serbi tentang Amanna Gappa," 20, 25–26.

106. Matthes, *Over de Wadjorezen met hun Handels- en Scheepswetboek*, 30–31.

107. Noorduyn, "The Wajorese Merchants' Community in Makassar," 496.

108. Noeroeddin Daeng Magassing, "Pegatan," *Sinar Selebes Selatan* 1, 1 (1941): 9; Matthes, ed., *Iyanaé sure powada-adaengi Undang-undangna sinina toWajoé*, 1, 42.

109. Sipman to Gov. Gen. van Swoll, 23.9.1714, NA, VOC 1853: 100.

110. Iranian migrants in early modern South and Southeast Asia also played a semi-administrative, semi-commercial role. See Sanjay Subrahmayam, "Iranians Abroad," 358.

4: Commerce

1. John Crawfurd, *A Descriptive Dictionary of the Indian Islands and Adjacent Countries* (London: Bradbury & Evans, 1856), 441.

2. Gerrit Knaap and Heather Sutherland, *Monsoon Traders: Ships, Skippers and Commodities in Eighteenth-century Makassar* (Leiden: KITLV Press, 2004), 64.

3. Ibid., 135, 137, 159.

4. Smout to Loten, 1.6.1744, NA, VOC 2628: 246–247.

5. Engseng Ho, *The Graves of Tarim: Genealogy and Mobility across the Indian Ocean* (Berkeley: University of California Press, 2006), 101–02.

6. Matthes, *Over de Wadjorezen met hun Handels- en Scheepswetboek*, 29.

7. Sutherland, "Eastern Emporium and Company Town," 114.

8. Ibid, p. 122.

9. The Malay term *orang asli*, literally meaning 'indigenous people,' refers to the indigenous non-Malay peoples residing on the Malay Peninsula.

10. The Malay term *orang laut*, literally meaning 'sea people,' refers to peoples residing along the rivers and coasts of the western Malay-Indonesian archipelago.

11. Knaap and Sutherland, *Monsoon Traders*, 28, 73, 91, 102.

12. P. D. Reub, "Het Westsumatraanse Goud Handel en Exploitatie in de Zeventiende Eeuw" (master's thesis, Leiden University, 1989), 7.

13. Christine Dobbin, *Islamic Revivalism in a Changing Peasant Economy, Central Sumatra, 1784–1847* (London and Malmö: Curzon Press, 1983) 72; Jane Drakard, *A Kingdom of Words*, 104 and 119.

14. Jane Drakard, *A Malay Frontier: Unity and Duality in a Sumatran Kingdom* (Ithaca: Southeast Asia Program, 1990), 14.

15. Eighteen copies of this legal code were held in the manuscript collection of the Yayasan Kebudayaan Sulawesi Selatan, which no longer exists as such, and numerous copies are held in the NBG collection held at the Leiden University Library. It has also been published in the original Bugis, Indonesian, Dutch, and English. See Matthes, ed., *Iyanaé sure powada-adaengi Undang-undangna sinina toWajoé*; O. L. Tobing, *Hukum Pelajaran dan Perdagangan Amanna Gappa* (Makassar: Jajasan Kebudajaan Sulawesi Selatan dan Tenggara, 1961); C. H. Thomsen, ed., *A Code of Bugis Maritime Laws with a Translation and Vocabulary, giving the Pronunciation and Meaning of Each Word* (Singapore: Mission Press, 1832); and Leonardus Johannes Jacobus Caron, *Het Handels- en Zeerecht in de Adatrechtsregelen van Rechtskring Zuid-Celebes* (Bussum: Van Dishoek, 1937). This analysis is based on Matthes, 1869.

16. C. C. Macknight and I. A. Caldwell, "Variation in Bugis Manuscripts," *Archipel* 61 (2001): 149.

17. On the date of Amanna Gappa's law code, see La Side, "Serba-serbi tentang Amanna Gappa," 11–12 and Noorduyn, "The Wajorese merchants' community in Makassar," 495–96.

18. Noorduyn, "The Wajorese Merchants' Community in Makassar," 483.

19. Ibid., 487.

20. Barbara Watson Andaya, "Orality, Contracts, Kinship and the Market in Pre-Colonial Island Southeast Asia," in *Ownership, Contracts and Markets in China, Southeast Asian and the Middle East: The Potentials of Comparative Study*, ed. Toru Miura (Tokyo: Islamic Area Studies Project, 2001), 8.

21. *Lontaraq Sukkuqna Wajoq*, 228.

22. The *lontaraq* (*Lontaraq Sukkuqna Wajoq*, 229) refers to "Java" but this actually refers to the western archipelago. See A. A. Cense, "Eenige aantekeningen over Makassaars-Boeginese geschiedschrijving," 49n23.

23. *Lontaraq Sukkuqna Wajoq*, 230–32.

24. Abdurrazak, *Sedjarah Wadjo*, 63.

25. Matthes, *Over de Wadjorezen met hun Handels- en Scheepswetboek*, 24.

26. The mosque was improved with lime, the well was deepened and a *menara* (tower) was built from which to make the call to prayer. See *Lontaraq Sukkuqna Wajoq*, 236.

27. Noorduyn, "The Wajorese Merchants' Community in Makassar," 480; KITLV, Or. 545 No. 182 *Stukken van Intje Moehammad*, VIII.

28. Although its meaning has changed, the term *sawi* is still in use. In eighteenth-century Dutch documents, it was defined as indigenous trading passengers. In the nineteenth century, it meant "crew member" and is now used in a variety of fields to denote clients who are dependent upon *punggawa* or patrons. See Abrah: Franzs contra Tombo Inlandse vrouw, 1728, ANRI, Makassar 333.2; and Pelras, *The Bugis*, 332.

29. Imbedded in relatively hierarchical societies, slavery in early modern Southeast Asia was arguably a less onerous institution than in the Atlantic world. On occasion, people voluntarily entered into slavery because it could be more advantageous than freedom. See Anthony Reid, ed., *Slavery, Bondage and Dependency in Southeast Asia* (St. Lucia: University of Queensland Press, 1983).

30. Matthes ed., *Iyanaé sure powada-adaengi Undang-undangna sinina toWajoé*, 70–72.

31. Ibid., 71–72.

32. Christian Pelras, "Patron-client ties among the Bugis and Makassarese of South Sulawesi," *BKI* 156, 3 (2000): 424–26.

33. Abrah: Fransz contra Tombo Inlandse vrouw, unpaginated.

34. While Karre Mangewai claimed that To Anko paid these expenses out of his profits from the sale of slaves, the court favored Abraham Franzson's testimony that To Anko paid them with part of the *sawi vragtloons* as they had agreed. Either way, Abraham Franzson was to reimburse To Anko, but using the *sawi*'s money is not in accordance with the spirit of Amanna Gappa's law code, which states that a captain must have money to invest in the maintenance of the ship.

35. The prosecutor (*Fiskaal*) was a core member of the Council that, together with the Governor General, was responsible for preserving order and administering justice within the VOC's establishments. See John Ball, *Indonesian Legal History 1602–1848* (Sydney: Oughtershaw Press, 1982), 9.

36. Andaya, "Orality, Contracts, Kinship and the Market," 30.

37. Although he had considerable Dutch support and simultaneously held the office of both ranreng Tua and arumponé, Arung Palakka's successor and nephew La Patauq (1696–1714) was unable to maintain his level of control over the various polities of South Sulawesi. Thereafter Bone's relations with the Dutch deteriorated in part because of the rapid succession of rulers. La Patauq's successor and daughter Batari Toja reigned from 1714 until 1715, briefly in 1720, and then again from 1724 until 1749. The non-continuous dates of her reign suggest political problems and instability, which were indeed prevalent at the time.

38. Sipman to Gov. Gen. van Swoll, 24.10.1717, NA, VOC 1894: 34.

39. Noorduyn, "The Wajorese Merchants' Community in Makassar," 482.

40. In 1737, Governor Sautijn reported that during the past 25–30 years, Boné had declined into a weak state. See Sautijn to Smout, 14.10.1737, NA, VOC 2409: 178.

41. Ibid., 244.

42. Ibid.

43. Sutherland, "Eastern Emporium and Company Town," 114, 122.

44. Smout to Loten, 1.6.1744, NA, VOC 2628: 259.

45. Gobius to van Arrewijne, 20.5.1728, NA, VOC 2100: 92–93.

46. Sutherland, "Trade in VOC Indonesia," 58.

47. Heather A. Sutherland and David S. Brée, "Quantitative and Qualitative Approaches to the Study of Indonesian Trade," in *Dari Babad dan Hikayat sampai Sejarah Kritis,* ., eds.(Yogyakarta: Gadjah Mada University Press, 1987), 397.

48. The text implies that they are Wajorese on folio 139.

49. Report of van Aldorss concerning clandestine trade, 28.12.1715, NA, VOC 1894: 133–35.

50. Ibid., 135–39.

51. Ibid., 135–36.

52. Sutherland and Brée, "Quantitative and Qualitative Approaches to the Study of Indonesian Trade," 404.

53. Noorduyn, *Een Achttiende-Eeuwse Kroniek van Wadjo',* 126.

54. Coolhaas, ed., *Generale Missiven,* VII, 173.

55. Voll to Boelen, 11.4.1768, NA, VOC 3243: unpaginated, document 16.

56. Sutherland and Brée, "Quantitative and Qualitative Approaches," 397–400.

57. York Fort Diary and Consultations Book, June 1695 to February 1696, SFR, III: 28.

58. Winter, "De familie Daing Mabella," 119.

59. The use of opium was common among the Bugis. When, in 1780, the Bugis stationed in Cawoor were unable to obtain the opium (and white rice) to which they were accustomed, they marched back to Bengkulu on their own. Marsden commented on the effects of opium in the eighteenth century: "The bugis soldiers, and others in the Malay bazars, whom we see most attached to it, and who use it to excess, commonly appear emaciated; but they are in other respects abandoned and debauched." See Harfield, *Bencoolen,* 249; and Bastin, *The British in West Sumatra,* 47n231.

60. Anthony Reid, "Economic and Social Change, c. 1400-1800," in Nicholas Tarling, ed. *Cambridge History of Southeast Asia,* (Cambridge: Cambridge University Press, 1999) Vol. 1, part 2, page 144.

5: Family Relations

1. *Lontaraq Sukkuqna Wajo,* 231. Interestingly enough, *A Short History of the Arrival of the Bugis in Samarinda Seberang* records La Maddukelleng making the same speech not when he departed Wajoq, but rather when he departed Samarinda to return to Wajoq.

2. Ho, *The Graves of Tarim,* 152–55.

3. Scott C. Levy, *The Indian Diaspora in Central Asia and its Trade, 1550–1900,* (Leiden: Brill, 2001), 180–222.

4. Tony Day, *Fluid Iron: State Formation in Southeast Asia* (Honolulu: University of Hawai'i Press, 2002), 38–39.

5. Vladmir Draginsky, *The Heritage of Traditional Malay Literature: A Historical Survey of Genres, Writings and Literary Views* (Leiden: KITLV Press, 2004), 128.

6. As Barbara Andaya notes in the first sustained study of the role of kinship in political history any Southeast Asian society, what Europeans perceived of as "kingdoms" were actually "cultural-economic unities comprised of a web of kinship-infused relationship." See Barbara Watson Andaya, *To Live as Brothers: Southeast Sumatra in the Seventeenth and Eighteenth Centuries* (Honolulu: University of Hawai'i Press, 1993), 213.

7. Anthony Reid, *Southeast Asia in the Age of Commerce 1450–1680*, (New Haven: Yale University Press, 1988), I, 6, 146 and 162.

8. Barbara Watson Andaya, "Gender, Islam and the Bugis Diaspora in Nineteenth- and Twentieth-Century Riau," *Sari* 21 (2003): 79.

9. Reid, *Southeast Asia in the Age of Commerce*, I, 151–54.

10. Andaya, *To Live as Brothers*, 28–29.

11. Barbara Watson Andaya, *The Flaming Womb: Repositioning Women in Early Modern Southeast Asia* (Honolulu: University of Hawai'i Press, 2006), 182

12. Bulbeck, *A Tale of Two Kingdoms*, 121.

13. Andaya, *The Flaming Womb*, 145.

14. Cummings, *Making Blood White*, 109–10.

15. H. Maier, "'We are Playing Relatives': Riau the Cradle of Reality and Hybridity," *BKI* 153 (1997): 673–74.

16. C. van Vollenhoven, *Het Adatrecht van Nederlandsch-Indië*, (Leiden: Brill, 1918), I, 298.

17. Andaya, *To Live as Brothers*, 57.

18. Peter Parkes, "Milk Kinship in Islam: Substance, Structure, History," *Social Anthropology* 13, 3 (2005): 310–11.

19. Andaya, *To Live as Brothers*, 35, 237.

20. Andaya, *The Flaming Womb*, 89, 129, 186.

21. Fritz Schulze, *Die Chroniken von Sambas und Mempawah: Einheimsche Quellen zur Geschichte West-Kalimantans* (Heidelberg: Julius Groos Verlag, 1991), 45.

22. Noorduyn, *Een Achttiende-Eeuwse Kroniek van Wadjo'*, 129.

23. On the status of women among the Bugis, see Shelly Errington, *Meaning and Power in a Southeast Asian Realm* (Princeton: Princeton University Press, 1989), chap 8. On the use of marriage as a means of determining status, see Millar, *Bugis Weddings*.

24. A notable exception to this bilateralism is the tendency to assign elite titles among patrilineal lines.

25. Bulbeck, *A Tale of Two Kingdoms*, 39.

26. Millar, *Bugis Weddings*, 6.

27. Tromp, "Eenige Mededeelingen omtrent de Boegineezen van Koetei," 172–73n1.

28. Andaya, "The Bugis-Makassar Diasporas," 122.

29. A. H. F. J. Nusselein, "Beschrijving van het Landschap Pasir," *BKI* 58 (1905): 566.

30. Report of Intje Jalani, Intje Pouassa and Intje Oeman regarding the situation in Kutai, 5.8.1728, NA, VOC 2100, 60–61.

31. According to Zainal Abidin and Alam, from 1723 to 1727 La Maddukelleng roamed with his (father) in-law Sultan Sumbawa Amas Madina who fought a war against the Balinese in Salaparang in Lombok but Dutch records describe Karaéng Bontolangka-

sa, rather than La Maddukelleng, as having married into the royal family of Sumbawa. See Zainal Abidin Farid and Alam, "La Maddukelleng, Pahlawan jang tak kenal menjerah," *Bingkisan* 1, 10, (1968): 30; and Memorie van Sautijn aan Smout, Makassar, 14.10.1737, NA, VOC 2409: 200–01.

32. Report of Intje Jalani, Intje Pouassa and Intje Oeman regarding the situation in Kutai, 5.8.1728, NA, VOC 2100: 60–61.

33. This tradition is echoed in the oral historical research conducted in Pegatan, in the extreme southeast corner of Borneo, across from Pulau Laut. See KITLV Or. 545, Nagelaten papieren en manuscripten van Prof. Dr. Anton Abraham Cense, XI Collectie Noeroeddin Daeng Magassing, 156 Borneo, Aantekeningen en bijlagen, stambomen in 3 blocnotes, VI: 28–35; and Noeroeddin Daeng Magassing, "Pegatan," 42–47.

34. According to legend, one of Daéng Menambong's descendants then founded Kubu near Pontianak and one of his daughters married the first sultan of Pontianak. The *Tuhfat al-Nafis* also states that Daéng Menambun married the daughter of the King of Matan, but identifies Daéng Menambun as a son of Daéng Rilaga, not a follower of La Maddukelleng. See G. Hamonic, "Les réseaux marchands bugis-makassar," in *Marchands et hommes d'affaires asiatiques dans l'Océan Indien et la Mer de Chine 13e-20e siècles*, Denys Lombard and Jean Aubin, eds. (Paris: Éditions de l'École des Hautes Études en Sciences Sociales, 1988), 258, 265n16; and Matheson and Andaya, eds., *The Precious Gift*, 28.

35. The *Tuhfat al-Nafis* confirms that Daéng Kamboja became the Yamtuan Muda, but relates a different background for him as Daéng Parani's son. See Matheson and Andaya eds., *The Precious Gift*, 92.

36. Examples include D. Adham's *Salasilah Kutai* (Jakarta: Departemen Pendidikan dan kebudayaan, 1981) and A. S. Assegaff's *Sejarah Kerajaan Sadurangas Atau Kesultanan Pasir* ([Tanah Grogot]: Pemerintah Daerah Kabupaten Daerah Tingkat II Pasir, 1982).

37. J. Dalton, "Remarks on the Exports of Coti," in *Notices of the Indian Archipelago, and Adjacent Countries*, J. H. Moor (Singapore: s.n., 1837), 55.

38. In the early eighteenth century, the polities of Simpang, Sukadana, and Matan in southwest Borneo formed a single united kingdom which was known according to the names of its successive capital cities: Sukadana, Matan, Muara Kajung, and Tanjung Pura. Like Brunei and the other coastal polities of western Borneo, it fell very much into the political sphere of the Malay world. See Matheson and Andaya eds., *The Precious Gift*, 327, folio 58n1.

39. Matheson and Andaya eds., *The Precious Gift*, 52. Other sources indicate that the marriage to Puteri Kesumba was a reward after the military campaign had succeeded. See P. J. Veth, *Borneo's Wester-afdeeling, geographisch, statistisch, historisch, voorafgegaan door eene algemeene schets des ganschen eilands*, (Zaltbommel: Joh Noman, 1854–1856), I: 241.

40. Veth, *Borneo's Wester-afdeeling*, I: 240.

41. Matheson and Andaya, eds., *The Precious Gift*, 51–52. The chronicles of Sambas and Mempawa identify the cannon as Si Genda. See Schulze, *Die Chroniken von Sambas und Mempawah*, 45.

42. Timothy P. Barnard, *Multiple Centres of Authority: Society and Environment in Siak and Eastern Sumatra, 1674–1827* (Leiden: KITLV Press, 2003), 56–65.

43. There are different accounts about the sources of this animosity. See also Mu-

hammad Yusoff Hashim, ed., *Hikayat Siak* [by Tengku Said], (Kuala Lumpur: Dewan Bahasa dan Pustaka, 1992), 124–25; Matheson and Andaya, eds., *The Precious Gift*, 49–50; and Barnard, *Multiple Centres of Authority,* 69.

44. Matheson and Andaya, eds., *The Precious Gift*, 49–50; M. Yusoff, ed., *Hikayat Siak*, 127; Barnard, *Multiple Centres of Authority*, 70.

45. As occurred elsewhere in the archipelago, the Bugis in Riau established an uneasy partnership with their Malay hosts. Malay rulers needed Bugis industry and enterprise to advance their kingdoms' commerce and the Bugis needed the sanctity of the ruler since the kingdom was held together by his person. See Matheson and Andaya, eds., *The Precious Gift*, 62–63; Leonard Y. Andaya, "Bugis Diaspora, Identity, and Islam in the Malay World." Unpublished paper presented at the conference on "The Bugis Diaspora and Islamic Dissemination in the 20th Century Malay-Indonesian Archipelago," in Makassar, June 6–8 ,2003.

46. E. Netscher, *De Nederlanders in Djohor en Siak, 1602–1865: Historische Beschrijving*, (Batavia: Bruining & Wijy, 1870), 63.

47. This tenuous alliance is described in Raja Kecik to du Quesne, undated, NA, VOC 2074: 70; Raja Kecik to Gov. of Melaka, undated, NA, VOC 2074: 62; du Quesne to Raja Kecik, undated, NA, VOC 2074: 68; Netscher, *De Nederlanders in Djohor en Siak,* 64; Barnard, *Multiple Centres of Authority*, 77–78.

48. R. O. Winstedt, "A History of Selangor," *JMBRAS*, 12, 3 (1934): 4–5. Andaya also mentions Daéng Parani's marriage to Tengku Tengah. See Andaya, "The Bugis-Makassar Diasporas," 127.

49. Matheson and Andaya, eds., *The Precious Gift*, 336.

50. To Passarai was the brother of the former Arumponé La Patauq, and thus the uncle of the reigning Arumponé Batari Toja. Following a dispute with Arung Mampu concerning women, To Passarai fled Boné around 1695 with a following of about 300 people. After brief stays at Mandar and Pulau Laut, he went to Banjarmasin where he and his followers remained for two years while earning their living mining diamonds. Then, alledgedly because of a dispute with La Patauq, he had to flee again. This time he went to Riau where Daéng Marewa and Daéng Manompoq were already established. He followed their orders for about two years, but they eventually grew suspicious of him and feared that he would try to take over their positions. As it was dangerous for him to stay in Riau, he relocated to Linggi with Daéng Marewa and Daéng Manompoq's approval. See Legal examination of Prince Topassarai, 27.7.1735, NA, VOC 2327: 1250–52.

51. Pasques de Chavonnes to Gov. Durven, 28.1.1732, NA, VOC 2194:7–8.

52. Matheson and Andaya, eds., *The Precious Gift*, 81–85.

53. Ibid., 81–82.

54. Ibid., 81–85.

55. Ibid., 84–85, 137.

56. Ibid., 87.

57. Noorduyn, *Een Achttiende-Eeuwse Kroniek van Wadjo'*, 129.

58. Winter, "De familie Daing Mabella, volgens een Maleisch handschrift," 317.

59. Helfrich, "De Adel van Bengkoelen en Djambi," 316–317.

60. Ibid.

61. Winter, "De familie Daing Mabella," 116–17.

62. Panganting to Snickers, recorded 8.1.1690, NA, VOC 1462: 483v.

63. *Lontaraq Bilang Wajoq 1711–1732*, No. 01/MKH/4/Unhas/UP, Rol 35 No. 4.

64. Daniel M. Swetschinski, "Kinship and Commerce: the Foundations of Portuguese Jewish Life in Seventeenth-Century Holland," *Studia Rosenthaliana*, 15, 1, (1981): 59.

65. See, for example, Gelina Harlaftis, "Mapping the Greek Maritime Diaspora from the Early Eighteenth to the Late Twentieth Centuries," in *Diaspora Entrepreneurial Networks*, Ina Baghdiantz McCabe et al., eds. (New York: Bloomsbury Academic, 2005),155–157, and Sebouh David Aslanian, *From the Indian Ocean to the Mediterranean: The Global Trade Networks of Armenian Merchants from New Julfa* (Berkeley: University of California Press, 2011), 146–49.

66. Claude Markovits, *The Global World of Indian Merchants, 1750–1947* (Cambridge: Cambridge University Press, 2008), 178; Francesca Trivellato, "Sephardic Merchants in the Early Modern Atlantic and Beyond: Toward a Comparative Historical Approach to Business Cooperation," in *Atlantic Diasporas: Jews, Conversos, and Crypto-Jews in the Age of Mercantilism, 1500–1800*, (Baltimore: The Johns Hopkins University Press, 2009), 106; Trivellato, *The Familiarity of Strangers*, 40–42.

67. Matthes, ed., *Iyanaé sure powada-adaengi Undang-undangna sinina toWajoé*, 20, 64.

68. Benjamin Arbel, *Trading Nations: Jews and Venetians in the Early Modern Eastern Mediterranean* (Leiden: E. J. Brill, 1995), 191.

69. Cense, "Old Buginese and Macassarese Diaries," 421.

6: Identity and Ethnicization

1. John A. Armstrong, "Mobilized and Proletarian Diasporas," *The American Political Science Review* 70, 2 (1976): 394–97; Rogers Brubaker, "The 'Diaspora' Diaspora," *Ethnic and Racial Studies* 28, 1 (2005): 6–7.

2. A pioneer in the study of ethnicity, Frederik Barth demonstrated that the cultural and social boundaries between two groups do not necessarily dissolve as a result of sustained contact with each other. Barth's work has inspired that of Eriksen who argues that ethnicity is "an aspect of a relationship, not a property of a group." See Frederik Barth, "Enduring and Emerging Issues in the Analysis of Ethnicity," in Hans Vermeulen and Cora Govers, eds., *The Anthropology of Ethnicity: Beyond Ethnic Groups and Boundaries*, (Amsterdam: Het Spinhuis, 1994); and Thomas Hylland Eriksen, *Ethnicity and Nationalism: Anthropological Perspectives* (Sterling: Pluto Press, 2002), 12.

3. Frederick Cooper with Rogers Brubaker, "Identity," in *Colonialism in Question: Theory, Knowledge, History*, ed. Frederick Cooper (Berkeley and Los Angeles: the University of California Press, 2005), 59–90.

4. Leonard Y. Andaya, *Leaves of the Same Tree: Trade and Ethnicity in the Straits of Melaka*, (Honolulu: University of Hawai'i Press, 2008), 237.

5. Heather Sutherland, *Imposing Identities: Self, Community and the State: Makassar as a Microcosm, 1660–2008*, (Amsterdam: Vrij Universiteit, 2008), unpaginated.

6. Christian Pelras, "Culture, Ethnie, Espace Sociale: Quelques réflexions autour du cas bugis," *ASEMI* 8, 2 (1977): 61.

7. Thus if two people of Wajorese origin meet outside of Sulawesi, they are likely to discuss their village and family affiliations, and to continue doing so until they locate a common relative. The fact that this remains true in the twenty-first century, even among Westernized Wajorese, attest to the enduring strength of the traditional ties holding the community together.

8. Pelras, "Culture, Ethnie, Espace Sociale," 58–60.

9. Ibid., 65.

10. Ibid., 58–65.

11. Velthoen, "Contested Coastlines," 200.

12. Gilbert Hamonic, "Autour de l'identité bugis," *Aséanie* 23 (2009): 147.

13. Pelras, "Culture, Ethnie, Espace Sociale," 59.

14. Henry Yule and A. C. Burnell, *Hobson-Jobson, A Glossary of Colloquial Anglo-Indian Words and Phrases, and of Kindred Terms, Etymological, Historical, Geographical and Discursive* (London: John Murray, 1903), 124.

15. Harfield, *Bencoolen*, 100–101.

16. Andaya, "The Bugis-Makassar Diasporas," 129.

17. Alternatively it can be implicit in an individual's name, such "To Ani Témpé" or "To Wajoq Wajoq."

18. Andaya, "The Bugis-Makassar Diasporas," 120.

19. Sheldon Pollack, "The Cosmopolitan Vernacular," *Journal of Asian Studies* 57, 1 (1998): 6.

20. Caldwell, "South Sulawesi A.D. 1300–1600," 169–171; Macknight, "The Emergence of Civilisation in South Celebes," 132.

21. While there are numerous Indian influences in the languages, belief systems, and technologies of South Sulawesi, the region did not undergo the profound social transformation of Indianization that, according to Coedes, is "characterized by Hinduist or Buddhist cults, the mythology of the Puranas, and the observance of the Dharmasastras" as expressed in the Sanskrit language. See Coedes, *The Indianized States of Southeast Asia*, 15–16.

22. See C. C. Macknight, "La Galigo in Comparative Perspectives," in N. Rahman, A. Hukma and I. Anwar, eds., *La Galigo: Menelusuri Jejak Warisan Sastra Dunia* (Makassar: Indonesia Cetakan Pertama, 2003), 351–52.

23. It its entirety, *I La Galigo* is said to be one and a half times the length of the *Mahabharata*. Most *I La Galigo* manuscripts, however, consist of only a couple episodes. A notable exception is the NBG 188 held in the Leiden University Library. At 2,851 pages, it is estimated to contain about a third of the entire *I La Galigo* corpus. See Sirtjo Koolhof, " 'The La Galigo': A Bugis Encyclopedia and its Growth," *BKI* 153, 3 (1999): 370.

24. Koolhof, " 'The La Galigo,' " 364, 371.

25. Mattulada, *Latoa: Satu Lukisan Analitis terhadap Antropologi Politik Orang Bugis,* (Yogyakarta: Gadjah Mada University Press, 1985), 19.

26. Pelras, *The Bugis*, 50; Koolhof, " 'The La Galigo,' " 369.

27. A. Mattulada, "Leadership and Democracy in the Tradition of Nusantara Society," *Lontara: Journal of Hasanuddin University* 1, 1 (1993): 44.

28. C. Pelras, "'Herbe Divine' Le riz chez les Bugis," *Etudes Rurales*, 53–56 (1974) : 360–62; Koolhof, " 'The La Galigo,' " 373–74.

29. On the spread of I La Galigo beyond South Sulawesi, see Zainal Abidin and C. C. Macknight, "The I La Galigo Epic of South Celebes and Its Diffusion," *Indonesia* 17 (1974): 160–69.

30. On the importance of these relations, see Pelras, "Patron-client ties."

31. Noorduyn, *Een Achttiende-Eeuwse Kroniek van Wadjo'*, 154–57.

32. This traditional story was first published in Bugis by Matthes in 1864, and it is on this version that the following summary is based. The story has recently been reprinted

in the original Bugis script and made available in South Sulawesi. "Pau pau ri kadong" is also a more general term for folktales which are intended to entertain and may contain a moral. See, for example, Nurdin Yusuf, *Lapagala*, (Makassar: Dipajaya, 1997), which is first in a series of Bugis folktales translated into Indonesian by Nurdin Yusuf.

33. Matthes, *Over de Wadjorezen met hun Handels- en Scheepswetboek*, 1–2.

34. Speelman to Gov. Gen. Maatsuijcker, 1.12.1667, NA, VOC 1267: 322–42.

35. *Lontaraq Sukkuqna Wajoq*, 218.

36. Andaya, *The Heritage of Arung Palakka*, 102.

37. Koolhof, " 'The La Galigo,' " 384. On the use of texts in Bugis society see Zainal Abidin, "Notes on the Lontara' as Historical Sources," 159–72, and Christian Pelras, "L'Oral et l'écrit dans la tradition Bugis." *Asie du Sud-Est et Monde Insulindien* 10 (1979): 271–97.

38. Smith, *The Ethnic Origins of Nations*, 22–30.

39. Andaya, *Leaves of the Same Tree*, 236.

40. Extract from Dag register 12.6.1728: Makassar 291.11 Compendium op de secrete papieren 1759, ANRI, Makassar 145a: 5.

41. Tromp, "Eenige Mededeelingen omtrent de Boegineezen van Koetei," 185.

42. Ibid., 182–183.

43. *Kampong Wajoq* was located on the coast and in time came to extend east to Jalan Yos. Sudarso (formerly Lajangweg), north to Jalan Satando (formerly Coehoorenweg), and south to Jalan Banda (Bandastraat) in the northwestern section of the town. See KITLV, Or. 545 No. 219 Stukken uit de Japanse tijd, h Hikajat Pendek District-Wadjo, 1; J.R. van Diessen and R.P.G.A. Voskuil, *Stedenatlas Nederlands-Indië*, (Pumerend: Asia Maior, 1998), 143.

44. The Wajorese house of worship (*langgar*) was replaced with a mosque during the administration of Amanna Gappa (1697–1723). A palace was then built during the administration of Matoa Amanna Moming (1723–1729) in Kampong Wajoq for the Arung Matoa La Saléwangeng To Tenrirua, as well as a village meeting hall (*baruga*) during the administration of Matoa To Dawéq (1732–1735). See Noorduyn, "The Wajorese merchants' community in Makassar," 482.

45. Ibid.

46. Ibid.

47. Matthes, *Over de Wadjorezen met hun Handels- en Scheepswetboek*, 34–35.

48. Hamonic, "Autour de l'identité bugis," 163.

49. Kathirithamby-Wells, "A Survey of the Effects of British Authority in Southwest Sumatra," 252.

50. Ball, *Indonesian Legal History*, 6.

51. Diary and Consultations, 17.10.1695, SFR, III: 143.

52. Gibbon to Bloome, 10.30.1689, SFR, II: 45–46.

53. C. R. Boxer, "War and Trade in the Indian Ocean and the South China Sea, 1600–1650," *The Great Circle, Journal of the Australian Association for Maritime History* 1, 2 (1979): 9, as reprinted in *Portuguese Conquest and Commerce in Southern Asia, 1500–1750* (London: Variorum Reprints, 1985).

54. Atkinson to Skingle, 27.7.1708, SFR, V: document no. 75.

55. Broughton to Eyton, 9.5.1699, unpaginated. (The volume in which this document is contained is not clearly noted in the CRL's copy of the SFR, yet it is presumably vol. 4.) While this presumably appeared odd to the EIC officials, it was not unusual within

the context of Sumatra where women were central to the domestic economy. See Barbara Watson Andaya, "Women and Economic Change: The Pepper Trade in Pre-Modern Southeast Asia," *Journal of Economic and Social History of the Orient* 38, 2 (1995): 172. Unfortunately there is no information available as to the origins of Sultan Selan's wife.

56. In the early 1720s, the British asked Daéng Makkullé to appoint four *datok* to represent the four districts of Bengkulu. In the event that these four *datok* were unable to settle a dispute among themselves, Daéng Makkullé was asked to intervene personally. If the case was still unable to be resolved, it was referred to the *pengeran* of Balai Buntar, and finally to the EIC. See Winter, "De familie Daing Mabella," 118.

57. Ibid., 119.

58. William Marsden, *The History of Sumatra* (London: Longman, 1811), 209.

59. Helfrich, "De Adel van Bengkoelen en Djambi," 321.

60. Andaya, *Leaves of the Same Tree*, 237.

61. Netscher, *De Nederlanders in Djohor en Siak*, 77–78; and Schulze, *Die Chroniken von Sambas und Mempawah*, 40.

62. Netscher, *De Nederlanders in Djohor en Siak*, 79.

63. Barnard, *Multiple Centres of Authority*, 93.

64. Matheson and Andaya, eds., *The Precious Gift*, 124.

65. Netscher, *De Nederlanders in Djohor en Siak*, 111.

66. Ibid., 132.

67. Barbara Watson Andaya, "The Installation of the First Sultan of Selangor in 1766," *JMBRAS* 47, 1, (1974): 55.

68. Matheson and Andaya, eds., *The Precious Gift*, 143–44; M. Yusoff, ed., *Hikayat Siak*, 175–77.

69. Barnard, *Multiple Centres of Authority*, 132.

70. Ibid., 217.

71. Matheson and Andaya, eds., *The Precious Gift*, 141.

72. M. Yusoff, ed., *Hikayat Siak*, 171, 177.

73. Barnard, *Multiple Centres of Authority*, 137.

74. Ibid.

75. M. Yusoff, ed., *Hikayat Siak*, 181–82.

76. Barnard, *Multiple Centres of Authority*, 139–43.

77. Matheson and Andaya, eds., *The Precious Gift*, 134. The exact nature of the dance is not specified in this text but it resonates with a Bugis *aruq*, a dance of allegiance that involves jumping with a kris and shouting about one's devotion.

78. Matheson and Andaya, eds., *The Precious Gift*, 143.

79. By her aunt Tengku Tih according to the *Tuhfat al-Nafis* or by a wife of Raja Ismail named Tengku Enid according to the *Hikayat Siak*. See Matheson and Andaya, eds., *The Precious Gift*, 144 and M. Yusoff, ed., *Hikayat Siak*, 175.

80. Matheson and Andaya, eds., *The Precious Gift*, 145.

81. M. Yusoff, ed., *Hikayat Siak*, 170.

82. Ibid., 169.

83. Schulze, *Die Chroniken von Sambas und Mempawah*, 45.

84. Matheson and Andaya, eds., *The Precious Gift*, 52; Schulze, *Die Chroniken von Sambas und Mempawah*, 46–47.

85. Harfield, *Bencoolen*, 81, 87; and F. C. Danvers, "The English Connection with Sumatra," *The Asiatic Quarterly Review*, 1 (1886): 420.

86. Daéng Mabéla to the Dutch in Batavia, received 3.8.1719, NA, VOC 1926: 118–19; and Kathirithamby-Wells, *The British West Sumatran Presidency*, 38–39.

87. Daéng Mabéla to the Dutch in Batavia, received 3.8.1719, NA, VOC 1926: 119.

88. Ibid., 120.

89. *Lontaraq Bilang Wajoq 1711–1732*, No. 01/MKH/4/Unhas/UP, Rol 35 No. 4.

90. Clifford Geertz, "Deep Play: Notes on the Balinese Cockfight," *Daedalus* 101, 1 (1972): 1–37.

91. Andaya, "Nature of War and Peace among the Bugis-Makassar People," *South East Asia Research*, 12, 1 (2004): 63–64.

92. Esther Velthoen, "'Wanderers, Robbers and Bad Folk': The Politics of Violence, Protection and Trade in Eastern Sulawesi 1750–1850," in *The Last Stand of Asian Autonomies Responses to Modernity in the Diverse States of Southeast Asia and Korea 1750–1900*, ed. Anthony Reid (Hampshire: Macmillan Press Ltd., 1997), 385n8.

93. Abdurrazak, *Sedjarah Wadjo*, 42; and Noorduyn, *Een Achttiende-Eeuwse Kroniek van Wadjo'*, 168–169.

94. *Lontaraq Bilang Wajoq*, 15.

95. A. S. Assegaff, *Sejarah Kerajaan Sadurangas Atau Kesultanan Pasir*, 56. See also M. Yusuf, *Awal Kerajaan Paser*, 91.

96. Noeroeddin, "Pegatan," 42.

97. According to Noeroeddin, in their customs and language resembled those used in Sulawesi two centuries previously. While his impression would have been difficult to verify, it suggests that there was a high degree of cultural preservation in Pegatan. See Noeroeddin, "Pegatan," 11.

98. Christian Pelras, "Ancestors' Blood: Genealogical Memory, Genealogical Amnesia and Hierarchy among the Bugis," in *The Potent Dead*, Henri Chambert-Loir and Anthony Reid, eds. (Honolulu: University of Hawai'i Press, 2002), 117.

99. See chapter 3, note 20.

100. Winter, "De familie Daing Mabella," 117.

101. Helfrich, "De Adel van Bengkoelen en Djambi," 317.

102. Winter, "De familie Daing Mabella," 117, 119.

103. Ibid.

104. Lewis, "A Commentative Digest of the Laws of the Natives of that part of the Coast of Sumatra," 283.

105. Ibid., 285.

106. Kathirithamby-Wells, "A Survey of the Effects of British Authority in Southwest Sumatra," 251.

107. Ibid., 256.

108. Winter, "De familie Daing Mabella," 119.

109. Noorduyn, "The Wajorese Merchants' Community in Makassar," 116.

110. D. Adham, *Salasilah Kutai*, 253–84.

111. Abdul Cadier to Gov. Sinkelaar, 2.3.1762, ANRI, Makassar 280, *Stukken handelende over den Panekischen Oorlog*, unpaginated.

112. Arung Timurung to Sautijn, 9.5.1736, NA, VOC 2409: 771.

113. Leid Cod Or 1923 VI: 15.

114. Brugman to Gov. Sinkelaar, 4.3.1762, ANRI, Makassar 280, *Stukken handelende over den Panekischen Oorlog*, unpaginated.

7: The Repatriate Arung Matoa

1. Noorduyn, *Een Achttiende-Eeuwse Kroniek van Wadjo'*, 127.
2. *Lontaraq Sukkuqna Wajoq*, 230–31.
3. Nusselein, "Beschrijving van het Landschap Pasir," 566.
4. Report of the Intje Jalani, Intje Pouassa and Intje Oeman regarding the situation in Kutai, 5.8.1728, NA, VOC 2100: 60–61.
5. Report of the commission to Banjermassin to Gov. Gen. de Haan, 14.11.1728, NA, VOC 2100: 176.
6. Coolhaas, ed., *Generale Missiven,* VIII, 76.
7. Report of the commission to Banjermassin to Gov. Gen. de Haan, 14.11.1728, NA, VOC 2100: 176–177.
8. Daily register kept by Arent van Broijel et al on their commission to Banjermassin, 5.10.1729, NA, VOC 2133: 316.
9. Van Broijel and de Broun to Gov. Gen. de Haan, 25.7.1729, NA, VOC 2133: 272.
10. Der Snippe to Gov. Gen. Durven, 8.4.1730, NA, VOC 2163: 2–3. Whereas To Assa and La Maddukelleng were not able to install themselves in Banjarmassin, their rival To Passarai was. The brother of Arumponé La Patauq and thus the uncle of Arumponé Batari Toja, To Passarai fled his homeland around 1695 because of a dispute with Arung Mampu over a woman. After a six-month stay at Pulau Laut, he and his following of about three hundred people went to Banjar. They spent two years there mining diamonds. His business was lucrative to support him and his following and to arouse the jealousy of his brother La Patauq. Fearing for his life, To Passarai proceeded further east. See Legal Examination of Prince To Passarai, 27.6.1735, NA, VOC 2327: 1250–51.
11. *Lontaraq Sukkuqna Wajoq*, 236. Zainal Abidin also writes about this missive. He writes that La Saléwangeng sent a secret letter to La Maddukelleng in 1735 via La Dallé Puanna Pabbola. La Saléwangeng asked La Maddukelleng to return home and promised to request pardon from the Arumponé on his behalf. But then in the same paragraph, Zainal Abidin writes that the Arumponé did not want to pardon La Maddukelleng when she did anyway, albeit grudgingly. He goes on to say that La Saléwangeng had already succeeded in purchasing arms from the British, and assembling 2,000 carbines and tens of cannons and wanted to liberate Wajoq from the oppression of the Bonéans. See Zainal Abidin and Alam, "La Maddukelleng, Pahlawan jang tak kenal menjerah," 1, 9: 31. H. A. Demang Kedaton's *A Short History of the Arrival of the Bugis in Samarinda Seberang* also states that a messenger from Wajoq came to Kalimantan to ask La Maddukelleng to return and rule Wajoq.
12. *Lontaraq Sukkuqna Wajoq*, 236–37.
13. One *lontaraq* specifies that La Maddukelleng's followers were not Wajorese, and would most likely have been local people from Pasir. See Leid Cod Or 1923 VI: 11.
14. Matthes, *Over de Wadjorezen met hun Handels- en Scheepswetboek*, 25.
15. *Lontaraq Sukkuqna Wajoq*, 241.
16. Sautijn to Smout, 14.10.1737, NA, VOC 2409: 192.
17. Bugis *lontaraq* also record La Maddukelleng attacking Sabutung. See Leid Cod Or 1923 VI: 10.
18. Sautijn to Council, 29.7.1736, NA, VOC 2381: 34–35.
19. Sautijn to Council, 29.7.1736, NA, VOC 2381: 53.
20. Arung Taq was a messenger of the reigning Arung Matoa La Saléwangeng. See Zainal Abidin and Alam, "La Maddukelleng, Pahlawan jang tak kenal menjerah," 1, 10: 28.

21. Leid Cod Or 1923 VI: 10.

22. Noorduyn, *Een Achttiende-Eeuwse Kroniek van Wadjo'*, 127.

23. Bloom to Patras, 24.2.1736, ANRI, Makassar 282a: 2c-2d.

24. Noorduyn, *Een Achttiende-Eeuwse Kroniek van Wadjo'*, 127–28.

25. Zainal Abidin and Alam, La Maddukelleng, "Pahlawan jang tak kenal menjerah," 1, 11: 29.

26. Noorduyn, *Een Achttiende-Eeuwse Kroniek van Wadjo'*, 128.

27. Ibid., 282–83.

28. 960 according to Zainal Abidin and Alam, "La Maddukelleng, Pahlawan jang tak kenal menjerah," 1, 11: 31. In contrast to these accounts, the Leid Cod Or 1923 VI does not mention La Maddukelleng attracting a following as he proceeded to trial. On the contrary, it states that he was refused entrance to Tosora because Wajoq was on Boné's side. This is in accordance with its exaggeration of La Maddukelleng's role in winning over Wajoq which is a distinguishing characteristic of this *lontaraq*. See Leid Cod Or 1923 VI: 12.

29. J. Noorduyn, "Arung Singkang (1700–1765): How the Victory of Wadjo' Began," *Indonesia* 13 (1972).

30. Ms. No. 126 of Nederlands Bijbel Genootschap's collection in the Leiden University library.

31. Noorduyn, "Arung Singkang," 66–67. For alternative lists of crimes and La Maddukelleng's replies to his accusers, see *Lontarak Wajoq*, III and Leid Cod Or 1923 VI: 12. That La Maddukelleng attacked To Passarai in the Tobunio river as revenge for having attacked Daéng Matekko in Selangor is attested to in Dutch records. See Legal examination of Prince To Passarai, 27.6.1735, NA, VOC 2327: 1250–51, 1256; Memorie van Sautijn aan Smout, Makassar, 14.10.1737, NA, VOC 2409: 192.

32. Zainal Abidin and Alam, "La Maddukelleng, Pahlawan jang tak kenal menjerah," 1, 12: 27.

33. Noorduyn, *Een Achttiende-Eeuwse Kroniek van Wadjo'*, 129; Noorduyn, "Arung Singkang," 64. Whereas some *lontaraq* state that the people of Pénéki asked La Maddukelleng to be their ruler and that the Bonéans left voluntarily, Dutch records suggest that La Maddukelleng may have captured Pénéki by force. See Leid Cod Or 1923 VI: 12–13; and Police Council Resolution, Makassar, 30 August, 1737, NA, VOC 2409: 157.

34. *Lontarak Wajo*, III: 372.

35. *Lontarak Wajo*, III: 380–88.

36. Noorduyn, *Een Achttiende-Eeuwse Kroniek van Wadjo'*, 129.

37. Steinmetz to Sautijn, 13.10.1736, NA, VOC 2409: 677–96.

38. Steinmetz to Sautijn, 26.10.1736, NA, VOC 2409: 718.

39. Sautijn to Smout, Makassar, 14.10.1737, NA, VOC 2409: 196–97.

40. Ibid., 176, 200–201.

41. Arung Timurung to Sautijn, 9.5.1736, NA, VOC 2409: 771.

42. Leid Cod Or 1923 VI: 15.

43. While more succinct, Leid Cod Or 1923 VI also recounts how La Saléwangeng resigned because he did not consider himself fit to wage war. See folio 14.

44. Zainal Abidin and Alam, "La Maddukelleng, Pahlawan jang tak kenal menjerah," 29. Leid Cod Or 1923 VI: 14, says 2 Rajab 1148 = November 18, 1735.

45. *Lontarak Wajo*, III: 381–82.

46. Thereafter he became known as La Essoé ri Pattujunna, òr Salaienngé Pattu junna. See *Lontarak Wajo*, III: 382.

47. Datu Baringeng to Sautijn, Wednesday 8 Saban 1736, NA, VOC 2409: 748–49.

48. *Lontarak Wajo*, III: 383.

49. *Lontarak Wajo*, III: 382. Zainal Abidin also lists Luwuq. See Zainal Abidin and Alam, "La Maddukelleng, Pahlawan jang tak kenal menjerah," 30.

50. Resolutions from Fort Rotterdam, Makassar, 19.3.1737, NA, VOC 2409: 300–01. This information was reported by the Makkedangng Tana.

51. Leid Cod Or 1923 VI: 14–16. Some of these attacks, such as the 1736 attack on Sidénréng, are confirmed in Dutch records. (Arung Timurung to Sautijn et al, 21 Ramadan, 1736, NA, VOC 2409: 765.)

52. *Lontarak Wajo*, III: 385–88.

53. *Lontarak Wajo*, III: 390–92; Leid Cod Or 1923 VI: 17–19; Noorduyn, *Een Achttiende-Eeuwse Kroniek van Wadjo'*, 130.

54. Leid Cod Or 1923 VI: 21–22.

55. Terms of peace of 11 June 1737 are found in Smout to Loten, Makassar, 1.6.1744, NA, VOC 2628: 253.

56. Leid Cod Or 1923 VI: 24; Noorduyn, *Een Achttiende-Eeuwse Kroniek van Wadjo'*, 131.

57. Plans for expelling the Dutch were delayed by a political crisis in Boné which is described in Noorduyn, "Arung Singkang," 63; John Splinter Stavorinus, *Voyages to the East Indies*, (London: G. G. and J. Robinson, Paternoster-Row, 1798), 221; and Noorduyn, *Een Achttiende-Eeuwse Kroniek van Wadjo'*, 132. La Maddukelleng's influence in this crisis make it clear that Soppéng and Boné were under his sway. Had it not been for the pocket of Arumponé Batari Toja's supporters in Makassar, he would have had effective political control over the Tellumpocco. His inability to control Batari Toja's supporters, however, was crucial and ultimately ruined his plan to expel the Dutch.

58. In 1737 the Makkedangng Tana reported that the Makassarese had plans to move against the Dutch. See Resolutions from Fort Rotterdam, Makassar, 19.3.1737, NA, VOC 2409: 302–03.

59. Smout to Valckenier, 26.10.1738, NA, VOC 2466: 3.

60. Extract from the Daily Register kept at Casteel Rotterdam, 7.10.1738, NA, VOC 2466: 12–14.

61. Extract from the Daily Register kept at Casteel Rotterdam, 25.10.1738, NA, VOC 2466: 15–18.

62. Smout to Valckenier, NA, VOC 2466: 6.

63. Smout's Instructions for Figera and Vol for their trip to Wajoq, Makassar, 5.11.1738, NA, VOC 2466: 18–21.

64. Arung Matoa to Honorable Gentleman, 15.11.1738, NA, VOC 2466: 45.

65. Report of Figera and Vol concerning their expedition to Wajoq, 20.11.1738, NA, VOC 2466: 43–44.

66. Relation of the sailor Lambregts concerning his imprisonment by the enemy, 27.11.1738, NA, VOC 2466: 49–52.

67. *Lontarak Wajo*, III: 396–97.

68. Leid Cod Or 1923 VI: 30.

69. Ibid., 23.

70. *Lontarak Wajo*, III: 399.

71. Leid Cod Or 1923 VI: 31–32.

72. *Lontarak Wajo*, III: 400–01; Noorduyn, *Een Achttiende-Eeuwse Kroniek van Wadjo'*, 134.

73. Leid Cod Or 1923 VI: 32–33.

74. Noorduyn, *Een Achttiende-Eeuwse Kroniek van Wadjo'*, 135.

75. Leid Cod Or 1923 VI: 33.

76. Noorduyn, *Een Achttiende-Eeuwse Kroniek van Wadjo'*, 131.

77. Ibid., 135. Leid Cod Or 1923 VI: 34–35.

78. *Lontarak Wajo*, III: 403, provides an interesting encounter between a Wajorese messenger representing La Maddukelleng and Boné. When La Maddukelleng perceives that the Arumponé and Karaéng Talloq are joining forces against Gowa, he sends a message to the Arumponé saying, "Greetings to my child Arumponé. I truly know the words of the Tellempocco from the meeting at Cenrana, and I know that the Tellumpocco is ruined because of the arrival of the Dutch. Before they arrived we helped each other, and did not destroy each other's glory. That is why I want to drive them out of Makassar." To this, the Arumponé replied that Arung Palakka had gone to Java and asked the Dutch to come here because of the bad things that Gowa was doing (i.e. treating its subjected lands harshly.)

79. Leid Cod Or 1923 VI: 26 and KITLV Or. 545 No. 219 Stukken uit de Japanse tijd, h Hikajat Pendek District-Wadjo, 1.

80. *Lontarak Wajo*, III: 403. There is, however, evidence that La Maddukelleng also used cannons mounted on ships.

81. Leid Cod Or 1923 VI: 34.

82. *Lontarak Wajo*, III: 405.

83. Noorduyn, *Een Achttiende-Eeuwse Kroniek van Wadjo'*, 294–97.

84. Noorduyn's version says that her name was Wé Togeq. See Noorduyn, *Een Achttiende-Eeuwse Kroniek van Wadjo'*, 296–97.

85. *Lontarak Wajo*, III: 406–07.

86. Leid Cod Or 1923 VI: 36; Matthes, *Over de Wadjorezen met hun Handels- en Scheepswetboek*, 26.

87. Andaya, *The Heritage of Arung Palakka*, 73.

88. The Wajorese attempts to pay redemption money are not recorded in Smout's report. He does, however, write about this desire to resolve the conflict peacefully.

89. Leid Cod Or 1923 VI: 36.

90. Smout to Loten, 1.6.1744, NA, VOC 2628: 250; Matthes, *Over de Wadjorezen met hun Handels- en Scheepswetboek*, 26.

91. Noorduyn, *Een Achttiende-Eeuwse Kroniek van Wadjo'*, 136, 296–97.

92. *Lontarak Wajo*, III: 407–08, Noorduyn, *Een Achttiende-Eeuwse Kroniek van Wadjo'*, 296–99.

93. Leid Cod Or 1923 VI: 37.

94. Smout to Loten, 1.6.1744, NA, VOC 2628: 251.

95. Leid Cod Or 1923 VI: 37–38

96. Leid Cod Or 1923 VI: 37.

97. Leid Cod Or 1923 VI: 37–39; Smout to Loten, 1.6.1744, NA, VOC 2628: 252.

98. Smout to Loten, 1.6.1744, NA, VOC 2628: 255–257.

99. Matthes, *Over de Wadjorezen met hun Handels- en Scheepswetboek*, 27.

100. Noorduyn, *Een Achttiende-Eeuwse Kroniek van Wadjo'*, 137.

101. That such a reference is made in a contemporary source, as opposed to just in the *lontaraq* which were written and recopied later lends credence to the antiquity and historical validity of the Wajorese motto.

102. Smout to Loten, 1.6.1744, NA, VOC 2628: 258.

103. Leid Cod Or 1923 VI: 40.

104. Heeres and Stapel, eds., *Corpus Diplomaticum Neerlando-Indicum*, V, 314–16.

105. Noorduyn, *Een Achttiende-Eeuwse Kroniek van Wadjo'*, 137–38.

106. Leid Cod Or 1923 VI: 42; Noorduyn, *Een Achttiende-Eeuwse Kroniek van Wadjo'*, 138.

107. Noorduyn, *Een Achttiende-Eeuwse Kroniek van Wadjo'*, 138.

108. *Lontarak Wajo*, III: 431.

109. Not enough council members were available to make a decision on such short notice. Those that were present decided to try to abide by La Maddukelleng's wishes but the Addatuang insisted that this was against adat.

110. *Lontarak Wajo*, III: 436–37 and 442–43. Different *lontaraq* provide different versions of how this conflict was resolved. According to Noorduyn's published chronicle, the Pillaq went to Boné and asked Boné to plea his case with Wajoq. Boné did, but the Arung Matoa would not pardon Pillaq La Gauq and the conflict lasted for four years, with both sides standing ready to fight. Finally there was a month of negotiations and peace was concluded. See Noorduyn, *Een Achttiende-Eeuwse Kroniek van Wadjo'*, 306–09.

111. *Lontarak Wajo*, III: 448–49.

112. *Bunga Rampai Lontaraq*, No. 01/MKH/27/Unhas/UP Rol 34, No. 27: 124–25.

113. Abdurrazak, *Sedjarah Wadjo*, 69–70; Noorduyn, *Een Achttiende-Eeuwse Kroniek van Wadjo'*, 139–40.

114. *Lontarak Wajo*, III: 455.

115. R. Blok, *History of the Island of Celebes* (Calcutta: Calcutta Gazette Press, 1817), 3–7.

116. *Lontarak Wajo*, III: 457.

117. Sinkelaar to Boelen, 28.2.1767, NA, VOC 3216: 39.

118. Instructions for Daéng Manjareekij, 21.2.1763, ANRI, Makassar 280, *Stukken handelende over den Panekischen Oorlog*, unpaginated.

119. For example, at one point the Bonéans argue that they could not attack Pénéki because the Dutch didn't deliver the straw they had promised, while there was straw readily available.

120. Brugman to Sinkelaar, 4.3.1762, ANRI, Makassar 280, *Stukken handelende over den Panekischen Oorlog*, unpaginated.

121. *Lontarak Wajo*, III: 457.

122. Brugman to Sinkelaar, 4.3.1762, ANRI, Makassar 280, *Stukken handelende over den Panekischen Oorlog*, unpaginated.

123. *Lontarak Wajo*, III: 457–59.

124. *Lontarak Wajo*, III: 460–61.

125. Letter from the ruler of Boné dated October, 1766, ANRI, Makassar 280, *Stukken handelende over den Panekischen Oorlog*, unpaginated.

126. *Lontaraq Sukkuqna Wajoq*, 327–28. There is reason to suspect that La Maddukelleng died five months after this meeting of the Tellumpocco but there may have been another meeting of the Tellumpocco at which his crimes were also discussed and from which five months are counted.

127. *Lontarak Wajo*, III: 451.

128. Sources are contradictory, sometimes even self-contradictory, as to whether or not la Maddukelleng was recalled or returned to Sulawesi on his own initiative.

129. P. J. Kooreman, "De feitelijke toestand in het Gouvernements-gebied van Celebes en Onderhoorigheden," *De Indische Gids*, 5, II (1883): 145–46.

8: The Wajorese in Comparative Perspective

1. B. F. Matthes, "Eenige opmerkingen omtrent en naar anleiding van dat gedeelte van Dr. J. J. de Hollander's Handleiding bij de Beoefening der Land- en Volkenkunde van Nederlandsch Oost-Indië, hetwelk handelt over het Gouvernement van Celebes en Onderhoorigheden," *BKI*, 19 (1872): 18.

2. Andaya, *Leave of the Same Tree*, 94. See also the classic work on Minangkabau migration, Tsuyoshi Kato, *Matriliny and Migration: Evolving Minangkabau Traditions in Indonesia* (Ithaca: Cornell University Press, 1982).

3. Leiden: Brill, 2002.

4. Trivellato, *The Familiarity of Strangers*, 40–42.

Bibliography

Archival Sources

The archival sources used for this study are from numerous collections. Bugis *lontaraq* from the microfilm collection assembled by a team from Hasanuddin University were viewed at ANRI Makassar, the Royal Netherlands Institute of Southeast Asian and Caribbean Studies (KITLV) in Leiden, and in Honolulu on inter-library loan from the Center for Research Libraries in Chicago. These sources are cited using the project's name, *Proyek Naskah Unhas*. Use was also made of *lontaraq* from the Dutch Bible Society's collection housed at the Leiden University Library and the Manuscript Collection at KITLV. United Dutch East India Company archives were found in both The Hague and Jakarta. Those from the National Archives of the Netherlands in The Hague are cited as VOC (*Vereenigde Oost-Indische Compagnie*) and those from the National Archives of Indonesia in Jakarta are cited as ANRI (Arsip Negara Republik Indonesia). English archival sources from the India Office Library in London were viewed in Kuala Lumpur at the University Malaya library and in Honolulu on inter-library loan from Chicago. Documents from the (English) Sumatra Factory Records are cited as SFR.

Printed Sources

Abdurrazak Daeng Patunru. *Sedjarah Wadjo.* Makassar: Jajasan Kebudajaan Sulawesi Selatan dan Tenggara, 1965.

Acciaioli, Greg. "Distinguishing Hierarchy and Precedence: Comparing Status Distinctions in South Asia and the Austronesian World, with special reference to South Sulawesi," in *Precedence: Social Differentiation in the Austronesian World*, ed. Michael P. Vischer, (Canberra: ANU ePress, 2009), 51–90.

D. Adham. *Salasilah Kutai.* Jakarta: Departemen Pendidikan dan Kebudayaan, 1981.

Alfian, T. Ibrahim et al., eds. *Dari Babad dan Hikayat sampai Sejarah Kritis*. Yogyakarta: Gadjah Mada University Press, 1987.

Aliamir. "Tinjuan Historis Politik Pemerintahan Kerajaan Puang Rimaggalatung di Wajo." Master's thesis. Universitas Hasanuddin, Makassar, 1993.

Ammarell, Gene. *Bugis Navigation.* New Haven: Yale Southeast Asian Studies, 1999.

———. "Bugis Migration and Modes of Adaptation to Local Situations." *Ethnology* 41, 1 (2002): 51–67.

Andaya, Barbara Watson. "The Installation of the First Sultan of Selangor in 1766." *JMBRAS* 47, 1 (1974): 41–57.

———. *To Live as Brothers: Southeast Sumatra in the Seventeenth and Eighteenth Centuries.* Honolulu: University of Hawai'i Press, 1993.

———. "Women and Economic Change: The Pepper Trade in Pre-Modern Southeast Asia." *Journal of Economic and Social History of the Orient* 38, 2 (1995): 164–90.

———. *Other Pasts: Women, Gender and History in Early Modern Southeast Asia.* Honolulu: Center for Southeast Asian Studies, 2000.

————. "Gender, Islam and the Bugis Diaspora in Nineteenth- and Twentieth-Century Riau." *Sari* 21 (2003): 77–108.

————. *The Flaming Womb: Repositioning Women in Early Modern Southeast Asia*. Honolulu: University of Hawai'i Press, 2006.

————, and Leonard Y. Andaya. *A History of Malaysia*. London: Macmillan Press Ltd., 1982.

Andaya, Leonard Y. *The Kingdom of Johor 1641–1728*. Kuala Lumpur: Oxford University Press, 1975.

————. "Treaty Conceptions and Misconceptions: A Case Study from South Sulawesi." *BKI*, 134 (1978): 275–95.

————. *The Heritage of Arung Palakka: A History of South Sulawesi (Celebes) in the Seventeenth Century*. Den Haag: Martinus Nijhoff, 1981.

————. "Local Trade Networks in Maluku in the 16th, 17th and 18th Centuries." *Cakalele* 2, 2 (1991): 71–96.

————. *The World of Maluku: Eastern Indonesia in the Early Modern Period*. Honolulu: University of Hawai'i Press, 1993.

————. "The Bugis-Makassar Diasporas." *JMBRAS* 68 (1995): 119–38.

————. "Bugis Diaspora, Identity, and Islam in the Malay World." Paper presented at the conference, "The Bugis Diaspora and Islamic Dissemination in the 20th Century Malay-Indonesian Archipelago," Makassar, June 6–8, 2003.

————. "Nature of war and peace among the Bugis-Makassar people." *South East Asia Research* 12, 1 (2004): 53–80.

————. *Leaves of the Same Tree: Trade and Ethnicity in the Straits of Melaka*. Honolulu: University of Hawai'i Press, 2008.

Anderson, Benedict. *Imagined Communities: Reflections on the Origins and Spread of Nationalism*. London: Verso, 1991.

Anonymous. "Verslag van het Verhandelde tot Regeling der Betrekkingen tusschen de Maleische en Boeginesche Nederzettingen aan de Koetei-Rivier onder den Vorigen Sultan van Koetei,—vertaald uit het Oorspronkelijke Maleisch." *TGB* 24 (1877).

Arbel, Benjamin. *Trading Nations: Jews and Venetians in the Early Modern Eastern Mediterranean*. Leiden: E. J. Brill, 1995.

Arena Wati, ed. *Silsilah Melayu dan Bugis*. Kuala Lumpur: Penerbitan Pustaka Antara, 1973.

Armstrong, John A. "Mobilized and Proletarian Diasporas." *The American Political Science Review* 70, 2 (1976): 393–408.

Aslanian, Sebouh David. *From the Indian Ocean to the Mediterranean: The Global Trade Networks of Armenian Merchants from New Julfa*. Berkeley: University of California Press, 2011.

Assegaff, A. S. *Sejarah Kerajaan Sadurangas Atau Kesultanan Pasir*. [Tanah Grogot]: Pemerintah Daerah Kabupaten Daerah Tingkat II Pasir, 1982.

Aswani, Shankar, and Graves, Michael W. "The Tongan Maritime Expansion: A Case in the Evolutionary Ecology of Social Complexity." *Asian Perspectives* 32, 2 (1998): 135–64.

Baghdiantz-McCabe, Ina. *The Shah's Silk for Europe's Silver: The Eurasian Silk Trade of the Julfan Armenians in Safavid Iran and India (1590–1750)*. Atlanta: Scholar's Press, 1999.

————, Gelina Harlaftis and Ioanna Pepelasis Minoglou, eds. *Diaspora Entrepreneurial Networks: Four Centuries of History*. New York: Berg, 2005.

Ball, John. *Indonesian Legal History 1602–1848.* Sydney: Oughtershaw, 1982.
———. *Indonesian Legal History: British West Sumatra 1685–1825.* Sydney: Oughtershaw, 1984.
Bastin, John. *The British in West Sumatra (1695–1825): A Selection of Documents, Mainly from the East India Company Records Preserved in the India Office Library, Commonwealth Relations Office, London.* Kuala Lumpur: University of Malaya Press, 1965.
Barnard, Timothy P. *Multiple Centres of Authority: Society and Environment in Siak and Eastern Sumatra, 1674–1827.* Leiden: KITLV Press, 2003.
Bell, David A. *The Cult of the Nation in France: Inventing Nationalism, 1680–1800.* Cambridge: Harvard University Press, 2001.
Berthomiere, William, and Christine Chivallon, eds. *Les diasporas dans le monde contemporain.* Paris: Karthala, 2006.
Bertling, C.T. "Een Hypothese omtrent de Sociale Structuur van Zuid-Celebes in Verband met de Stichtingsmythe van Wadjo." *BKI* 98 (1939): 489–95.
Bienstock, Gregory. *The Struggle for the Pacific.* New York: Macmillan, 1937.
Blok, R. *History of the Island of Celebes.* Calcutta: Calcutta Gazette Press, 1817.
Boxer, C. R. "War and Trade in the Indian Ocean and the South China Sea, 1600–1650." *The Great Circle, Journal of the Australian Association for Maritime History* 1, 2 (1979):. 3–17. As reprinted in Boxer, C. R., *Portuguese Conquest and Commerce in Southern Asia, 1500–1750.* London: Variorum Reprints, 1985.
Bonnemaison, Joel. "The Tree and the Canoe: Roots and Mobility in Vanuatu Societies." *Pacific Viewpoint* 26, 1 (1985): 30–62.
Braginsky, Vladmir. *The Heritage of Traditional Malay Literature: A Historical Survey of Genres, Writings and Literary Views.* Leiden: KITLV Press, 2004.
Broeze, Frank, ed. *Brides of the Sea: Port Cities of Asia from the 16th-20th Centuries.* Kensington: New South Wales University Press, 1989.
Bulbeck, Francis David. "A Tale of Two Kingdoms: The Historical Archaeology of Gowa and Tallok, South Sulawesi, Indonesia." PhD diss., Australian National University, Canberra, March 1992.
———. "The Landscape of the Makassar War." *Canberra Anthropology* 13, 1 (1990): 78–99.
———. Review of *A Chain of Kings: The Makassarese Chronicles of Gowa and Talloq* by William P. Cummings, ed. and trans., *Review of Indonesian and Malaysian Affairs* 42, 1 (2008): 207–20.
———, and Caldwell, Ian. *Land of Iron: The Historical Archaeology of Luwu and the Cenrana Valley.* Hull and Canberra: Center for South-East Asian Studies and School of Archaeology and Anthropology, 2000.
Brubaker, Rogers. "The 'Diaspora' Diaspora." *Ethnic and Racial Studies* 28, 1 (2005): 1–19.
Caldwell, Ian. "South Sulawesi A.D. 1300–1600: Ten Bugis Texts." PhD diss., Australian National University, Canberra, April, 1988.
———. "Power, State and Society Among the Pre-Islamic Bugis." *BKI* 151, 3 (1995): 394–421.
———. "The Myth of the Exemplary Centre: Shelly Errington's Meaning and Power in a Southeast Asian Realm." *JSEAS* 22, 1 (1991):109–18.
Caron, Leonardus Johannes Jacobus. *Het Handels- en Zeerecht in de Adatrechtsregelen van Rechtskring Zuid-Celebes.* Bussum: Van Dishoek, 1937.

Cense, A. A. "Eenige aantekeningen over Makassaars-Boeginese geschiedschrijving." *BKI* 107 (1951): 42–60.

———. "Makassaars-Boeginese Prauwvaart op Noord-Australië." *BKI* 108 (1952): 248–64.

———. "Old Buginese and Macassarese Diaries." *BKI* 122, 4 (1966): 416–28.

Chabot, H. Th. *Kinship, Status and Gender in South Celebes.* Leiden: KITLV Press, 1996.

Chambert-Loir, Henri, and Anthony Reid. *The Potent Dead.* Honolulu: University of Hawai'i Press, 2002.

Chappell, David A. "Transnationalism in Central Oceanian Politics: A Dialectic of Diasporas and Nationhood?" *The Journal of the Polynesian Society* 108, 3 (1999): 277–303.

Coedes, G. *The Indianized States of Southeast Asia.* Honolulu: University of Hawai'i Press, 1968.

Cohen, Abner. "Cultural Strategies in the Organization of Trading Diaspora." In *The Development of Indigenous Trade and Markets in West Africa*, edited by Claude Meillassoux. Oxford: Oxford University Press, 1971.

Cohen, Robin. *Global Diasporas: An Introduction.* Seattle: University of Washington Press, 1997.

Conrad, Joseph. *The Rescue.* London: Dent, 1920.

Coolhaas, W. Ph., ed. *Generale Missiven van Gouverneurs-Generaal en Raden van Heeren XVII der Verenigde Oostindische Compagnie*, Den Haag: Martinus Nijhoff, 1960–. . .

Cooper, Frederick, ed. *Colonialism in Question: Theory, Knowledge, History.* Berkeley and Los Angeles: the University of California Press, 2005.

Crawfurd, John. *A Descriptive Dictionary of the Indian Islands and Adjacent Countries.* London: Bradbury & Evans, 1856.

Cummings, William. "The Melaka Malay Diaspora in Makassar, c. 1500–1669." *JMBRAS* 71, 1 (1998): 106–21.

———. "'Only One People but Two Rulers': Hiding the Past in Seventeenth-Century Makasarese Chronicles," *BKI* 155 (1999): 97–120.

———. *Making Blood White: Historical Transformations in Early Modern Makassar.* Honolulu: University of Hawai'i Press, 2002.

———. *A Chain of Kings: The Makassarese Chronicles of Gowa and Talloq.* Leiden: KITLV Press, 2007.

Curtin, Philip D. *Cross-cultural Trade in World History.* Cambridge: Cambridge University Press, 1984.

Danvers, F. C. "The English Connection with Sumatra." *The Asiatic Quarterly Review* 1 (1886): 410–31.

Davies, Sharyn Graham. *Gender Diversity in Indonesia; Sexuality, Islam and Queer Selves.* Oxon and New York: Routledge, 2010.

Day, Tony. *Fluid Iron: State Formation in Southeast Asia.* Honolulu: University of Hawai'i Press, 2002.

De Haan, F. *Oud Batavia.* Batavia: G. Kolff, 1922.

Dobbin, Christine. *Islamic Revivalism in a Changing Peasant Economy, Central Sumatra, 1784–1847.* London and Malmö: Curzon Press, 1983.

Drakard, Jane. *A Malay Frontier Unity and Duality in a Sumatran Kingdom.* Ithaca: Southeast Asia Program, 1990.

————. *A Kingdom of Words: Language and Power in Sumatra.* Shah Alam: Oxford University Press, 1999.

Druce, Stephen C. *The Lands West of the Lakes: A History of the Ajattappareng Kingdoms of South Sulawesi 1200 to 1600 CE.* Leiden: KITLV Press, 2009.

Dufoix, Stéphane. "Généalogies d'un lieu commun: 'diaspora' et sciences sociales." *Actes de l'histoire de l'immigration* 2, (2003): http://barthes.ens.fr/clio/revues/AHI/articles/preprints/duf.html.

————. *Diasporas.* Berkeley and Los Angeles: University of California Press, 2008.

————. *La Dispersion: Une Historie des Usages du Mot* Diaspora. Paris: Editions Amsterdam, 2011.

Eriksen, Thomas Hyland. *Ethnicity and Nationalism: Anthropological Perspectives.* London: Pluto Press, 1993.

Errington, Shelly. *Meaning and Power in a Southeast Asian Realm.* Princeton: Princeton University Press, 1989.

Fagan, Brian M. *People of the Earth: An Introduction to World Prehistory.* New York: HarperCollins, 1999.

Franklin, Cynthia et al., eds. *Navigating Islands and Continents: Conversations and Contestations in and around the Pacific.* Honolulu: College of Languages, Linguistics and Literature, University of Hawai'i and the East-West Center, 2000.

Fox, James J. and Sather, Clifford, eds. *Origins, Ancestry and Alliance: Explorations in Austronesian Ethnography.* Canberra: Research School of Pacific and Asian Studies, 1996.

Geertz, Clifford. "Deep Play: Notes on the Balinese Cockfight." *Daedalus* 101, 1 (1972): 1–37.

————. *Negara: The Theater State in Nineteenth-Century Bali.* Princeton: Princeton University Press, 1980.

Gellner, Ernest. *Nations and Nationalism.* Ithaca: Cornell University Press, 1983.

Gershon, Ilana. "Viewing Diasporas from the Pacific: What Pacific Ethnographies Offer Pacific Diaspora Studies." *The Contemporary Pacific* 19, 2 (2007): 474–502.

Hageman, J. "Geschiedkundige aanteekeningen omtrent zuidelijk Borneo." *TNI* 23, 1 (1861): 199–233.

Hamonic, Gilbert. *Le langage des dieux: cultes et pouvoirs pre-Islamiques en pays Bugis, Célèbes-Sud, Indonésie.* Paris: Centre National de la Recherche Scientifique, 1987.

————. "Autour de l'identité bugis." *Aséanie* 23 (2009): 145–80.

Harfield, Alan. *Bencoolen: A History of the Honourable East India Company's Garrison on the West Coast of Sumatra (1685–1825).* Hampshire: A & J Partnership, 1995.

Hau'ofa, Epeli. "Our Sea of Islands." *The Contemporary Pacific* 6, 1 (1994): 147–61.

Healey, Christopher. "Tribes and States in 'Pre-Colonial' Borneo: Structural Contradictions and the Generation of Piracy." *Social Analysis* 18 (1985): 3–39.

Helfrich, O. L. *Adatrechtbundels, XXII: Gemengd,* 's-Gravenhage: Martinus Nijhoff, 1923.

Heeres, J. E. and Stapel, F. W., eds. *Corpus Diplomaticum Neerlando-Indicum. Verzameling van Politieke contracten en verdere Verdragen door de Nederlanders in het Oosten gesloten, van Privilegebrieven, aan hen verleend, enz.* The Hague: Martinus Nijhoff, 1907–1955.

Ho, Engseng. *The Graves of Tarim: Genealogy and Mobility across the Indian Ocean.* Berkeley: University of California Press, 2006.

Hollinger, David A. *Postethnic American: Beyond Multiculturalism*. New York: Basic Books, 1995.

Holt, Claire, ed. *Culture and Politics in Indonesia*. Ithaca: Cornell University Press, 1972.

Israel, Jonathan. *European Jewry in the Age of Mercantilism 1550–1750*. Oxford: Clarendon Press, 1989.

——. *Diasporas within a Diaspora: Jews, Crypto-Jews and the World Maritime Empires* (1540–1740). Leiden: Brill, 2002.

Kagan, Richard L. and Philip D. Morgan. *Atlantic Diasporas: Jews, Conversos, and Crypto-Jews in the Age of Mercantilism, 1500–1800*. Baltimore: The Johns Hopkins University Press, 2009.

Kathirithamby-Wells, J. "A Survey of the Effects of British Authority in Southwest Sumatra (1685–1824)." *BKI* 129 (1973): 283–68.

——. "The Inderapura Sultanate: The Foundations of its Rise and Decline, from the Sixteenth to the Eighteenth Centuries." *Indonesia* 21 (1976): 64–84.

——. *The British West Sumatran Presidency 1760–1785 Problems of Early Colonial Enterprise*. Kuala Lumpur: Penerbit Universiti Malaya, 1977.

——and Muhammad Yusoff Hashim. *The Syair Mukomuko: Some Historical Aspects of a Nineteenth Century Sumatran Court Chronicle*. Kuala Lumpur: Art Printing Works Sdn. Bhd., 1985.

——and Villiers, John, eds. *The Southeast Asian Port and Polity: Rise and Demise*. Singapore: Singapore University Press, 1990.

Kato, Tsuyoshi. *Matriliny and Migration: Evolving Minangkabau Traditions in Indonesia*. Ithaca: Cornell University Press, 1982.

Kawashima, Midori, Kazuhiro Arai, and Hiroyuki Yamamoto, eds. *Proceedings on the Symposium on Bangsa and Umma: A Comparative Study of People-grouping Concepts in the Islamic Areas of Southeast Asia*. Tokyo: Institute of Asian Cultures, Sophia University, 2007.

Kelly, David and Reid, Anthony, eds. *Asian Freedoms: The Idea of Freedom in East and Southeast Asia*. Cambridge: Cambridge University Press, 1998.

Khoo Kay Kim. "Raja Lulu/Sultan Salehuddin: The Founding of the Selangor Dynasty." *JMBRAS* 58 (1985): 1–13.

Kiefer, Thomas M. *The Tausug: Violence and Law in a Muslim Society*. Prospect Heights: Waveland Press, Inc., 1972.

King, Victor T. *The Peoples of Borneo*. Oxford: Blackwell, 1993.

Knaap, Gerrit, and Heather Sutherland. *Monsoon Traders: Ships, Skippers and Commodities in Eighteenth-Century Makassar*. Leiden: KITLV Press, 2004.

Kooreman, P. J. "De feitelijke toestand in het Gouvernements-gebied van Celebes en Onderhoorigheden," *De Indische Gids*, 5-I: 171–204, 358–84, 482–98, 637–55, 5-II: 135–69, 346–58.

Koolhof, Sirtjo. "The 'La Galigo': A Bugis Encyclopedia and its Growth." *BKI* 155, 3: 363–87.

Kumar, Ann and McGlynn, John H., eds. *Illuminations: The Writing Traditions of Indonesia*. New York and Tokyo: Weatherhill, Inc., 1996.

La Side. "Serba-serbi tentang Amanna Gappa dan Penangkatan Matowa Wadjo di Makasar dalam abad ke-17." *Bingkisan* 2, 8, (1969):11–28.

Le Roux, C. C. F. M. "Boegineesche Zeekaarten van den Indischen Archipel." *Tijdschrift van het Aardrijkskundige Genootschap* 52 (1935): 687–714.

Levy, Scott C. *The Indian Diaspora in Central Asia and its Trade, 1550–1900.* Leiden: Brill, 2001.

Lewis, Dianne. *Jan Compagnie in the Straits of Malacca, 1641–1795.* Athens, OH: Ohio University Center for International Studies, 1995.

Lewis, H. R. "A Commentative Digest of the Laws of the Natives of that part of the Coast of Sumatra, immediately dependent on the Settlement of Fort Marlborough and practised in the Court of that Presidency." *Adatrechtbundel VI*, Den Haag: Martinus Nijhoff, 1913.

Lieberman, Victor, ed. *Beyond Binary Histories: Re-imagining Eurasia to c. 1830.* Ann Arbor: University of Michigan Press, 1997.

Lineton, Jacqueline. "An Indonesian Society and Its Universe: A Study of Bugis of South Sulawesi (Celebes) and Their Role within a Wider Social and Economic System." PhD diss., University of London, 1975.

———. "Pasompe 'Ugi': Bugis Migrants and Wanderers." *Archipel* 10 (1975):173–201.

Lombard, Denys, and Aubin, Jean, eds. *Marchands et hommes d'affaires asiatiques dans l'Océan Indien et la Mer de Chine 13ᵉ-20ᵉ siècles.* Paris: Éditions de l'École des Hautes Études en Sciences Sociales, 1988.

Macknight, C. C. *The Voyage to Marege': MacassanTrepangers in Northern Australia.* Carlton: Melbourne University Press, 1976.

———. "The Rise of Agriculture in South Sulawesi before 1600." *RIMA* 17 (1983):92–116.

———, and Caldwell, I. A. "Variation in Bugis Manuscripts," *Archipel* 61 (2001): 139–54.

———, and Mukhlis. *The Chronicle of Boné.* forthcoming.

Maier, H. "'We are Playing Relatives': Riau the Cradle of Reality and Hybridity." *BKI* 153, 4 (1997): 672–98.

Markovits, Claude. *The Global World of Indian Merchants, 1750–1947.* Cambridge: Cambridge University Press, 2008.

Marsden, William. *The History of Sumatra.* Kuala Lumpur: Oxford in Asia Historical Reprints, 1966.

Matheson, Virginia and Barbara Watson Andaya, eds. and trans. *The Precious Gift (Tuhfat al-Nafis)* [by Raja Ali Haji ibn Ahmad]. Kuala Lumpur: Oxford University Press, 1982.

Matthes, B. F., ed. *Boegineesche Chrestomathie, Oorspronkelijke Boeginesche geschriften in proza en poëzij.* Vol. I, Makassar:Het Nederlandsch Bijbelgenootschap op Celebes, 1864.

———. *Over de Wadjorezen met hun Handels- en Scheepswetboek.* Makassar: P. van Hartrop, 1869.

———, ed. *Iyanaé sure powada-adaengi Undang-undangna sinina toWajoé, iya nawinrué matowana to-Wajoé ri Junpandang riyasengé Amanna Gappa,* Makassar: Van Hartrop Jr., 1869.

———. "Eenige Opmerkingen omtrent en naar Aanleiding van dat Gedeelte van Dr. J. J. de Hollander's Handleiding bij de eoefening der Land- en Volkenkunde van Nederlandsch Oost-Indië, het welk handelt over het Gounernement van Celebes en Onderhoorigheden." *BKI*, 19 (1872): 1–91.

———. *Kort Verslag aangaande alle mij in Europa bekende Makassaarsche en Boeginesche Handschriften.* Amsterdam: C. A. Spin & Zoon, 1875.

Mattulada. *Latoa: Satu Lukisan Analitis terhadap Antropologi Politik Orang Bugis.* Yogyakarta: Gadjah Mada University Press, 1985.

————. "Leadership and Democracy in the Tradition of Nusantara Society." *Lontara: Journal of Hasanuddin University* 1, 1 (1993): 37–54.

Mees, Constantinus Alting. *De Kroniek van Koetai: Tekstuitgave met Toelichting.* Santpoort: N. V. Uitgeverij, 1935.

Meillassoux, Claude, ed. *The Development of Indigenous Trade and Markets in West Africa.* Oxford: Oxford University Press, 1971.

Millar, Susan Bolyard. *Bugis Weddings: Rituals of Social Location in Modern Indonesia.* Berkeley: Center for South and Southeast Asia Studies, 1989.

Milner, A. C. *Kerajaan: Malay Political Culture on the Eve of Colonial Rule.* Tucson: University of Arizona Press, 1982.

Mishra, Vijay. "The Diasporic Imaginary: Theorizing the Indian Diaspora." *Textual Practice* 10, 3 (1996): 421–47.

Miura, Toru, ed. *Ownership, Contracts and Markets in China, Southeast Asian and the Middle East: The Potentials of Comparative Study.* Tokyo: Islamic Area Studies Project, 2001.

Moertono, Soemarsaid. *State and Statecraft in Old Java: A Study of the Later Mataram Period, 16th to 19th Centuries.* Ithaca: Modern Indonesia Project, 1963.

Mohd. Yusof Md. Nor, ed. *Salasilah Melayu dan Bugis* [by Raja Ali Haji Ibn Ahmad]. Shah Alam: Fajar Bakti, 1997.

Moor, J. H., ed. *Notices of the Indian Archipelago, and Adjacent Countries: Being a Collection of Papers Relating to Borneo, Celebes, Bali, Java, Sumatra, Nias, The Philippines Islands, Sulus, Siam, Cochin China, Malayan Peninsula . . .* Singapore:[s.n.], 1837.

M. Noor. *Sejarah Pemerintahan Kabupaten Berau dari Masa ke Masa.* [Samarinda]: [the author], 1996.

————. *Perlawanan Terhadap Imperialisme dan Kolonialisme di Kerajaan Berau, Kutai dan Pasir.* Samarinda, 1997.

M. Yusuf. *Awal Kerajaan Paser.* Pasir: Kanwil Dep Dikbud, 1993.

Muhammad Yusoff Hashim, ed. *Hikayat Siak* [by Tengku Said]. Kuala Lumpur: Dewan Bahasa dan Pustaka, 1992.

Mundy, Rodney, ed. *Narrative of Events in Borneo and Celebes down to the Occupation of Labuan: from the Journals of James Brooke, Esq. Rajah of Sarawak and Governor of Labuan.* London: John Murray, 1848.

Netscher, E. *De Nederlanders in Djohor en Siak 1602–1865: Historische Beschrijving.* Batavia: Bruining & Wijt, 1870.

Noeroeddin Daeng Magassing. "Pegatan." *Sinar Selebes Selatan* 1, 1 (1941): 9–13, and 2: 42–47.

Noorduyn, J. *Een Achttiende-Eeuwse Kroniek van Wadjo': Buginese Historiografie.* 's-Gravenage: H. L. Smits, 1955.

————. "De Islamisering van Makasar." *BKI,* 117 (1956): 254–56.

————. "Arung Singkang (1700–1765): How the Victory of Wadjo' Began." *Indonesia,* 13 (1972): 61–68.

————. "The Wajorese Merchants' Community in Makassar." *BKI* 156, 3 (2000): 473–98.

Nusselein, A. H. F. J. "Beschrijving van het Landschap Pasir." *BKI* 58 (1905):532–74.

Nur Asiah. *Ensiklopedia Pahlawan Nasional Indonesia.* Jakarta: Mediantara, 2009.

Nurdin Yusuf. *Lapagala.* Makassar: Dipajaya, 1997.

Parkes, Peter. "Milk Kinship in Islam: Substance, Structure, History." *Social Anthropology* 13, 3 (2005): 307–29.

Peddemors, M. "Wadjo. Een federatieve Staat in Celebes." *Mededeelingen der Vereeniging der gezaghebbers in Nederlandsch-Indie* 42 (1937): 24–28.

Pelras, Christian. "Hiérarchie et pouvoir traditionnels en pays Wadjo.'" *Archipel* 1 (1971): 169–91; 2 (1971): 197–224.

———. "Les fouilles et l'histoire à Célèbes Sud." *Archipel*, 3 (1972): 205–12.

———. "'Herbe divine' le riz chez les Bugis." *Etudes Rurales* 53–56 (1974): 357–74,

———. "Culture, ethnie, espace sociale : Quelques réflexions autour du cas bugis." *ASEMI* 8, 2 (1977): 57–79.

———. "Les premières données occidentales concernant Célèbes-Sud." *BKI* 133 (1977): 227–60.

———. "L'Oral et l'écrit dans la tradition Bugis." *Asie du Sud-Est et Monde Insulindien* 10 (1979): 271–97.

———. *The Bugis.* Cambridge: Blackwell, 1996.

———. "Patron-client ties among the Bugis and Makassarese of South Sulawesi." *BKI* 156, 3 (2000): 393–432.

Pheng Cheah and Bruce Robbins, eds. *Cosmopolitics: Thinking and Feeling Beyond the Nation.* Minneapolis: University of Minnesota Press, 1998.

Pickus, Noah M. J., ed. *Immigration and Citizenship in the Twenty-first Century.* Lanham, MD: Rowman and Littlefield, 1998.

Pollack, Sheldon. "The Cosmopolitan Vernacular." *Journal of Asian Studies* 57, 1 (1998): 591–625.

Pouchepadass, J. and Stern, H., eds. *De la Royauté à l'Etat: Anthropologie et Histoire du Politique dans le Monde Indien.* Paris: Ecole des Hautes Etudes en Sciences Sociales, 1991.

Rahilah Omar. "The History of Boné A.D. 1775–1795: The Diary of Sultan Ahmad as-Salleh Syamsuddin." PhD diss., University of Hull, 2003.

Rahman, N., A. Hukma, and I. Anwar, eds. *La Galigo: Menelusuri Jejak Warisan Sastra Dunia,* Makassar: Indonesia Cetakan Pertama, 2003.

H. Aji Rahmatsyah. *Sejarah Raja-Raja Berau.* Tanjung Redeb: Yayasan Kesejahteraan Kerabat Kesultanan Gunung Tabur, 2010.

Reid, Anthony. "A Great Seventeenth-century Indonesia Family: Matoaya and Pattingalloang of Makassar." *Masyarakat Indonesia* 8, 1 (1981): 1–28.

———. "The Rise of Makassar." *RIMA* 17 (1983): 117–60.

———, ed. *Slavery, Bondage and Dependency in Southeast Asia.* St. Lucia: University of Queensland Press, 1983.

———. *Southeast Asia in the Age of Commerce 1450–1680,* Vol. 1. New Haven: Yale University Press, 1988.

———, ed. *The Last Stand of Asian Autonomies Responses to Modernity in the Diverse States of Southeast Asia and Korea 1750–1900.* Hampshire: Macmillan Press Ltd., 1997.

———. "Pluralism and Progress in Seventeenth-century Makassar." *BKI* 156, 3 (2000): 433–49.

———, and Castles, Lance, eds. *Pre-colonial States Systems in Southeast Asia: The Malay Peninsula, Sumatra, Bali-Lombok, South Celebes.* Kuala Lumpur: Perchetakan Mas, 1975.

Reub, P. D. *Het Westsumatraanse Goud Handel en Exploitatie in de Zeventiende Eeuw.* Master's thesis, Leiden University, 1989.

Schulze, Fritz, ed. and trans. *Die Chroniken von Sambas und Mempawah: Einheimsche Quellen zur Geschichte West-Kalimantans.* Heidelberg: Julius Groos Verlag, 1991.

Schutte, Gerrit, and Heather Sutherland, eds. *Papers of the Dutch-Indonesian Historical Conference held at Lage Vuursche.* Leiden/Jakarta: Bureau of Indonesian Studies, 1982.

Skinner, C., ed. *Sja'ir Perang Mengkasar: The Rhymed Chronicle of the Macassar War by Entji'Amin.* Den Haag: Martinus Nijhoff, 1963.

Smith, Anthony D. *The Ethnic Origins of Nations.* Oxford: Blackwell, 1986.

Soedjatmoko et al. *An Introduction to Indonesian Historiography.* Ithaca: Cornell University Press, 1965.

Soemersaid Moertono. *State and Statecraft in Old Java: A Study of the Late Mataram Period 16th to 19th Century.* Ithaca: Cornell Modern Indonesia Project, 1968.

Southall, Aidan W. "The Segmentary State in Africa and Asia." *Comparative Studies in Society and History* 30, 1 (1988): 52–82.

Stapel, F. W. *Het Bongaais Verdrag.* Leiden: University of Leiden, 1922.

———. *Cornelis Janszoon Speelman.* Den Haag: Martinus Nijhoff, 1936.

Stavorinus, John Splinter. *Voyages to the East Indies.* London: G. G. and J. Robinson, Paternoster-Row, 1798.

Subrahmanyam, Sanjay. "Iranians Abroad: Intra-Asian Elite Migration and Early Modern State Formation." *Journal of Asian Studies* 51, 2 (1992): 340–63.

Sutherland, Heather. *Imposing Identities: Self, Community and the State: Makassar as a Microcosm, 1660–2008.* Amsterdam: Vrij Universiteit, 2008.

Swetschinski, Daniel M. "Kinship and Commerce: the Foundations of Portuguese Jewish Life in Seventeenth-Century Holland." *Studia Rosenthaliana* 15, 1 (1981): 52–74.

Tambiah, S. J. *World Conqueror and World Renouncer: A Study of Buddhism and Polity in Thailand against a Historical Background.* Cambridge: Cambridge University Press, 1976.

Tambiah, Stanley Jeyaraja. *Culture, Thought, and Social Action: An Anthropological Perspective.* Cambridge: Harvard University Press, 1985.

Teaiwa, Teresia. "L(o)osing the Edge." *The Contemporary Pacific* 13, 2, (2001): 343–65.

Tobing, O. L. *Hukum Pelajaran dan Perdagangan Amanna Gappa.* Makassar: Jajasan Kebudajaan Sulawesi Selatan dan Tenggara, 1961.

Tölölyan, Kachig. "The Nation State and Its Others: In Lieu of a Preface." *Diaspora* 1, 1 (1991): 3–7.

Thomsen, C. H., ed. *A Code of Bugis Maritime Laws with a Translation and Vocabulary, Giving the Pronunciation and Meaning of Each Word.* Singapore: Mission Press, 1832.

Thongchai Winichakul. *Siam Mapped: A History of the Geo-Body of a Nation.* Honolulu: University of Hawai'i Press, 1994.

Trivellato, Francesca. *The Familiarity of Strangers: The Sephardic Diaspora, Livorno, and Cross-Cultural Trade in the Early Modern Period.* New Haven: Yale University Press, 2009.

Tromp, S. W. "Eenige Mededeelingen omtrent de Boegineezen van Koetei." *BKI* 36 (1887): 167–98.

———. "Uit de Salasila van Koetai." *BKI* 37 (1888): 1–108.

Van der Brink, H. *Dr. Benjamin Frederik Matthes: Zijn Leven en Arbeid in Dienst van het Nederlandsch Bijbelgenootschap.* Amsterdam: Nederlandsch Bijbelgenootschap, 1943.

Van Mens, Lucie. *De Statusscheppers Sociale Mobiliteit in Wajo, 1905–1950.* Amsterdam: Centre for Asian Studies, 1989.

Van Vollenhoven, C. *Het Adatrecht van Nederlandsch-Indië.* Leiden: Brill, 1918.

Velthoen, Esther J. *Contested Coastlines: Diasporas, Trade and Colonial Expansion in Eastern Sulawesi, 1680–1905.* PhD diss., Murdoch University, 2002.

Vermeulen, Hans, and Cora Govers, eds. *The Anthropology of Ethnicity: Beyond Ethnic Groups and Boundaries.* Amsterdam: Het Spinhuis, 1994.

Veth, P. J. *Borneo's Wester-afdeeling, geographisch, statistisch, historisch, voorafgegaan door eene algemeene schets des ganschen eilands.* Zaltbommel: Joh Noman, 1854–1856.

Warren, James Francis. *The Sulu Zone 1768–1898: The Dynamics of External Trade, Slavery, and Ethnicity in the Transformation of a Southeast Asian Maritime State.* Singapore: Singapore University Press, 1981.

Whitten, Anthony; Mustafa, Muslimin and Henderson, Gregory. *The Ecology of Sulawesi.* Yogyakarta: Gadjah Mada University Press, 1987.

Winstedt, R. O. "A History of Selangor." *JMBRAS* 12, 3 (1934): 1–35.

[Winter]. "De familie Daing Mabella, volgens een Maleisch handschrift." *Tijdschrift voor Nederlandsch-Indie*, 3, 2 (1874): 115–21.

Wolters, O. W. *The Fall of Srivijaya in Malay History.* Ithaca: Cornell University Press, 1971.

———. *History, Culture, and Region in Southeast Asian Perspectives.* Singapore: Institute of Southeast Asian Studies, 1982.

Yule, Henry and A. C. Burnell. *Hobson-Jobson, A Glossary of Colloquial Anglo-Indian Words and Phrases, and of Kindred Terms, Etymological, Historical, Geographical and Discursive.* London: John Murray, 1903.

Zainal Abidin. "Notes on the Lontara' as Historical Sources." *Indonesia* 12 (1971): 159–72.

———. *Persepsi Orang Bugis Makasar tentang Hukum, Negara dan Dunia Luar.* Bandung: Penerbit Alumni, 1983.

———. *Wajo' Abad XV-XVI: Suatu Penggalian Sejarah Terpendam Sulawesi Selatan dari Lontara.'* Bandung: Penerbit Alumni, 1985.

———and Alam. "La Maddukelleng, Pahlawan jang tak kenal menjerah." *Bingkisan* 1, 9 (1967) 25–31; 1, 10 (1968): 28–31; 1, 11 (1968): 28–32; 1, 12 (1968): 27–31; 1, 13 (1968): 27–31; 1, 14 (1968): 31–36; 1, 15 (1968): 32–36.

———and C. C. Macknight. "The I La Galigo Epic of South Celebes and Its Diffusion." *Indonesia* 17 (1974): 161–69.

Index

Index